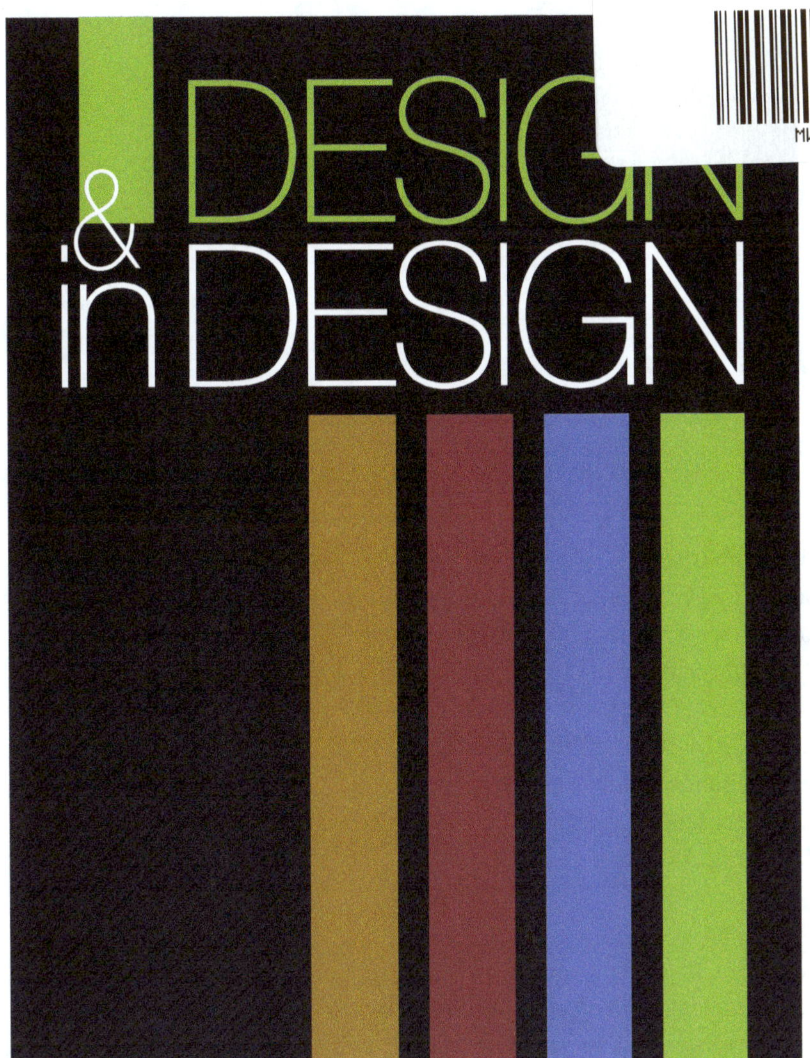

Written, illustrated & designed
by Scott Farrand

Bassim Hamadeh, Publisher
Michael Simpson, Vice President of Acquisitions
Christopher Foster, Vice President of Marketing
Jessica Knott, Managing Editor
Stephen Milano, Creative Director
Kevin Fahey, Cognella Marketing Program Manager
Becky Smith, Acquisitions Editor
Sarah Wheeler, Project Editor
Erin Escobar, Licensing Associate

First published in the United States of America in 2012 by University Readers, Inc.

15 14 13 12 11 1 2 3 4 5

Printed in the United States of America

ISBN: 978-1-60927-020-9

www.cognella.com 800.200.3908

DESIGN & in DESIGN

CONTENTS

Meet the author

1 Designing with a purpose

Chapter 1

9 Designing from the beginning

Chapter 2

17 Designing with basic shapes

Chapter 3

CONTENTS

CONTENTS

Partnership with the author

During my early years, I got a fine arts degree in print making and drawing. I spent the next 20 years as a graphic artist and editor, pioneering the use of Apple computers to create informational graphics and newspaper design. I have spent the last decade at the University of South Carolina, teaching students all aspects of visual communication to include print design, video, audio, informational graphics, flash animation, and multimedia journalism.

Each step along my career, I was faced with the struggle of learning new theories, new media, and new technologies. Recently, I added up all the computer software I have learned during my career and it was daunting. Just adding up all the numbers of versions of Illustrator, Photoshop, QuarkXPress, and InDesign was shocking. I wondered how I have had time to eat and sleep.

Recently I took on learning a new creative program and tried just sitting down and figuring it out, and that soon failed. I tried getting the book, which was really big, and found myself drowning in information. Next I tried video tutorials, and soon became blurry-eyed and lost. Why was I having such problem learning? In the early 1980s some of my creative programs had 15-25 tools. In contrast, today's creative programs can produce incredible content but have hundreds of tools and techniques. No wonder those wanting to learn today's communication software programs often find themselves lost, intimidated, and fustrated.

Here to help you

So, what I am offering you is not just book, but a partnership to learn design and InDesign. I have worked hard to not teach you everything about the desktop publishing program but only the most important tools and techniques to get you going and give you confidence. The instructions are written as if I am talking to you and use a balance of words and visuals to make it easy. Each lesson comes with all the material needed to produce the design projects.

Here to help faculty

Having taught visual communication myself and to many college professors across the southeast and as far away as Dubai, I have learned firsthand the challenges faculty are

The book is fondly dedicated to Renee, my wife, who was a gift from God and has spent many hours editing the book and encouraging me to be my best.

Also thanks to my sons, Roy and Emory, for their sacrifices.

Cognella website

For more information about book materials go to https://titles.cognella.com

having when trying to teach communication theories, design theories, and any software skills . . . it is almost impossible.

What I am offering you is a partnership to help with your class.Using this supplemental text is like using me as your teaching assistant. I have created InDesign lessons that introduce a couple of new tools with each lesson but continue to use those introduced earlier. Because of the differences of many colleges' programs, I have created two different lessons for each chapter (one with an advertising, public relations emphasis and the other with a journalism emphasis). Each chapter begins with discussing design theories that are used in the lesson, and is followed by detailed illustrated instructions. Each lesson comes with all the materials needed to create the InDesign projects. I use this book in my own classes. I give 15 minutes of instruction at the beginning of each lesson and the book does the rest of the teaching.

More help for you

I have worked with the book publisher to make it easy for you to go to their website and download all the lessons' materials, which often include templates and images.

More help for faculty

I have also worked with the publisher to make it easy for you to get access to all the supplemental material. You will have a separate log-in for this secure material. It includes:

- InDesign lesson templates (created in InDesign 4 and 5).
- Lesson images (copyright free).
- Grading sheets (for each lesson).
- Lesson instructional tips on how I have used the lessons successfully.
- A blog site where you can communicate with me easily for additional help.

Acknowledgments

The author is sincerely grateful to the following people whose assistance made this book possible:

Terence Young – A good friend and accomplished S.C. musician who was kind enough to offer great material for the CD lesson.

David Weintraub – A collegue and great photographer whose San Francisco images were a great help.

Paul Bowers – A former journalism student who allowed me to use his excellent cobbler story and photographs.

Denise McGill – An excellent photojournalist and collegue who took a great portrait of me on a recent study abroad class we taught together.

Dr. Carol Pardun – Who gave me the inspiration to think big and pursue writing a book.

Dr. Augie Grant, Bonnie Drewniany, and Dr. Keith Kenney – Colleagues who shared their valuable book experience.

Carmen Maye – Who shared some great legal and book publishing insight.

Van Kornegay and Bruce Konkle – Visual Communication collegues who gave constant encouragement.

Doug Fisher – A journalism faculty collegue who helped me in the clasroom and gave me a lot of guidance and encouragent along the way.

USC, School of Journalism and Mass Communication faculty – Many thanks to Dean Charles Bierbauer and the many others who gave me encouragement along the way.

The Cognella and University Readers staff – Thanks to Jessica Knott, Becky Smith, Amy Wiltbank, Kevin Fahey, and Sarah Wheeler, for their guidance and help along the way.

DESIGNING with a purpose

"**Design** is to create a message that is perceived and understood."

Why learn design?

Does it not make sense that if you can learn to create a message that is noticed by more, comprehended faster, and has greater impact, you should?

Why learn InDesign?

It is great to be able to create words, but the true power lies in the ability to create a message and disseminate it to hundreds, thousands, or even millions of people.

Why learn them both at the same time?

Many have asked me that question, and the answer I give is that it works. Being a university professor has given me the ability to try different techniques and test them on a class. If they did not work, I had new students in six months to refine my techniques and try again. The result is a set of InDesign lessons that build upon each other as they introduce new software tools and design skills. At the end of the lessons, you will be amazed how comfortable you have become with InDesign and how good you are at designing an effective message.

Let's get started

More than decorating

The common perception is that designers make things look pretty, much like decorating a cake. However, even the best cake decorators go far beyond adding some sprinkles and colorful icing to their cakes. A master baker starts with choosing the appropriate size and shape of the dessert. Then, the perfect flavor must be selected before the cake is baked, cooled, and skillfully decorated using a wide variety of techniques to match the client's specific needs. It is far more than just making something pretty looking.

So what is graphic design?

Many days I struggle to fully understand this simple yet complex term.

If you ask my parents what their son does for a living, they will pause and say that he does something with art–they think. My first job was at a newspaper, and when my boss (the editor) introduced me, he would say, "This is Scott, the creative "doodler." Even the reporters at the newspaper would pause when introducing me and then describe what I did was make things (their words) look good. I knew then that I would spend my career defining this term and my career.

Some dictionaries describe design as a method of combining words, symbols, and images together to create a visual message. But it is much more than this definition:

Designing is when you give greater impact to information.

Designing is simplifying a message for mass media consumption.

Designing is arranging words, images, and other elements in a logical manner to create a clear message for a target audience.

Designing is collaborating with a client to visually communicate their message to their specific customers or audiences.

You will discover that design is all of this and much more.

Design is a science

Make no mistake, that when you are designing it is much more than a feeling or using a color that you like. It is not enough to be skilled in the tools, like InDesign, but you need to also understand the theories, principles, and science of communication to fully be able to create an effective message. This seems easy enough, but the problem is that society is constantly changing. Technology is constantly changing. Thus, the designer needs to be constantly adapting and creating new ways to communicate. Today's visual communicators are facing some of the greatest challenges in history because society is changing at an incredible pace.

Your notes

Your notes

■ **Today's audience is spoiled**
Society has spoiled two generations of Americans giving them hundreds of new movies each year, a multitude of vehicles to choose to drive, and a vast array of other superior services and products. The result is an audience that expects the best for little or no cost.

– The designer will have to learn to create quicker, cheaper and better communications products to appeal to this demanding audience.

■ **Today's audience is very sophisticated**
What do I mean by this? The average person is bombarded with hundreds of messages in a day from a wide variety of media. The result is that they have become very visually literate and will often dismiss the simple messages that worked five year ago.

– Communicating to today's audience requires much more sophisticated approaches, methods, and tools.

■ **Today's audience is incredibly mobile**
They do not want information at a set time like TV and newspapers still like to think. This new audience is constantly moving and they want information when and where they are at any given time of day or night. The proof of this fact is the quick adoption of the mobile phone, which has reached about 97 percent of the American population now owning one of these devices. But now these are not good enough, and people are upgrading to smart phones and other portable devices like iPads at alarming rates to enable them to access even more information.

– Designers now must learn to design on a wide variety of media using new technologies and techniques to deliver their communication to the mobile audience.

■ **Today's audiences are multitaskers**
When was the last time you did only one thing at a time? You are not alone! It is not uncommon to go down the highway and observe someone listening to the radio, munching on a burger while attempting to drive. Gone are the days when the TV viewer sat tentatively for 30 minutes watching the evening news.

– The challenge now is to create information that is simpler, louder, and has greater impact to compete for attention from numerous other sources.

Is this challenge a lost cause? No! However, anyone who wants to succeed as a communicator needs to arm themselves with the best knowledge and technologies if they hope to effectively communicate to today's audience. The first step is mastering the basics of design and InDesign.

Why this approach to learning InDesign?

During my first years as a college professor, I was assigned the journalism school's basic design class where I would lecture in the classroom twice a week on design theories. My 45 students then would have to attend one of the of three 55-minute computer lab classes where I would teach them all aspects of the desktop publishing program. The results:
– Students forgot or just skipped lab sessions.
– Some hated the time of day the labs were held.
– Some were bored because they already knew InDesign.

Understanding convergence

Also during my first years at USC, I was introduced to Kerry Northrup, who was working with newspapers around the world experimenting and developing new journalism techniques. He introduced me to a new concept called "convergence." Northrup pointed out that most newspapers and other media companies simply try to adopt new technologies but do not consider new media uses. Convergence, applied here to newspapers, is the merging of different elements (technology, stories, and media) together to create new story forms that are significantly better and communicates more effectively to the changing audiences.

Over the next few months I repeatedly found convergence to work so I thought, why not try to apply it to my classes by combining design theories with applied uses. I created self-paced InDesign lessons that followed the theories learned in class. Each lesson building upon each other by using the design theories, introducing several new InDesign tools/techniques, and repeating the use of previously learned InDesign tools. The result was that my new class of 150 students outperformed my former classes of 45. The new large class got better test scores, had more advanced InDesign skills, and gave the class higher evaluations.

Introduction to the book

The publication contains eight chapters, five of which contain lessons that teach new InDesign skills. Each chapter starts with an introduction, followed by a few pages that explain some design theories and end with an InDesign skill lesson that includes simple step-by-step instructions.

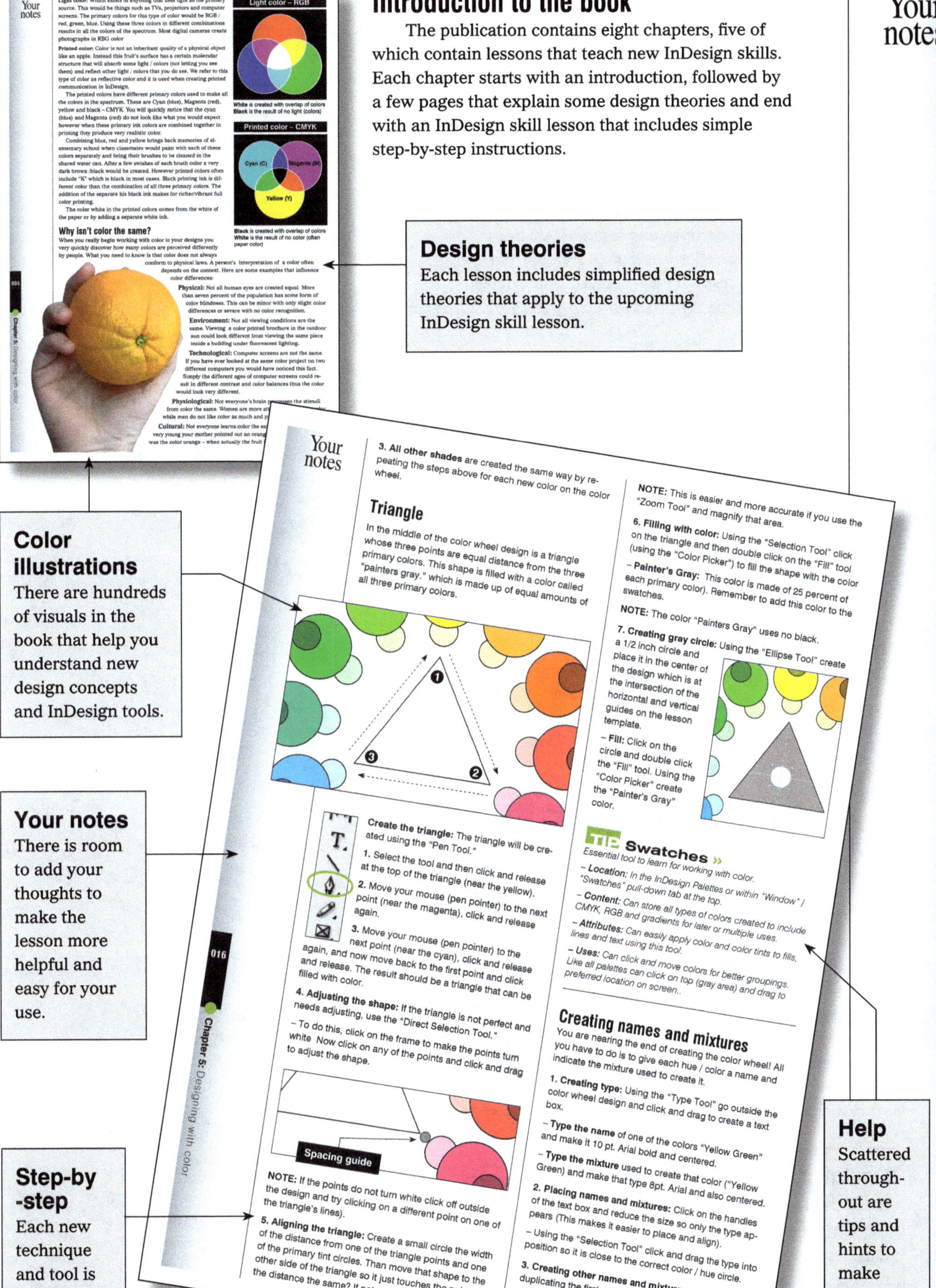

Your
notes

Light color: Which exists in anything that uses light as the primary source. This would be things such as TVs, projectors and computer screens. The primary colors for this type of color would be RGB / red, green, blue. Using these three colors in different combinations results in all the colors of the spectrum. Most digital cameras create photographs in RBG color

Printed color: Color is not an inheritant quality of a physical object like an apple. Instead this fruit's surface has a certain molecular structure that will absorb some light / colors (not letting you see them) and reflect other light / colors that you do see. We refer to this type of color as reflective color and it is used when creating printed communication in InDesign.

The printed colors have different primary colors used to make all the colors in the spectrum. These are Cyan (blue), Magenta (red), yellow and black – CMYK. You will quickly notice that the cyan (blue) and Magenta (red) do not look like what you would expect however when these primary ink colors are combined together in printing they produce very realistic color.

Combining blue, red and yellow brings back memories of elementary school when classmates would paint with each of these colors separately and bring their brushes to be cleaned in the shared water can. After a few swishes of each brush color a very dark brown /black would be created. However printed colors often include "K" which is black in most cases. Black printing ink is different color than the combination of all three primary colors. The addition of the separate his black ink makes for richer/vibrant full color printing.

The color white in the printed colors comes from the white of the paper or by adding a separate white ink.

Light color – RGB

White is created with overlap of colors
Black is the result of no light (colors)

Printed color – CMYK

Cyan (C)
Magenta (M)
Yellow (Y)

Black is created with overlap of colors
White is the result of no color (often paper color)

Why isn't color the same?

When you really begin working with color in your designs you very quickly discover how many colors are perceived differently by people. What you need to know is that color does not always conform to physical laws. A person's interpretation of a color often depends on the context. Here are some examples that influence color differences:

Physical: Not all human eyes are created equal. More than seven percent of the population has some form of color blindness. This can be minor with only slight color differences or severe with no color recognition.

Environment: Not all viewing conditions are the same. Viewing a color printed brochure in the outdoor sun could look different from viewing the same piece inside a building under fluorescent lighting.

Technological: Computer screens are not the same. If you have ever looked at the same color project on two different computers you would have noticed this fact. Simply the different ages of computer screens could result in different contrast and color balances thus the color would look very different.

Physiological: Not everyone's brain processes the stimuli from color the same. Women are more at[...] while men do not like color as much and p[...]

Cultural: Not everyone learns color the sa[...] very young your mother pointed out an orang[...] was the color orange – when actually the fruit [...]

004

Chapter 5: Designing with color

Your
notes

3. All other shades are created the same way by repeating the steps above for each new color on the color wheel.

Triangle

In the middle of the color wheel design is a triangle whose three points are equal distance from the three primary colors. This shape is filled with a color called "painters gray," which is made up of equal amounts of all three primary colors.

Create the triangle: The triangle will be created using the "Pen Tool."

1. Select the tool and then click and release at the top of the triangle (near the yellow).

2. Move your mouse (pen pointer) to the next point (near the magenta), click and release again.

3. Move your mouse (pen pointer) to the next point (near the cyan), click and release again, and now move back to the first point and click and release. The result should be a triangle that can be filled with color.

4. Adjusting the shape: If the triangle is not perfect and needs adjusting, use the "Direct Selection Tool."

– To do this, click on the frame to make the points turn white. Now click on any of the points and click and drag to adjust the shape.

Spacing guide

NOTE: If the points do not turn white click off outside the design and try clicking on a different point on one of the triangle's lines).

5. Aligning the triangle: Create a small circle the width of the distance from one of the triangle points and one of the primary tint circles. Than move that shape to the other side of the triangle so it just touches the point. Is the distance the same? If not adjust the triangle shape.

NOTE: This is easier and more accurate if you use the "Zoom Tool" and magnify that area.

6. Filling with color: Using the "Selection Tool" click on the triangle and then double click on the "Fill" tool (using the "Color Picker") to fill the shape with the color

– Painter's Gray: This color is made of 25 percent of each primary color). Remember to add this color to the swatches.

NOTE: The color "Painters Gray" uses no black.

7. Creating gray circle: Using the "Ellipse Tool" create a 1/2 inch circle and place it in the center of the design which is at the intersection of the horizontal and vertical guides on the lesson template.

– Fill: Click on the circle and double click the "Fill" tool. Using the "Color Picker" create the "Painter's Gray" color.

TIP Swatches »

Essential tool to learn for working with color.

– Location: In the InDesign Palettes or within "Window" / "Swatches" pull-down tab at the top.

– Content: Can store all types of colors created to include CMYK, RGB and gradients for later or multiple uses.

– Attributes: Can easily apply color and color tints to fills, lines and text using this tool.

– Uses: Can click and move colors for better groupings. Like all palettes can click on top (gray area) and drag to preferred location on screen..

Creating names and mixtures

You are nearing the end of creating the color wheel! All you have to do is to give each hue / color a name and indicate the mixture used to create it.

1. Creating type: Using the "Type Tool" go outside the color wheel design and click and drag to create a text box.

– Type the name of one of the colors "Yellow Green" and make it 10 pt. Arial bold and centered.

– Type the mixture used to create that color ("Yellow Green) and make that type 8pt. Arial and also centered.

2. Placing names and mixtures: Click on the handles of the text box and reduce the size so only the type appears (This makes it easier to place and align).

– Using the "Selection Tool" click and drag the type into position so it is close to the correct color / hue circle.

3. Creating other names and mixtures: Is easiest by duplicating the first color.

– Highlighting the name and typing the new color.

– Next highlight the color mixture and type in the new

016

Chapter 5: Designing with color

Design theories

Each lesson includes simplified design theories that apply to the upcoming InDesign skill lesson.

Color illustrations

There are hundreds of visuals in the book that help you understand new design concepts and InDesign tools.

Your notes

There is room to add your thoughts to make the lesson more helpful and easy for your use.

Step-by-step

Each new technique and tool is explained in simple written instructions.

Help

Scattered throughout are tips and hints to make learning InDesign easier.

Your
notes

Your notes

Introduction to the lessons

The book contains five chapters with InDesign lessons which start very simple but get more complex. Each lesson introduces a few new tools and skills while reinforcing the ones learned in the previous lesson, which is one of the reasons for the success of the book.

Two ways to approach lessons

If you are more advanced, just read the lesson instructions and begin. If you need more help, follow the simple step-by-step instructions until you get more comfortable.

Self-paced Skill Lesson A

SCOTT FARRAND
DESIGN & InDESIGN

Designing WITH Typography

Creating an ad

Well, the advertising department lost the artwork for this magazine ad, so we need your help. Like always, the publication is going to press in a couple of days, so we need that ad ASAP. The goal is to make your work look EXACTLY like the current ad. This lesson will require you to learn new InDesign tools, so you will need to get started soon to meet the pending deadline.

BowWow! Magazine

SAVE 47% OFF THE COVER PRICE

12 ISSUES FOR JUST $21.99

Start my BowWow! subscription

Start one for my friend

MY SUBSCRIPTION:

Name City E-mail Address Zip State

SEND MY GIFT TO:

Name City E-mail Address Zip State

Bill me

Payment enclosed

This is the guaranteed lowest rate at these terms, excluding special business rates. All prices in U.S. funds. For Canada, $21. For all other countries, $29. Sales tax required for magazines sent to D.C., 5.75%; and S.C., 7% Canadian price includes GST. If you prefer to send payment now please place this reply card and your check in envelope and mail to BowWow! Magazine, Box 33031, Atlanta, GA 33660. Please allow weeks for delivery of your first issue.

LSABQ11

letter spacing added.

Hint: To match the rules within the ad use lines that are in size.

Specifications

- **Size:** The ad must be 6.6 inches wide by 4.9 inches deep. Ad shown is correct depth but the width is off about .25 inch.
  – You will need to adjust / align this content visually.
- **Template:** You need to start the lesson using the template provided. On the template are two images. You will need to create the outside frame and center it on the page.

NOTE: This template / lesson includes images. It is important that this file and images be kept within the same folder to print correctly. When images are used a link is created and if you rename any of the files the link will be broken.

The final product

- The final printout will need to be on a standard paper with the ad centered on the paper.
- Include your name on the lower left corner of

Assessment criteria

- Does the ad contain all the information
- Is the ad the correct size and centered
- Does the ad look exactly like the example
- Does the type faces (serif and sanserif), leading, body and spacing correct? Are the type faces
  – Remember one the dimensions have requiring you to visually adjust the pla
- Are the lines straight and evenly s
- Is it clean, pre

Overview

Each lesson includes an introduction outlining the project objectives.

Design & InDesign objectives

Each lesson includes criteria to access the success of your work.

What do you need to get started?

Computer: The good news is it does not matter what computer you use. The program InDesign works the same on both. However, there are a few key stroke differences between Apple and Windows computers, depending on the age of the computer. In most cases I avoid teaching basic InDesign using key strokes because of this difference and to keep instructions simple and visually oriented at first.

– **The lesson instructions are based on using an Apple computer** and will refer to the "Shift" in a few cases, which is the same key on most kinds of computers. The "Option," "Apple," and "Command" keys are referred to in limited cases, and these keys are different on various computers.

Software: The only need here is the InDesign software. It does not matter if it was part of an Adobe Creative Suite or if you have only the InDesign program. I have created the lessons to work with any recent version of the software that includes InDesign 3, InDesign 4, and InDesign 5.

Content: The book includes several lessons that use templates to help you get started. These InDesign lesson templates have been created in InDesign 3 and InDesign 5 so that they can be used with any of the recent three versions of InDesign.

– **Images** are also used in several of the lessons. These files are either Illustrator EPS, Illustrator TIFF or Photoshop TIFF files. You do not need either Illustrator or Photoshop to use these files.

– **Copyright:** The photographic images, illustrator files, and other content used in the book lessons are copyright materials and are not to be used for any other uses not connected to the InDesign lessons.

Some terminology you need to know

I have worked to simplify the wording in this book, and have reduced the amount of specific terminology dealing with design. However, many who use InDesign also will have their work printed, so I have included some printing terminolgy to get you familiar with this area of communication.

InDesign: It will be very important in the first few chapters to take the time to learn the InDesign interface, palettes, and tool names so that the step-by-step instructions are helpful.

Book terminology: I have created a rather unique terminology to simplify the instructions dealing with multiple steps, extended tabs, mouse click steps, and the many drop-down menus used in InDesign.

– **I put quotes** around the tool, palette, and menu names.

– **There will be slashes** between steps, mouse click steps, or different menu pull-outs.

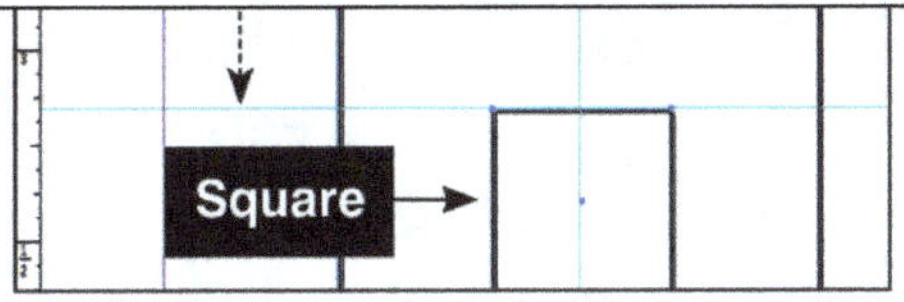

rulers and drag a guide and align it so it runs thru the center of the rectangle. This will be the position of the arrow point later.

– Now select the square and go to the top rulers and drag a guide so it is aligned with the top of the square. This will become the arrow points later.

3. Setting up the "Pen Tool": Now the easy part of drawing the arrow using the "Pen Tool." We will be using the tool much like the early childhood games of dot-to-dot drawing.

– **Set fill and stroke:** First select the "Pen Tool" from the "Too Palette. Next, go to the top "Control Strip" and select "Windows" / "Color" / "Swatches" where you will also find the "Fill" and "Stroke" tools.

– **Cick on the "Stroke"** and make black by clicking on the black square.

– **Cick on the "Fill"** tool and make the fill none by click-

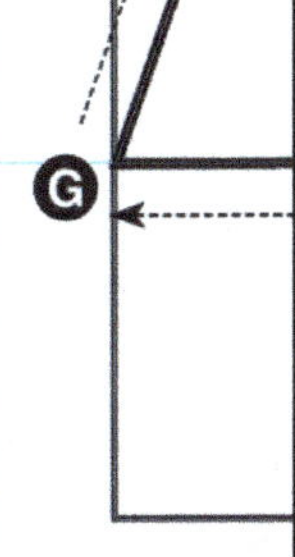

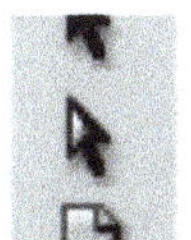

3. E
likely
try. T
lect
to click on any
white to allow e
preferred positi

4. Adjusting a
ered your arow
easy to adjust.

– **Using the "D**

Your notes

Your notes

Summary

While I have been fascinated and studied design most of my life, I must admit I still seem like I am new to this discipline and am constantly learned new techniques and skills. What I have learn is that communication is constantly changing and the technology needs are changing even faster.

Can design really make a difference? Yes and no! Design alone cannot but teamed up with good information it can really make a difference.

I once was asked by a colleague if I had a student who could help him "jazz up" some of his research data on South Carolina's libraries. He wanted a one-page, B&W handout to give to the S.C. legislators. I looked over his data and replied that I had several students who could do a great job, but would he be interested in letting me team up with him on this project. He agreed and gave me the many pages of data.

Two weeks later I presented him with a small, full-color trifold brochure, which I had significantly simplified and made visual. He was shocked, but pleased. When he showed the project to his colleagues at a few of the libraries, they found additional funding to increase the printing from 500 to 10,000 copies so it could also be given to all S.C. businesses, libraries, and interested residents in the state.

A year later the state legislators increased South Carolina libraries' funding by over 20 percent.

Design can make a difference.

DESIGNING from the beginning

"First you must learn to see before you can design."

Recently I began learning a new software program, and was reminded how intimidating it is to sit down at the computer and launch a new program, not knowing the first thing about it. I will give you the same advice I give my students (and myself) – take a deep breath and just give it a try. Try not to be perfect the first, time but know you will feel a bit uncomfortable until you get through the first lesson. After each lesson, you will get more confident.

What I need for you to do in the next few pages is to briefly look over how InDesign is set up and get familiar with the tools. You do not need to memorize them all, but I would like for you to have some knowledge with the "Tool Palette" (especially the selection arrows) and the other major interfaces of InDesign so I can lead you through the first lesson successfully.

The good news is that if you get confused during the lesson you can always refer back to this section until you remember some of the basic tools.

OK, enough of this, let's get up the courage and give this a try!

Why InDesign?

So why am I learning this program?

The truth is, that knowing this desktop publishing program beats:

- Spending a day writing and coding text to send it off to be transformed into paper columns.
- Spending hours marking photo prints and sending them off to be made into negatives.
- Sizing and coding headlines, deck headlines, quotes and many other items.
- Getting all the content back the next day and discovering you sized some things incorrectly and made a couple of misspellings. Now you spend hours making corrections and send off the content again.
- Spending another day cutting and gluing all the pieces together into a masterpiece design to discover at the end of the day the editor/client decided they want to make more changes.
- Now you spend yet another day writing, coding, cutting, designing, gluing . . . you get the picture.

Now I can't promise that some days you might be also doing the same thing over and over, but the development of desktop publishing programs has made design much faster, easier, and better.

In 1984 Apple debuted the Macintosh (Mac) with 128K and a B&W screen. This was followed up with the Mac Plus, Mac SE (my fourth Apple computer pictured above) and countless other Apple portable computers enabled the masses (you and me) to be creative and do desktop publishing.

It all began in a faraway land many years ago . . . not quite the truth.

As far as I am concerned, it began in the early 1980s when Apple created the desktop computer. This put a powerful tool into my hands and the hands of many others, allowing us to create. While some of the first software programs like MacDraw were great, there were other significant developments that allowed graphic designers the ability to go further into desktop publishing.

- **Aldus gave us the PageMaker** software (ability to do entire pages of content).
- **Adobe created the Postscript language** (ability to create sophisticated content digitally).
- **Cannon and Hewlett-Packard** technologies (desktop printers).

Your notes

So, why are we not using Microsoft Word or PageMaker?

While PageMaker was great at doing single pages and small projects, there was a need for more and larger projects.

First, let's address Word, which came out in 1998 as Multi-Tool Word and has now evolved to Microsoft Word 11, available for Window and Mac computers. This program is great for writing, editing and even fixing grammar and spelling problems. It is not the best for designing sophisticated communication projects.

Now PageMaker was great at creating word content, much like Microsoft Word, but this program included additional tools that enabled the user to also design the words and photographs into very nice-looking single pages and small projects. However, as digital technology advanced, designers wanted to be able to create bigger and better communications.

A company called Quark soon developed their layout program called QuarkXPress in 1987 with the tools to do large, sophisticated publishing projects. This now enabled large newspapers and magazines to produce their publications digitally. During the early 1990s PageMaker and QuarkXPress battled in what is known by some as the "Desktop Publishing War" for market shares in the vastly growing digital communication industry.

It soon became evident that the PageMaker software did not have the ability to progress, to meet new demands . . . thus came InDesign in 1999, which was developed by Adobe Systems after buying PageMaker. This program took the best features of PageMaker and QuarkXPress and added more features to become an excellent desktop publishing program. In 2002, InDesign was the first native software to work with Apple's new computers. Adobe also began bundling this program with their Creative Suite programs (Illustrator and Photoshop).

Today both software programs have loyal fans and command significant portions of the publishing market. I use both, and my students have found if you learn one you can easily switch to the other in the future if needed.

Ready to get started? Maybe not.

How do I get the program?

First you can go to the Adobe site and download a 30-day trial. This is great, but you will find that the 30 days goes fast.

Next you can purchase InDesign at many places (online sources to local stores) for around $699.*

InDesign Creative Suite is a better deal and includes: InDesign, Illustrator (drawing program), Photoshop (working digital images), Acrobat 9 Pro (creating PDF files) $1,299.*

Do you need the latest version of InDesign?

No. While each new version offers many new tools and features, it is not essential that you have the latest version. I will often only purchase every other version to save costs. However, if you do a lot of freelance work you may need to upgrade more often to stay compatible with clients. The good news is that upgrades are cheaper! InDesign CS5 upgrades start at $199.* Creative Suite 5 Design Standard upgrades start at $499.*

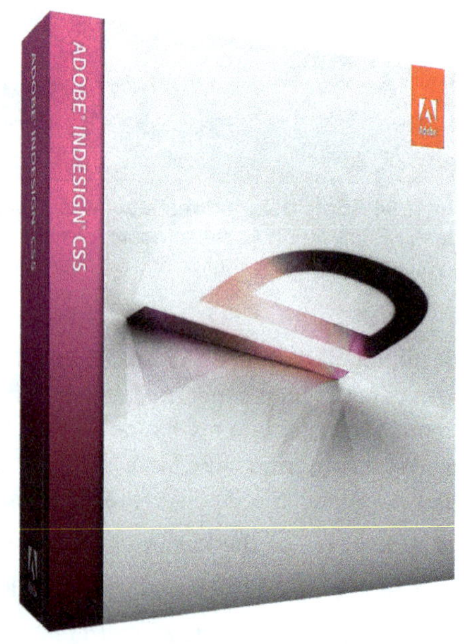

Good news for students and teachers!

While you are a full-time student, you can purchase the software for about 60%–75% off actual retail prices. This is fully licensed software! The bad news is that while you are a student you do not get cheaper upgrade prices.

Remember, when purchasing software make sure your computer can handle the basic requirements. Check your computer stats against the software. Also the Mac and Windows versions of the software are different, so make sure you specify which one you need.

Now that we have the technical stuff out of the way, let's learn good design and InDesign.

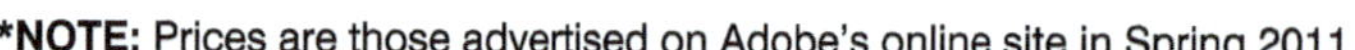

***NOTE:** Prices are those advertised on Adobe's online site in Spring 2011.

Getting started

Launching the software

The InDesign application can be found in the "Dock" (strip at the bottom or left with other programs / utilities). Remember : Your screen may look different at times if you are using a Windows computer or a different version of InDesign. While the examples are created in InDesign 5, using InDesign 4, 3, or 2 will be no problem.

Launch InDesign

The program can be found here or in your computer's "Application" folder.

Trash / eject

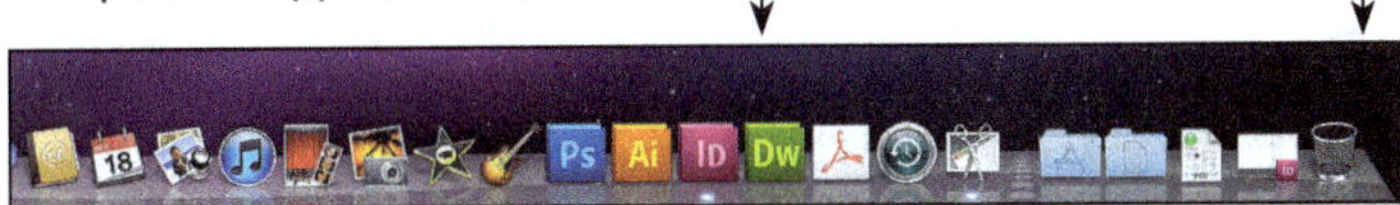

Creating a new document

Select "File / New / Document." Give the document a name: **Lesson 1_Your Name.ind**. It is important to follow the naming example so that you can remember your file name later and the file can be opened in Mac and window computers successfully.

More info »

To obtain the correct template / See "Partnership with the author" section.

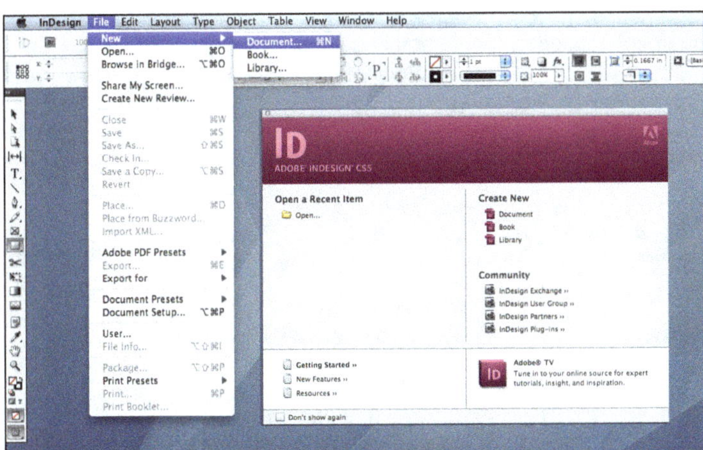

1. Select number of pages for this assignment.

2. Select correct page size for the project. For most assignments, select "Letter." Also select page orientation.

3. Select number of columns. This sets up the type columns for the page. Most lessons will start with one and change later if needed.

4. Setting the margins. This is determined by what your printer can print safely and your design. For most assignments, set at 0.5 in. (half inch from image area to sides of paper).

5. Facing pages and master text frame are used for large multi-page projects. This does not need to be selected for most lessons in this book.

6. Select "OK." Now you have a blank page to create your great communication project.

"Tool Palette"

These tools are used to create, edit, and manipulate all content. You need to learn each of these tools' names and their attributes to effectively use the program. **Remember, a black arrow** next to the tool symbol indicates more versions of the tools are available (click and hold to view additional tools).

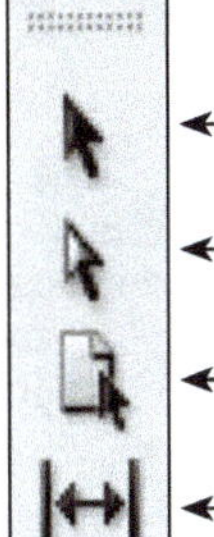

Selection tool: Selects, moves, and resizes items

Direct selection tool: Used to edit content

Page tool: Changes page dimensions

Gap tool: Measures between objects

Type tool: Creates type and text boxes

Line tool: Creates all lines

Pen tool: Used for drawing simple or complex shapes and lines

Pencil tool: Draws lines with a pencil

Rectangle frame tool: Creates shapes for images

Rectangle tool: Creates rectangular shapes and more

Scissor tool: Used to cut portions of lines and shapes

Free transform tool: Resizes elements and more

Gradient swatch tool: Used to create gradient tonal blends

Gradient feather tool: Creates sophisticated gradients

Note tool: Makes project notes for you or printer

Eyedropper tool: Identifies colors & more tools

Hand tool: Moves the position of the page

Zoom tool: Used to change page view

Fill & stroke tool: Modifies fills or strokes of an element

Formatting affects container

Apply tool: Used to quickly apply color, no color, or gradient

Project views: Normal, preview, bleed, and more

Your notes

Your notes

Understanding the tools

Using the "Control Strip"

The items in the InDesign control strip are content sensitive. That means they change depending on the item selected.

Rotation & shear
Enter values to rotate element or shear at an angle.

Lines
Select size and type of line or frame.

Frame / Content
Fill frame and fill content controls frame.

Control Strip settings
Select the control bar tools you like.

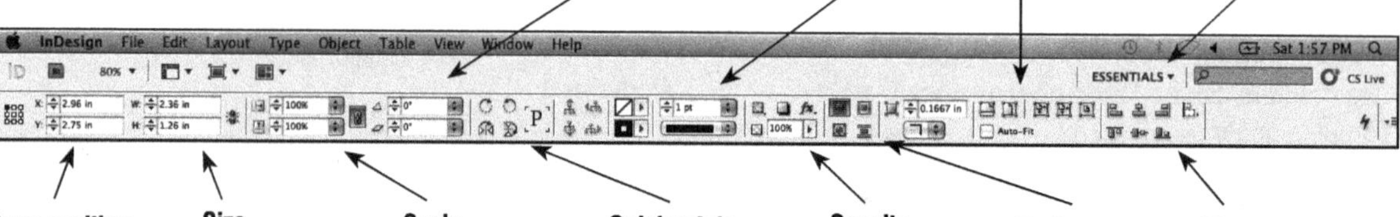

Page position
Coordinates of element on the document (X and Y).

Size
Width and height of item created (W and H).

Scale
Enter a value to scale horizontally or vertically.

Quick rotate & flip
Quickly rotate 90 degrees or flip element.

Opacity
Select percentage of opacity of element.

Text wraps
Four text wrap formats.

Align
Align two or more objects tool.

Understanding the InDesign document window

Here are some of the basic functions of the publication design interface.

Ruler Origin
Enables you to reposition ruler starting point. Click and drag to desired position if needed.

Document Name
Displays title of document created.

Horizontal Ruler
Click and drag to obtain guides hidden in ruler.

Moving Document
Click and drag on any gray portion to move window.

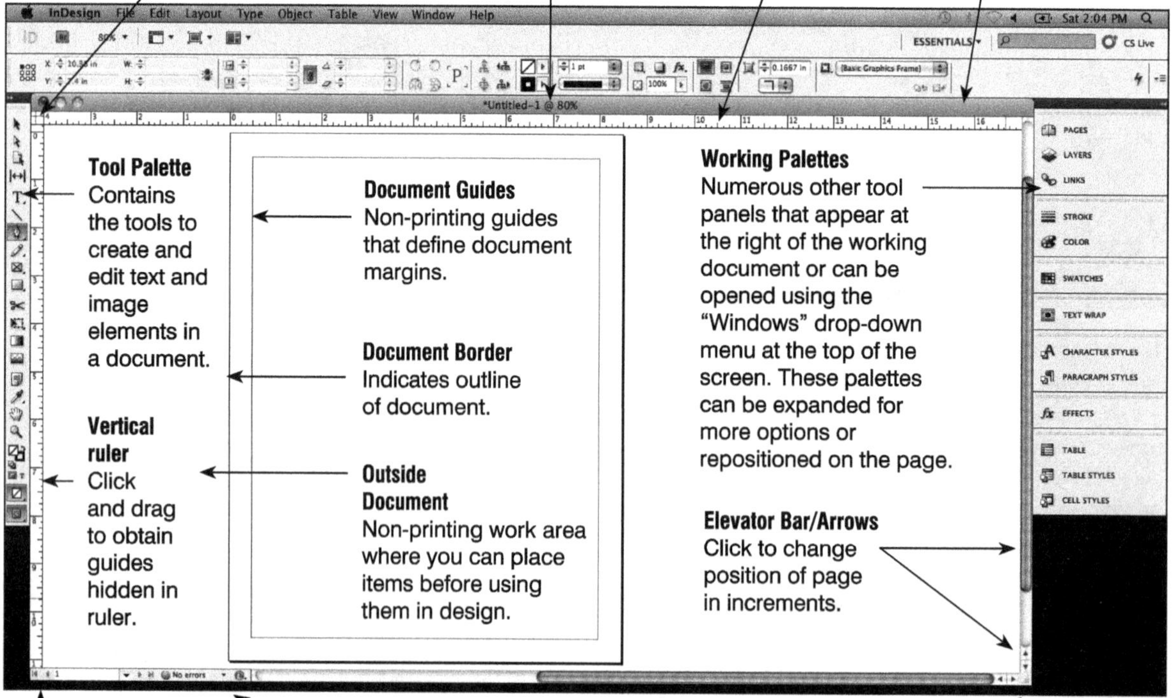

Tool Palette
Contains the tools to create and edit text and image elements in a document.

Document Guides
Non-printing guides that define document margins.

Working Palettes
Numerous other tool panels that appear at the right of the working document or can be opened using the "Windows" drop-down menu at the top of the screen. These palettes can be expanded for more options or repositioned on the page.

Document Border
Indicates outline of document.

Vertical ruler
Click and drag to obtain guides hidden in ruler.

Outside Document
Non-printing work area where you can place items before using them in design.

Elevator Bar/Arrows
Click to change position of page in increments.

Page view
Current magnification of page.

Page Indicator
Helpful when working on a multiple page document.

Elevator Bar
Move to change position of document.

Window Resizing
Drag the corner of window to resize document window.

New document basics

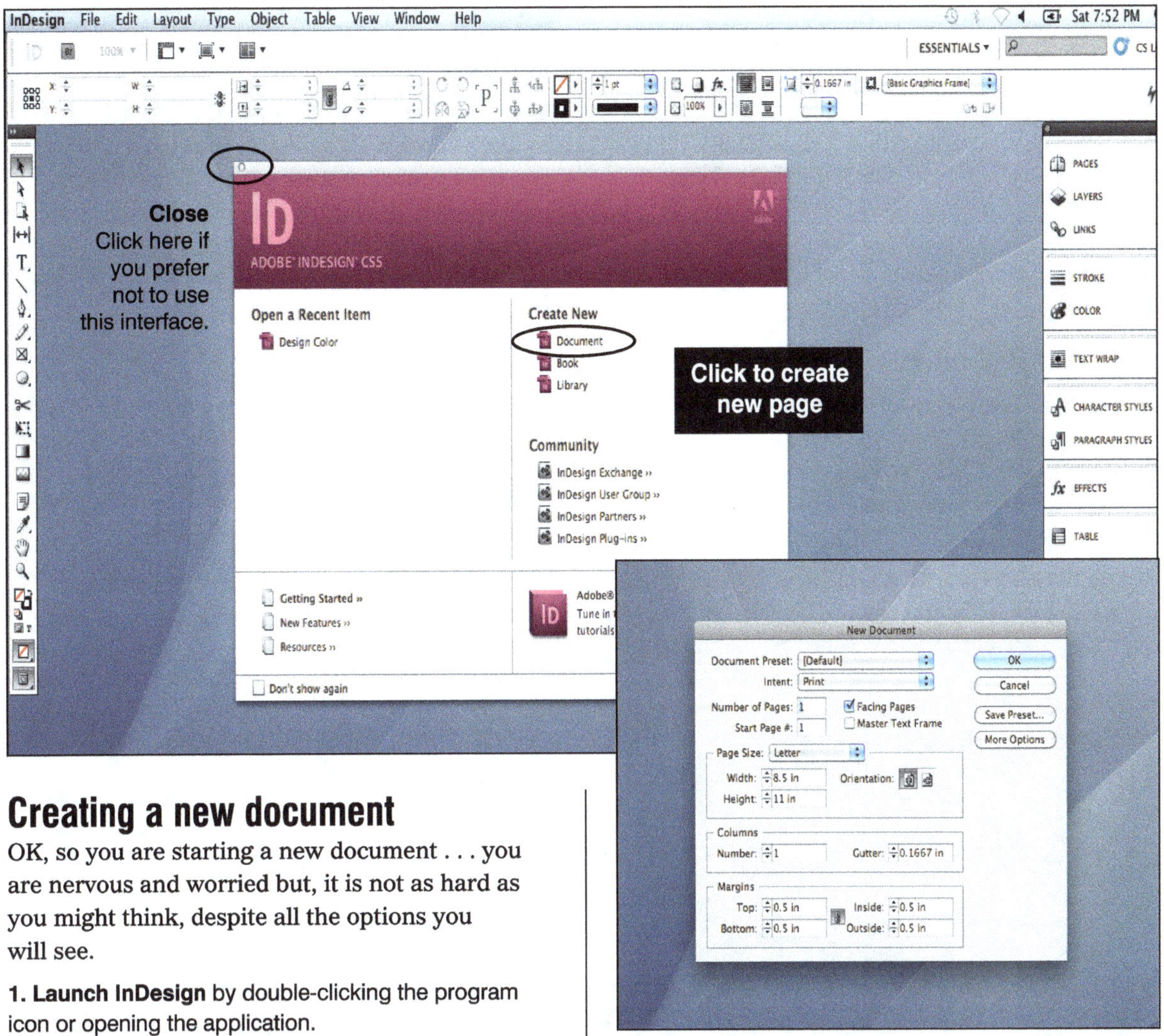

Close
Click here if you prefer not to use this interface.

Click to create new page

Creating a new document

OK, so you are starting a new document . . . you are nervous and worried but, it is not as hard as you might think, despite all the options you will see.

1. Launch InDesign by double-clicking the program icon or opening the application.

– **An Adobe InDesign CS5 window** will appear that will enable you to quickly open a recent file or create a new document simply by clicking on that selection.

– **New document:** I often do not use the InDesign window (indicated above) but, prefer to close the window and go to the top and select "File" / "New Document."

2. Page and document option: There are many options to choose depending if you are creating a one-page flyer or a multi-page custom-sized magazine.

– **These are the settings** I suggest for a single-page project (same as several upcoming lessons):

■ **Number of pages (1)**

■ **Facing pages (None)**
Unselect for just one page.

■ **Orientation (vertical)**
Select vertical or horizontal.

■ **Page size (letter)**
Select a standard paper size or enter any size you want.

■ **Columns and gutter (no change–default)**
Can set these now or later if needed.

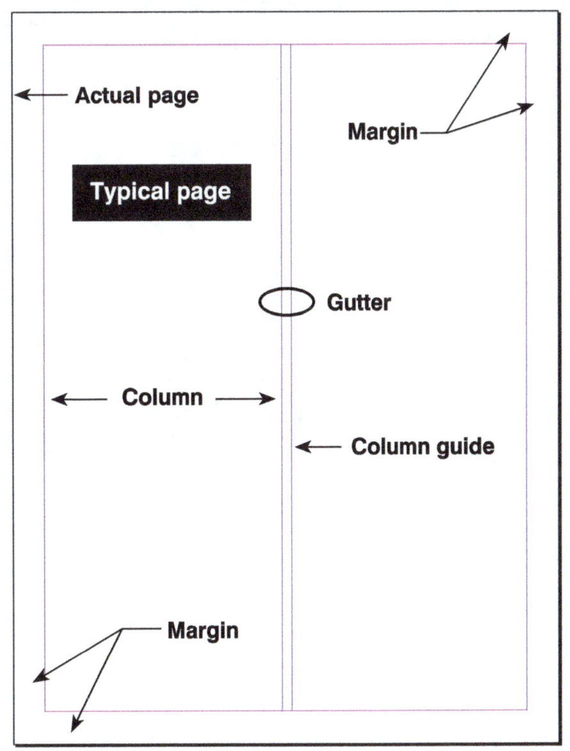

Your notes

Your notes

■ **Margins (0.5 in)**
Set to your design or to the printing area–many printers cannot print to the paper's edge (called bleeds).

Saving your document

This step is the easy part compared to creating the content. Saving the file incorrectly could give you big problems later.

■ **Go to the top and select "File / Save,"** which will bring up a pop-up window. Set these simple but important settings:

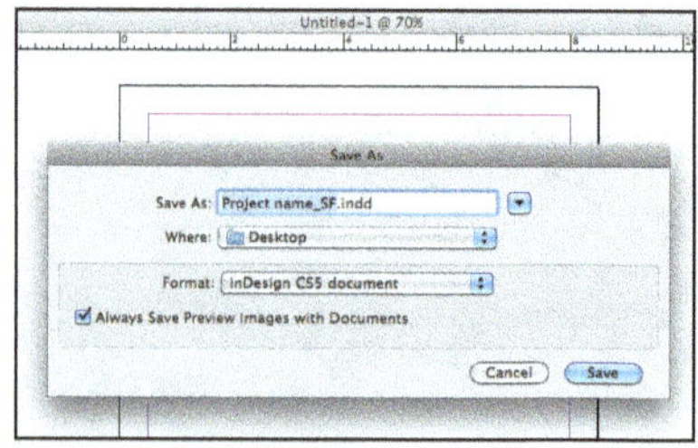

■ **Save As:** Give your project a name. I usually suggest keeping the name as short as possible (under 11 characters), because long names could be incomplete in many directory searches.

– **Follow the name by an underscore.** You can substitute the underscore for a space or other element if you like. I use the underscore because it helps separate some of the name, yet does not conflict with those using Windows computers or Web applications, that other symbols or key strokes do.

– **Next include your last name or initials.** Include this because often you will forget some of the file names. You most likely will not forget your name anytime soon. Now you stand a chance of finding the file later by doing searches for your initials or last name.

■ **Where:** The location is everything! Most locations are good as long as you remember what you have done. I suggest saving a document to your desktop or specific project folder.

TIP saving files »

Failure to save a file correctly can mean that it might not print or open later–potentially losing all the content.

– ***File extension:*** *Make sure your InDesign file name includes the ".indd" at the end. This tells the computer the type of file and is usually created automatically. Every software program creates a unique file extension.*

– ***Where:*** *Save the file to a location you can find–I would suggest to your desktop. Avoid saving a file to a thumbdrive! I have seen many files go bad that are worked on or saved directly to these small external drives.*

– ***Format:*** *Chose InDesign CS5 document (the default).*

Summary

I know that was a lot of new information about InDesign to comprehend, but remember I have taught hundreds of students, many of whom had never used any computer software except a Word program. In the upcoming lessons I have simplified the design theories and InDesign tools to help you learn faster and get confident quicker.

I hope that when we complete the upcoming lessons you will become another one of those persons who tells me how good they have become.

Trust me, you will soon be bragging about things you are creating that you never thought possible.

DESIGNING with basic shapes

"**Good design** is when you take the complicated and make it simple."

Some say that good graphic design is when you arrange things so they feel right . . . that's a little bit true.

Others have said you have to be creative to make something designed well . . . this again is partly correct.

A few state that good design is just when it works . . . and that has some validity.

Some of my academic colleagues have said that good graphic design is when you combine text and visuals into a simple message that effectively communicates to an audience . . . and that is true.

The truth is that excellent graphic design is all of these and much more, but becomes much less.

It is the convergence of the written word and visuals using many basic tools and principles to create a powerful simple message.

When you have created an excellent design you will become invisible and the audience will not talk about your design, but rather what you have said. In the coming pages you will be introduced to some of these simple basic tools and principles.

Design elements

Your notes

Basics do not have to mean simple

What I am referring to is that there are basic elements and tools that are used in design. These basics are not only used by those learning to communicate, but are part of the most sopisticated and polished communication projects. These elements are the basic building blocks of graphic design, publication design, web design, and many other forms of design in other disciplines and media.

I have seen many designs that at first glance appear brilliant, but then something seems to bother you. Upon closer examination you will usually find one of the basic elements or tools was either neglected or used poorly. The result is communication that is not clear, or worse, destroyed because of the lack of understanding the basics.

What are the basic designer tools?

You may think I am refering to my computer mouse, ruler, or drawing pencil. Well, the basics go far beyond the physical tools. Many of these are going to be familiar to you, but do not discount their use and power. Many of these basics you will find as tools in InDesign. Just remember, it is the understanding, use, and manipulation of these basics that will make it possible to create effective communication.

Point

Often the smallest of the elements are sometimes overlooked. You have spent many years in elementary school learning that the simplest use of this tool appears as a dot at the end of a sentence and means "stop." But put a point in the hands of a designer, and you will see many more uses of this simple element.

Some designer uses:

– **A larger version at the beginning of text becomes a bullet** and means "stop and look" and brings emphasis to the content.

– **A series of points** means something else . . . continuation.

– **Points are not always graphical.** They can become the optical center of a design, serving to bring emphasis and movement to the design.

Your notes

Line

I learned in the early 1980s, with my first Apple computer's dot matrix printer, that a series of dots becomes a line. While you are very familiar with this element, have you considered all the lines' different forms and how they might function in graphic design? Common types include: dashed, wavy, dotted lines.

Some designer uses:

– **A free form line** can create a path or movement

– **Horizontal or vertical lines** can help seperate elements

– **Lines with arrows** can connect content

Invisible lines

What do I mean by this? Well, let me use a highway sign to break down the lines into three basic types to illustrate this concept.

Contour lines

Visible or invisible lines. In this case lines that create a shape or container.

Index lines

Invisible line
In this case creates a distinctive line of sight. You will look ahead in direction.

Graphic lines

Visible lines. In this case they create a symbol that indicates a turn ahead.

Frame

Artists understand that if you put several lines together you can make a frame that sets apart the content from its environment. However, I caution you to use restraint when using this tool at first, because I often see beginning designers framing all the content. What this does is emphasizes everything and often the result is that nothing is emphasize.

Some designer uses:

– **A dashed frame** is a symbol to many consumers to clip out the information.

– **A frame can be white space** which is often used in advertising to set the content physically apart from competing advertisments.

Shape

This is commonly understood as the outline of an object that is tangible or invisible. Our knowledge of shapes comes from our youth when we were given a coloring book and given strict instructions to put color only within the shapes (lines). What you need to know is that shape is much more. Some shapes have significant power in designs that must be controlled.

Some designer uses:

– **Geometric shapes** like circles, squares, rectangles and triangles are very recognizable, thus, they have a lot of power. Be careful when using perfect circles and squares, because often the shape can overpower the content or design. You have heard of the power of the triangle–it is true!

– **Irregular shapes** like polygons and organic shapes can act as frames for content and convey meaning with the symbolism of the shape itself.

nulpa adi berem enima pernatquam volo blaudig endelic temoditium, consectotam, sequatq uidenis non nem dolorpos dolesequam sus, quam ium amus dolendi tiatem dolorest volor ad et laut ut dolo bea si cusa doleni as exped que et, num fugiaeris ea nus volupiet repudae volor atur? Qui odis porpos autatia il illit facearum harum ditiust, solorer umquatustem necaecto corum natempores min consequide volorrum con con consequundit hario corem volupta netum incia dolupta-tem comnihi lignietur, tota nest parchil-lore aliqui te pellautem. Dit ipsus ero eat mo quo totatemqui aut excero cupientiur aborum volesseque

Tone

Tone is the relative lightness and darkness of an area, shape, line, text, or other element. When adding tone to a shape, it begins to add a dimension that reveals the width and depth. When adding tone to the apple outline, it now has a surface. Adding tone often adds more emphasis.

Texture

This element reveals yet another dimension to the design. It is like tone, but often more descriptive and simulates the sensation of feeling to a one-dimension element. Using the apple shape again:

– **A bumping, course texture** added to the apple denotes an apple that may be less than perfect and thought to be lacking in appeal.

– **A shiny texture** (like the wax-coated expensive ones found in your grocery store) donotes a smooth, slick surface of a prized, good-tasting apple.

Color

One of the most powerful tools at the designer's disposal, but often the most misused. One important use for color in a design is to add information. Here is an example of how color adds information:

Using green tells you it might be a spring sour apple.

Using red indicates a sweet-tasting apple.

Using yellow indicates another type of apple.

Using brown will refer to an apple that is going bad!

Some designer uses:

– **Mood** can be created when specific color combinations are used.

– **Symbolism** is an important tool, and using colors that are associated with specific cultural icons or elements can invoke additional meanings.

To learn more about **color uses** */ Chapter 5*

Proportion / size

We are referring to the size relationship of different elements. This will be an easy tool for those beginning, because most have understood this concept since their early childhood when often the biggest package at the birthday party was the coveted attraction.

Some designer uses:

– **Hierarchy** can be created with the use of smaller to larger objects.

– **Contrast** is created simply by creating one significantly larger element next to small content.

Movement

One big mistake that beginners make is that they have little or no movement in their design–the viewer looks at the design for a short period and leaves. A good design will create movement from one element to another, thus increasing the time the viewer spends with the content. The result will be a stronger message.

Some designer uses:

– **Graphical lines** or index lines can help a design create visual eye movement.

– **Color** can help create movement by using bright vs. dull colors or little color vs. a lot of color.

You will discover that all the designer tools can help create movement in design if used properly.

Your notes

Beyond the basics

InDesign is more than meets the eye

By now you most likely are thinking, "Lets forget the basics and get to the good stuff." But really learning to use the basic tools and understanding the initial design concepts will take you much further than you might think. Most people seldom use InDesign's basic tools to their fullest potential. Instead, they are content designing projects using common rectangular text boxes and rectangle image containers.

InDesign, the creative tool

While InDesign was created to be a powerful desktop publishing program capable of producing high-quality magazines, newspapers, and books, it also can become a creative tool.

In 1984 I was using my first Apple computer (called Lisa) with its great 5-inch B&W screen, a new attachment called a mouse, and the Mac Paint program. This first Mac program came with just a few tools that enabled me to make a line, rectangle, and circle. While this may seem limiting to you, I was just happy I could make something more than a line of type. During the months, I experimented with these basic tools and discovered hundreds of things I could create. I learned to look at objects and designs as basic shapes to discover their origins and simplicity.

This illustration demonstrates what you can create in 30 minutes using InDesign basic shapes.

Summary

Most of the basic design tools covered in this chapter (point, line, frame, shape, tone, texture, color, proportion, and movement) were things you most likely have come across before, but now I will challenge you to learn to use them in expanded ways.

You are about to begin the first lesson, which will require you to locate and use most of the basic InDesign tools. I know this will seem intimidating and fustrating at times, but I have included illustrated instructions to help. Remember, like you, I still get nervous learning a new program. Just take a deep breath and know it will get easier . . . let's begin!

DESIGNING with basic shapes

LESSON A . . .

What InDesign skills will you learn?

- Methods to create many different types of lines
- How to create basic shapes (circles, squares)
- Working with fills, strokes, and simple type
- Skills to create illustrations using basic shapes
- Creating more complex shapes using the Pen Tool

SCOTT FARRAND

DESIGN & in DESIGN

Designing with Basic Shapes

Overview

One of the most effective tools of a visual communicator is the symbol. They often can overcome cultural, age, gender, and language differences. Many symbols can be created with basic shapes and tools–circles, rectangles, triangles, lines. This assignment is designed to introduce you to the basic tools of InDesign.

Lines

Create these types of lines as seen:

■ The last line should align with the bottom of the vertical rule seen at right.

■ Each line should be .125 inch from the verticle rule on the template, created 1.85 inches long and spaced 0.25 inch apart.

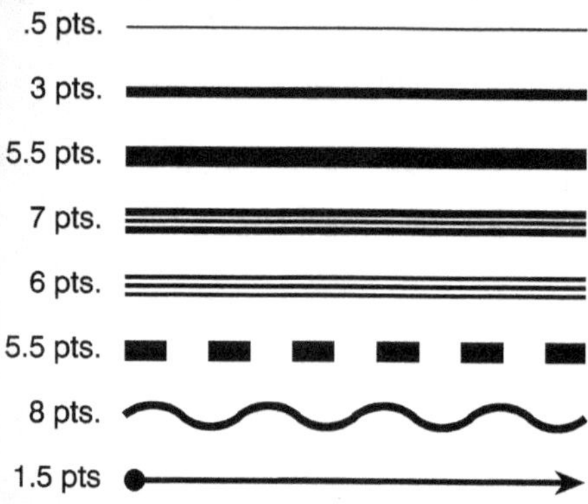

Rectangles

Create a rectangle with a width of 2.32 inches and a height of 1.5 inches.

■ Box placement: Visually place it in the position shown.

■ Finally, give the rectangle a fill of 15% black and a 1.8 pts.stroke (frame).

Circle

Create a perfect circle that is 1.5 inches wide.

■ The center of the circle should be placed at these coordinates: X= 7" and Y= 4.38."

■ Give the circle a fill of none and a 1 pt. stroke (frame).

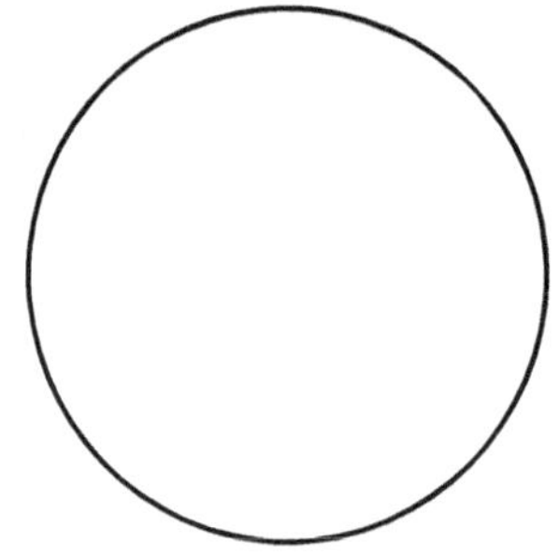

Triangle

Create a triangle width: 1.8" by height: 1.8"

■ The placement should be as shown (0.5 inch from the bottom horizontal rule on template and 0.15 inch from the vertical rule).

■ Finally, give the triangle a fill of 11% black and a 5 pts. frame of 50% black.

Creating an illustration

Within this 4-inch square, recreate one of the illustrations shown to the left, using only basic shapes (rectangles, circles, triangles, and lines).

NOTE: Match proportional sizes and tones to create an exact duplicate of illustration.

Assessment criteria

■ Do all the elements match the requirements?

■ Is the illustration an exact match of the smaller version?

Your Name

Type

Create your first and last name. Place it as shown (be accurate).

■ Use 33 pts., Times type, adjust tracking, and kern letters (make it look good).

Instructions Designing with Basic Shapes

Locating lesson template

For this lesson you will be using a precreated InDesign template named "Design Shapes_A template." I have created this template to give you a head start so you can complete the lesson quicker and easier.

More info »

To obtain the template / See "Partnership with the author."

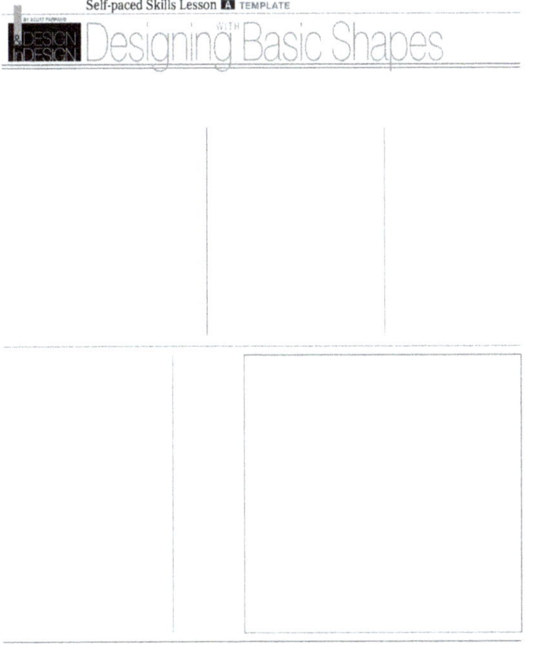

Getting started

Remember, you might find yourself confused and fustrated at some point during this lesson. This process is perfectly normal learning a new computer program. So just take a few deep breaths and continue on–it will get much easier and make more sense the further you progress. The result will be an empowered visual communicator – you.

Found the template!

Before you get started, make sure the InDesign template file is located on your computer desktop.

■ **NOTE: If transferring the file using a thumb drive,** make sure you dragged a copy to your computer desktop first. Never open and work on a file that is located on your thumb drive. Failure to remember this could result in a file that goes bad and will not open later.

Next, highlight the word "template" and replace it with your last name. This will ensure you are always working on your copy and can find the file later if needed.

Open file

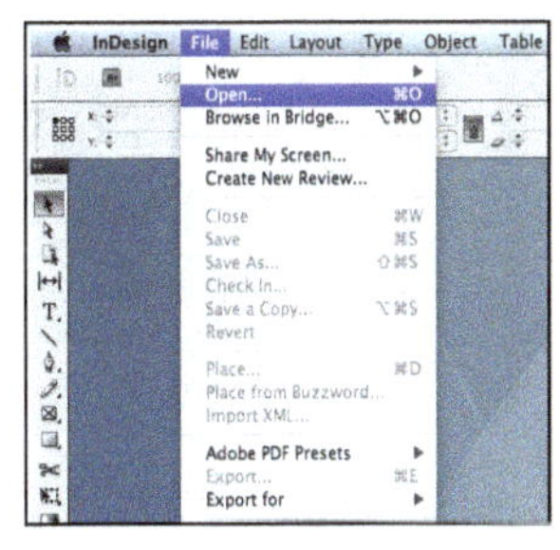

1. Launch your InDesign program (double-click icon if using a an Apple computer).

2. Go to top pull-down tabs and select "File / Open" and locate your lesson template on your desktop.

Creating the lines

1. Use guides to help: The instructions ask for eight lines to be created in the first column and the last line should be aligned with bottom of the vertical rule. The easiest way to do this is to create guides.

– **Go to the tool bar** and click on the top tool "Selection Tool."

– **Place your mouse arrow within the rulers** at the top of the document. Now click / hold and drag the guide until it aligns with the bottom of the vertical rule. Now you have determined the placement of one of the lines.

TIP using guides »

Guides are lines that help you align objects. These lines are only visible to you and will not appear when printing.

– ***Location:*** *In the document rulers.*

– ***Access:*** *Using the "Selection Tool" click / hold in the middle of the ruler and drag to the preferred location.*

– ***Changes:*** *To hide guides, lock guides, or snap to guides, go to the "Control Strip." Using the pull-down menus, select "View / Grids & Guides" to make changes.*

– ***Delete:*** *Using the "Selecton Tool," click / hold and drag back to ruler or click on guide and hit the "delete" key (this will not work if guides are locked).*

2. Create another guide: Next, the instructions indicate all the lines should align .125 inch from the vertical rule on the template. We could use the rulers to determine this location . . . but my math has been questionable at times, so I often use a simple method.

– **Select the "Rectangle Tool"** in the tool bar. Click and drag using this tool anywhere on the page and create a box that is .125 inch wide. If you have trouble getting the exact width, go to the "Control Strip" (at the top) and enter .125 in the "W" box (width).

– Now click (on a side of the box, not the handles) and

Your notes

SAVE

*– **Reminder:** All you have to do is lose all your work once because of a software glitch, power interruption, or any other unforeseen disaster, and you will know how important it is to save your work. Since you are new to design, I will remind you occasionally as you proceed along the lessons.*

Methods:

– "File" / "Save"

– Keyboard "command," "S"

Your notes

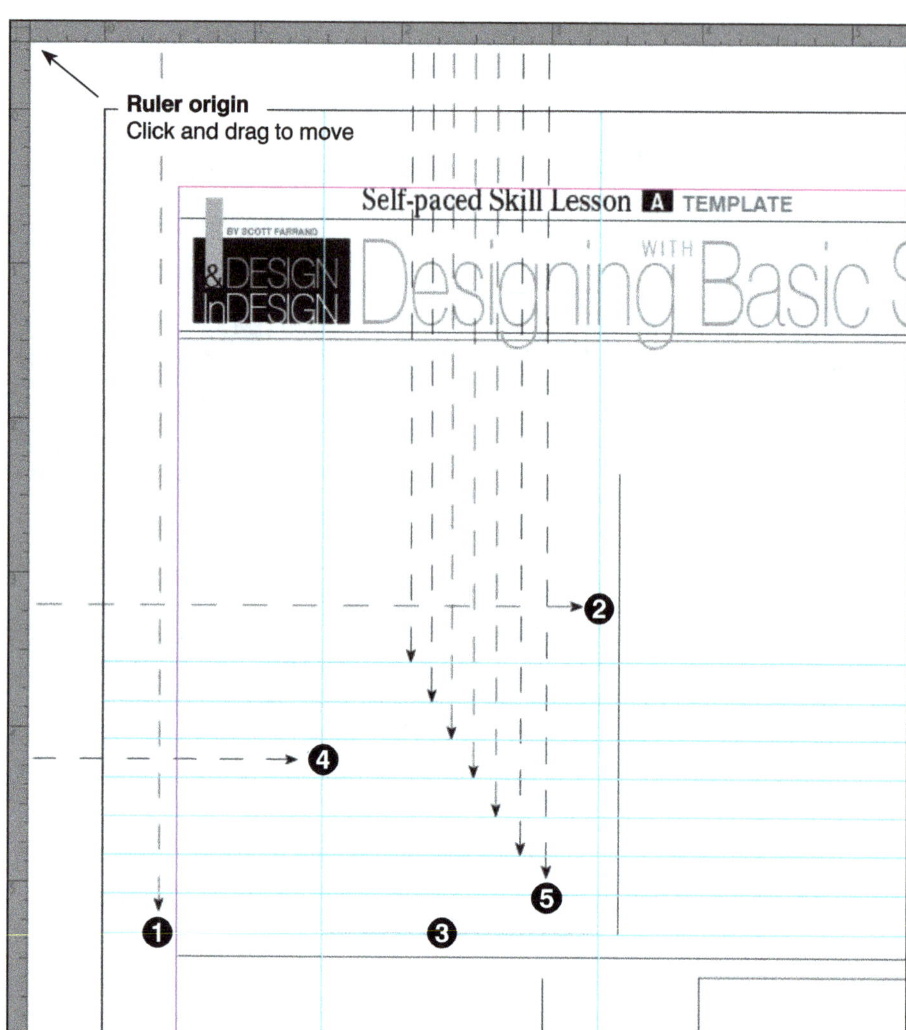

created.

– **Hold the "Shift" key** while creating the line to ensure you make a straight line.

– **Make the line 1.85 inches wide** by dragging until you get the desired length (indicated as you drag in the box that appears). A simple way to get an exact size is to create a line (any length) and then go to the "Control Strip" and locate the "Line Length" box and type in the desired size.

4. Create another guide: To ensure all your lines are the correct length, lets create another guide that aligns with the left side of the line. Remember, use the "Selection Tool," click, and drag within the left ruler to create the guide.

5. Space lines evenly: The instructions indicate each line should be .25 inch from each other. To do this accurately, you will need to create more guides.

– **Move ruler origin:** To do this easily, we will move the ruler measurements. This is done by moving the "0" origin from its current location with zero at the corner of the document. Using your "Selection Tool," put your arrow in the upper left-hand corner, where both rulers meet. Now click and drag the ruler "0" point to the left end point of the first line created. Now you can easily see .25" increments in the ruler that reflect your line.

– **Go to the top ruler and drag a guide** and place it .25 inch above the first line (when doing this you will see your guide location indicated in the ruler to the left. Now create six more guides (one for each line).

– **Return ruler origin:** When all guides are created, you will need to move the ruler origin back to the corner of the document. Place your selection arrow back at the "0" origin (corner where both arrows meet) and click and drag to the corner of the document.

6. Creating the lines: With the line locations identified, it is now time to create all the different lines.

– Click on the line tool and move your mouse to the intersection of two of the guides. Now click and drag to create a line to extend to the other guide.

NOTE: Holding the "Shift" key while creating a line makes a perfect staight line!

7. Creating the correct type lines: With the line select-

drag the box so one side aligns with the vertical line on the template.

– **Using the "Selection Tool," click within the rulers** to the left and drag another guide and align it with the left side of the box you placed on the template. Now you know how wide to extend the lines! When the guide is correctly in place, click on the box and delete (using delete key).

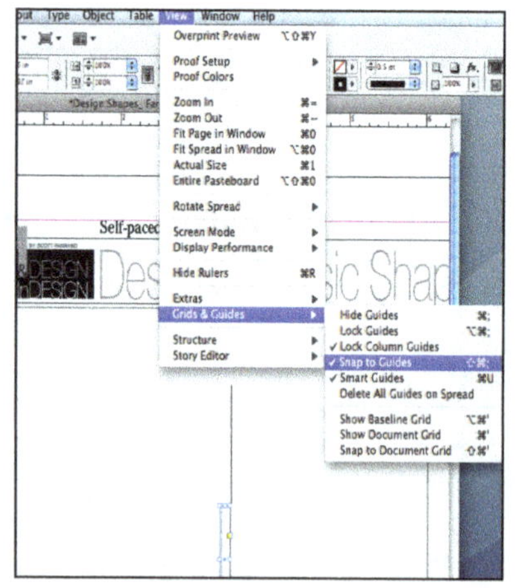

■ **Note: "Snap to Guide."** You will notice that whenever you are close to an edge or line, InDesign assumes you want to align that object and will snap to the point. This is because of a feature called "Snap to Guide."

You can turn this feature on or off by going to the pull-down tabs at the top and click on "View" / "Grids & Guides" / "Snap to Guides."

3. Create the first line: Click on the "Line Tool" from the "Tool Palette" and start your line by clicking and dragging from the intersection of the two guides you

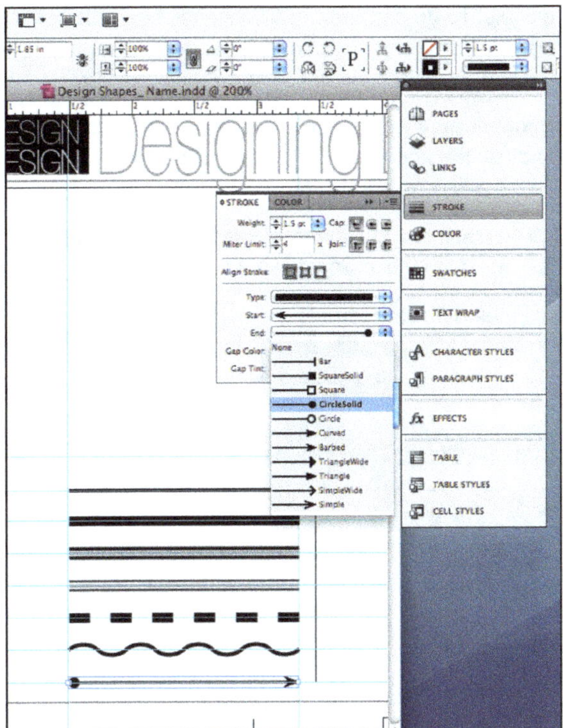

ed, go to the "Working Palettes" to the right and click on the "Stroke" palette. If you do not see this selection, go to the "Control Strip" at the top of the page and select "Window / Stroke."

– With the "Stroke" palette open, select the correct line weight (or just type the desired weight and hit the "Return" key on the keyboard).

– Next select the "Type" of line (solid, dashed, etc.)

– Select the correct "Start" and End" when creating an arrow.

8. More lines: Repeat the above process to create all the lines (Steps 6 & 7). Look closely at the size and the types of lines to create the correct ones.

Creating the rectangle

1. Select the "Rectangle Tool" from the "Tool" palette and go the top of the middle section of the template. Click and drag to create a rectangular shape.

2. Size: Click and drag on one of the corner handles of the rectangle to adjust the desired size. The size can be seen changing in the control strip.

NOTE: An easier way to get an exact size of an object is to type the size (width and height) in the "Control Strip."

3. Location: To get the rectangle in the correct location on the page, click on the rectangle's frame (not the handles) using the "Selection Tool" and drag it. Match

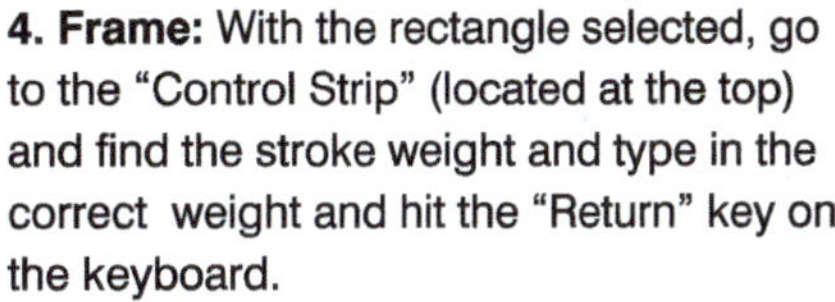

the position seen on the lesson sheet.

4. Frame: With the rectangle selected, go to the "Control Strip" (located at the top) and find the stroke weight and type in the correct weight and hit the "Return" key on the keyboard.

5. Fill tone: With the rectangle still selected, use the "Selection Tool," and double-click on the "Fill" box at the bottom of the "Tool Palette." The "Color Picker" palette will appear. Type 15% in the "K" box at the bottom and click on the "OK" button.

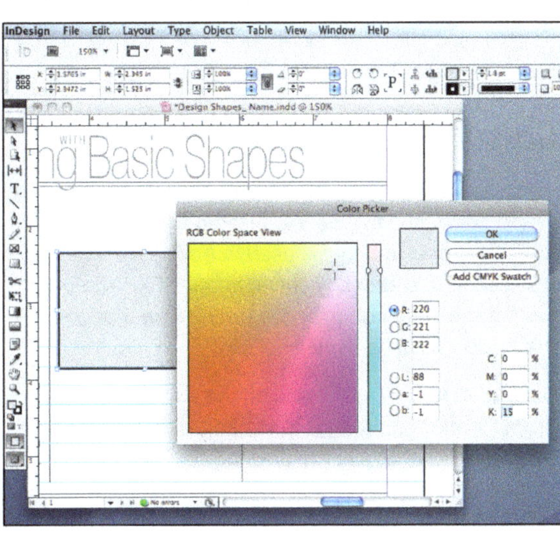

TIP fill & stroke »

Using these tools can modify the stroke and fill of anything created.

*– **Location:** Bottom of the "Tool palette."*

*– **Access:** Select an element, then double-click either the fill or the stroke tool and the "Color Picker" palette will appear.*

*– **Options:** Using the "Color Picker," you can move your mouse over the large color block and click to select a color. You can also move your mouse and click on any area of the color vertical bar to select a color. Finally, you can either type in the colors in any of the three color modes (we will be using print color C M Y K).*

Creating the circle

1. Select the "Ellipse Tool" from the tool palette. This tool is often not visible because it is one of the additional tools hidden by the "Rectangle Tool."

NOTE: Any tool that has a small black triangle next to the icon has additional tools hidden. Click and hold down on the mouse to discover the additional tools.

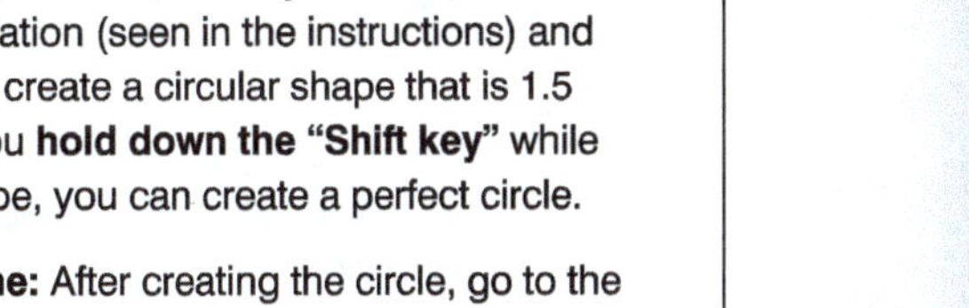

– **After selecting the tool, move your mouse** to the general circle location (seen in the instructions) and click and drag to create a circular shape that is 1.5 inches wide. If you **hold down the "Shift key"** while creating this shape, you can create a perfect circle.

2. Adding a frame: After creating the circle, go to the "Control Strip" and click on the "Stroke" and select 1 pt.

– Next, go to the "Tool Palette" and double-click the "Stroke" icon and set the color of the frame to K: 100%.

Your notes

Your notes

SAVE

– ***Reminder:*** *You may want to save your work.* ***Save often!***

3. Circle location: The instructions require that the circle be located at these cooridinates X: 7" and Y: 4.38."

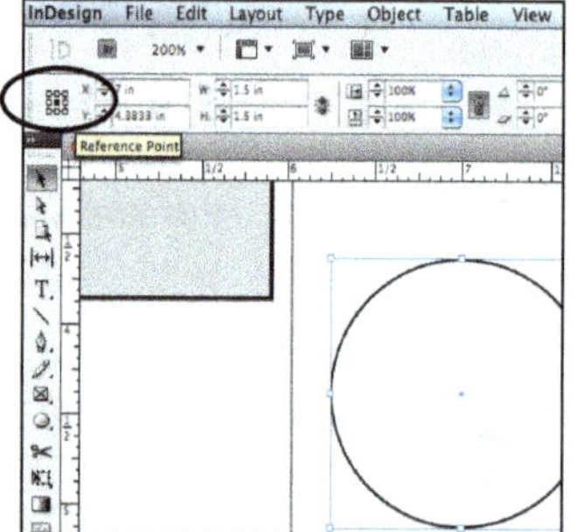

– With the circle still selected, you will need to **set the "Reference Point"** to the center. This is located in the "Control Strip" (far left).

– Using the "Selection Tool," click on the circle and set the **"X" and "Y" cooridinates in the "Control Strip"** located at the top. Remember after typing each setting to hit the "Return" key to set that amount.

Creating the triangle

1. To create this shape, you will be introduced to a new tool–**"Pen tool."** This a powerful tool that is used in Adobe Illustrator and Photoshop to create any shape imaginable. The tool can be simple or complex depending how it is used. For this lesson it will be kept simple.

SUGGESTION: Double-click on the stroke box in the "Tool Palette" and make the stroke black. This makes it easier to see what you are drawing.

2. Select the tool and move to the lower left-hand portion of the lesson page and click once at what will be the tip of the triangle **(position "A")** and let up. Now move your mouse to **position "B"** (another corner of the triangle) and click once and let up. Do the same to **position "C."** To end the shape, move and click on the starting point **(position "A").**

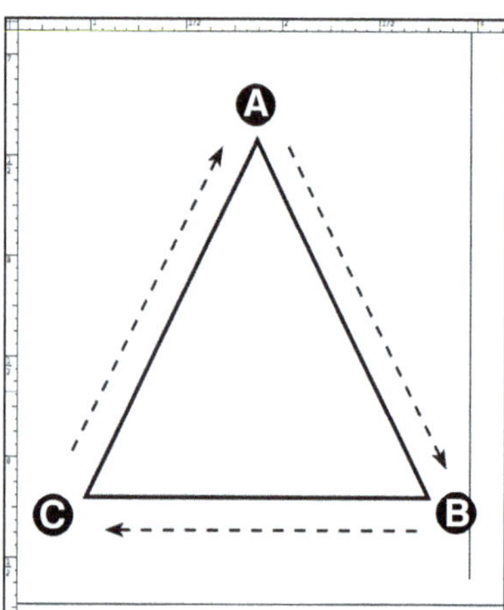

3. Edit shape: If you are like me, it is very likely the triangle shape is not perect with the first try. To adjust the shape, to make a perfectly symmetrical triangle, use the "Direct Select" tool in the "Tool Palette." Using this tool, click on any point (should turn white to allow editing) and drag to the preferred position.

4. Edit size: You can move the ruler origin and check the size. You also can click on one of the points with the "Direct Select" arrow and move a point while watching the measurement. But an easier way is to go to the "Control Strip" at the top and locate the width and height boxes and type in the required sizes.

5. Triangle location: The instructions indicate the triangle should be 0.5 inch from the bottom of the vertical rule. To do this, make a 0.5 inch tall box and align it with the bottom of the rule. Now move the triangle until it touches the top of the box, and it should be correct.

Suggestion: I would click on an edge of the triangle and use the arrow keys to move this element; often it is easier and quicker!

– **You will need to visually move** the triangle horizontally to match the lesson example (see lesson page).

6. Fill and stroke: Repeat the steps learned in the rectangle and the circle exercise to get the desired size, location, stroke, and fill for the triangle.

TIP zoom tool »

This tool enables you to magnify an area to see it better to perform many tasks . . . I use it often!

– ***Location:*** *In the tool palette.*

– ***Use:*** *Select the "Zoom Tool" and move your mouse over the area you are working on and click once. Click a second time to enlarge more!*

– ***Changes:*** *To reduce the view, hold down the "Option" key on the keyboard and click once.*

– ***In trouble:*** *If you clicked too much you might find yourself lost. A quick way to get back to normal is to go to the "Control Strip" and click on "View" / "Fit Page in Window."*

Creating an illustration

The object is to create an illustration with the tools that you have just learned. Pick one of the illustrations from the lesson and recreate it in the 4 inch box at the bottom of the page.

IMPORTANT: A portion of the lesson is also about learning to see. Can you reproduce the illustration EXACTLY as seen?

– **Pay attention to spacing, shading, and size of lines** and remember that you are enlarging the illustration over three times the size as the original seen (thus, lines must be thicker strokes to match).

■ **There are several more skills** that you will be introduced to in this exercise. All of the illustrations require you to know how to move elements to different layers. Often, you will create elements that you may want to move in front or back of other elements.

TIP working with layers »

This is an important feature of InDesign and allows you the ability to not have to worry about what order you create elements!

– ***What is it?*** *Everything created is on a individual layer based on when it was created.*

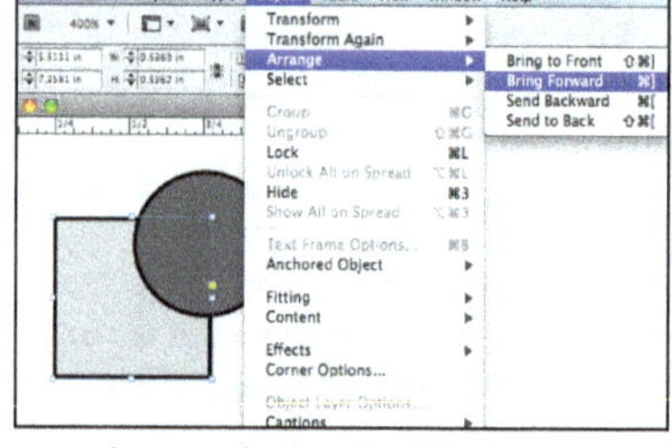

– ***Use:*** *To move elements, you simply have to select an element (using the "Selection Tool") and go to the "Control Strip" and select "Object" / "Arrange" / "Bring to Front" or select other choices.*

Creating the hourglass

This illustration uses the same basic shapes you previously have learned to make with the addition of an oval for the top.

1. Bottom & top: Create a rectangle and place it at the bottom. Try to size it correctly (as seen in illustration).

– **Rather than drawing another rectangle,** just duplicate the first rectangle. Go to top and select "Edit" / "Duplicate."

– **Align** this with the bottom rectangle, and use the arrow keys on your keyboard to move toward the top.

2. Sides: Create another rectangle that extends to the bottom and top rectangles. Notice it is the same thickness as the previously created rectangles. Duplicate this rectangle for the other side.

3. Center: You will see this is created using two triangles that are the same size.

– **Flip:** Select one of the triangles and go to the Control Strip at the top, and click on the "Flip Vertical" icon to flip your shape. Now just align the two triangles.

4. Top details: You will be creating an oval and circle and overlapping them as seen below.

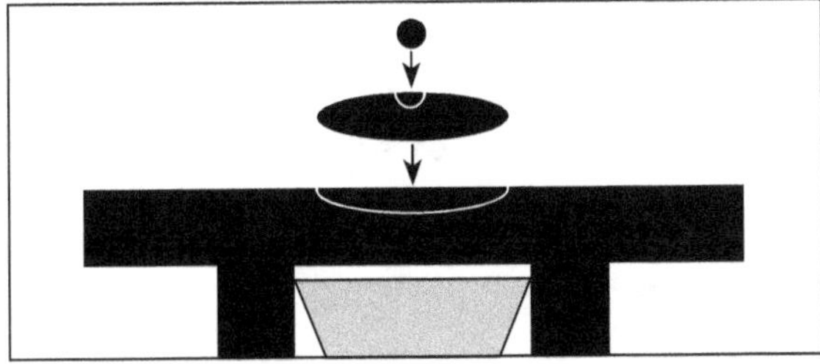

5. Edit work: Review spacing, sizes, and shading to make it match the illustration I have given you!

Creating the landscape

This illustration also uses the same basic shapes you previously have learned to make in this lesson. The only new technique comes when creating the moon.

1. Bottom: Create a rectangle, fill it with black, and place it at the bottom.

2. Mountains: These are made with different-sized triangles.

3. Background: You will need to create six lines and evenly space them. Now give each line a different stroke to match the illustration.

4. Moon: This is created with two same-size circles that are placed on top of each other (one moon is offset).

NOTE: To finish this illustration, you will need to select the outline box (supplied on template) and move it to the front to cover the white circle. To do this, go to the "Control Strip" and select "Object" / "Arrange" / "Bring to Front."

Creating the dog

Are you up for a challenge? This illustration is the hardest, but also the most fun. The good news is this illustration still uses basic shapes along with the pen tool, and I give you a lot of good instructions to help.

1. Head: This looks complicated, but it is made up of

Your notes

Your notes

one large oval with two small ovals for the dog's jaws on top.

2. Eyes: These consist of three different ovals for each eye. Create one eye then group elements and duplicate to make second eye.

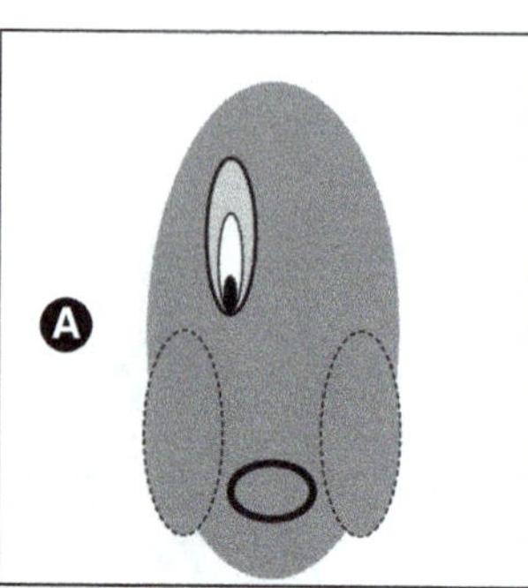

3. Mouth: First an oval is created with a thick stroke of black for the mouth (A).

– A rectangle is created and placed on top of a portion of the oval (B).

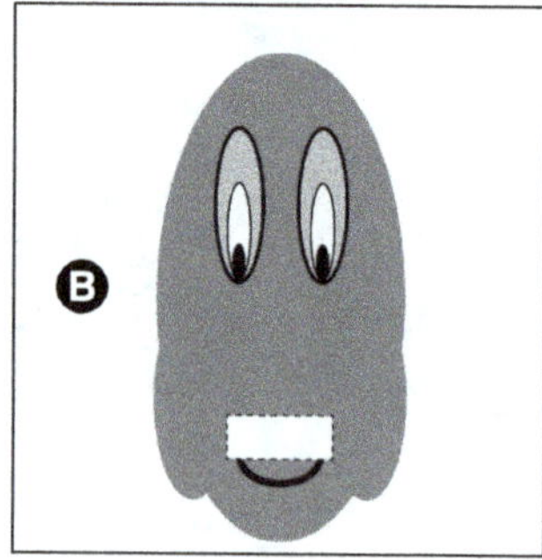

– Next, the oval is filled with the same tone as the background shapes to hide a portion of the oval to form the dogs mouth.

– To finish the mouth and nose a vertical line and another oval were added on top (C).

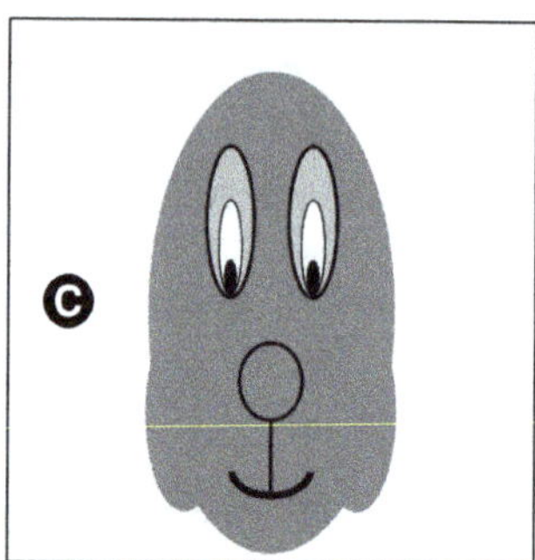

4. Dog ears: These are created by drawing an oval and overlapping with a triangle shape.

– Next these two **shapes are filled** with black and grouped together to form one shape.

5. Group dog ears: Use the "Selection Tool" and click on one shape and then holding down the **"Shift"** key, select the other shape.

– Now go to the top and select the "Object" drop-down tab at the top of the window and **select "Group."**

– Now the ear needs to be sent behind the dog's head to match the illustration. Using the "Selection Tool," click on the grouped shapes and go to the drop-down tabs at the top and select **"Object"** / **"Arrange"** / **"Send to Back."**

6. Duplicate ears: No need to draw another ear, just duplicate the shape. Select the ear using the "Selection Tool" and go to the "Edit" drop-down tab and select "Duplicate."

7. Flip ear: With the ear duplicated, it is now facing the wrong direction. Click on the ear using the "Selection-Tool," and go to the **"Control Strip" and select "Flip Horizontal."**

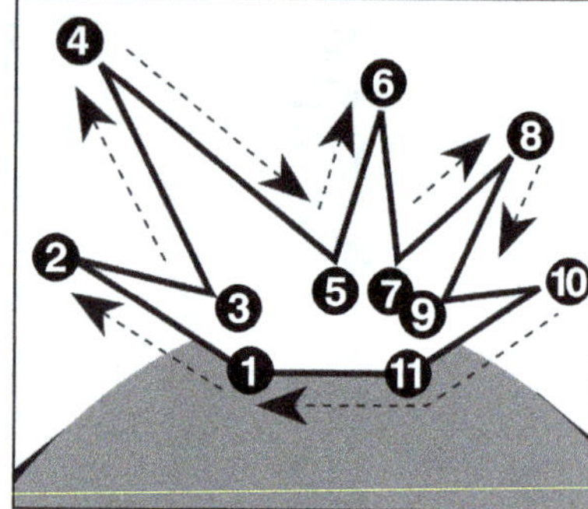

8. Dog hair: OK, the dog does not have much, but you still have to draw that tuft of hair at the top of his head! The secret is to use the "Pen Tool," much like the triangle, but with many more points.

– **Select the "Pen Tool,"** to create the irregular shape that makes the dog's hair.

– **Start by** clicking on one point, letting up, and then moving the mouse to the next point. Click and repeat the process until all points are created and you have clicked on the starting point.

– **Do not worry that the shape does not look perfect.** Select the "Direct Selection Tool" (white arrow key) and click on one of the points in the shape (the points will turn white). Now you can click and drag on any of the points to adjust the shape.

– **The final step** is to fill the shape with tone and using the "Selection Tool," move the shape into place.

– ***Reminder:***
You may want to save your work.

Always save before you print!

DESIGNING with basics

LESSON . . .

What InDesign skills will you learn?

- Draw types of lines
- How to create basic shapes (circles, squares)
- Working with fills
- Skills to create illustrations using basic shapes
- Ways to create shapes using the "Pen Tool"
- Creating placeholder text for designs

SCOTT FARRAND

DESIGN & in DESIGN

Designing WITH Basic Shapes

Overview

One of the most effective tools of a visual communicator is the symbol. Symbols often can overcome cultural, age, gender, and language differences. Many symbols can be created with basic shapes and tools–circles, rectangles, triangles and lines. This assignment is designed to introduce you to the basic tools of InDesign.

Text

Create a text box that is 1.75 inches square and is filled with placeholder text.

- Place 0.25 inch from first vertical rule on the template page. Type should also align with bottom of the vertical rule to the right.
- "Story to come" is 12 pt. Helvetica.

Story to come conest eatemporio quibus. Puditat aut et volorum erion pa corepratur sim ipsanimus quist que comnis ratur sit ea pra solum la sinihitat quis dolorporera nos resci nat et ventur ant oditatia que sum quibusd

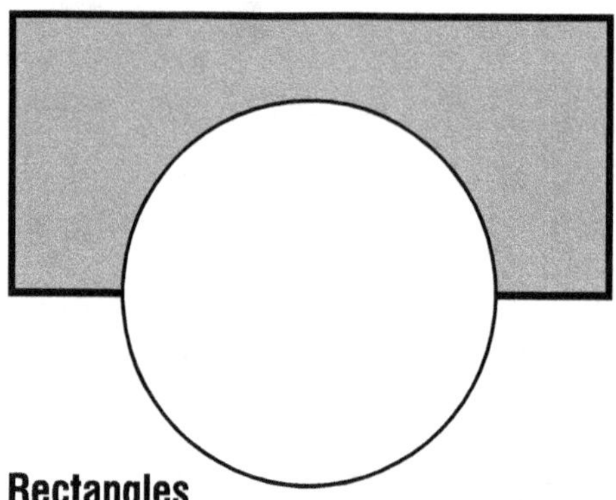

Rectangles

Create a rectangle with a width of 2.4 inches, height of 1.1 inches, stroke (frame) of 2 pts., and filled with 30% black.

- Create a circle with a 1.5 inch radius and has a 1 pt. stroke (frame).
- Placement: Visually position rectangle and circle as shown above.

Lines

Create these 5 types of lines:

- The last line should align with the bottom of the vertical rule to the left.
- Lines should be 0.16 inches from the verticle rule on the template, created 1.5 inches wide, and spaced 3/8 inches apart from each other.

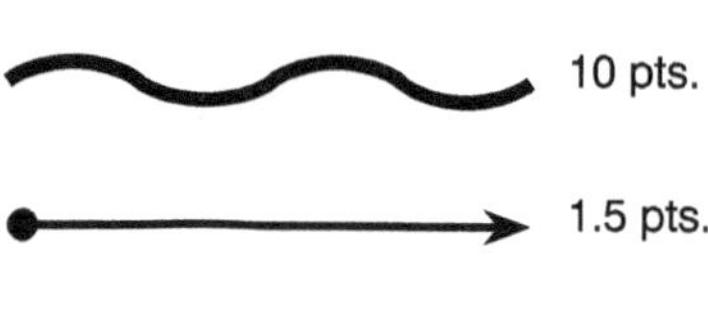

Arrow

This should be 1.3 inches wide and 2.25 inches tall.

- Give the arrow a 4 pt. frame that is 50% black and a fill of 15% black.
- The placement should be as shown.

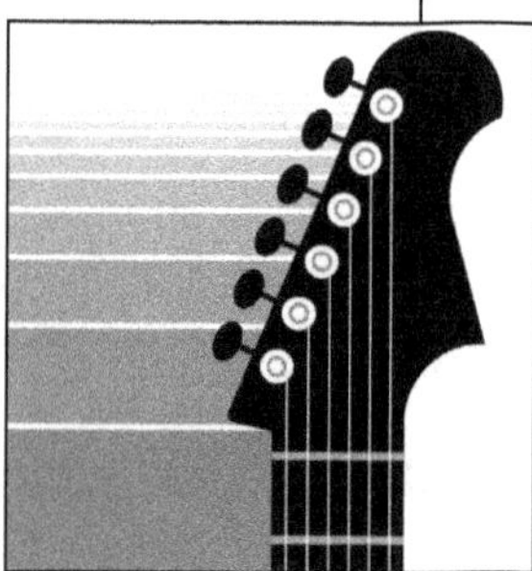

Creating an illustration

Within this 4 inch square, recreate one of the illustrations shown above, using basic shapes (rectangles, circles, triangles, lines, etc.).

NOTE: Match proportional sizes and tones to create an exact duplicate of illustration.

Assessment criteria

- Do all the elements match the requirements?
- Is the illustration an exact match of the smaller version?

YOUR NAME

Your name

- Create it as shown (be accurate) on top a 0.65 inch tall, 50% gray box.
- Use 42 pts. Arial type, adjust tracking (-40), and kern letters to look good.

Your notes

Locating lesson template

For this lesson, you will be using a precreated InDesign template named "Design Shapes_B template." I have created this template to give you a head start so you can complete the lesson quicker and easier.

More info »

To obtain the template / See "Partnership with the author."

Getting started

Remember, you might find yourself confused and fustrated at some point during this lesson. This is perfectly normal, learning a new computer program. Just take a few deep breaths and continue on. As you progress, InDesign will get much easier and make more sense. Eventually, you will be a powerful visual communicator.

Found the template!

Before you get started, make sure the InDesign template file is located on your computer desktop.

■ **NOTE: If transferring the file using a thumb drive,** make sure you dragged a copy to your computer desktop first. Never open and work on a file that is located on your thumb drive. Failure to remember this could result in a file that goes bad and will not open or print later.

Next, highlight the word "template" and replace it with your last name. This will ensure you are always working on your copy of the lesson and can find the file later if needed.

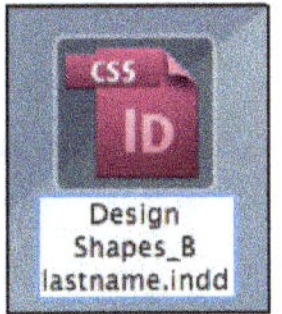

Open file

1. Launch your InDesign program (double-click icon if using a an Apple computer).

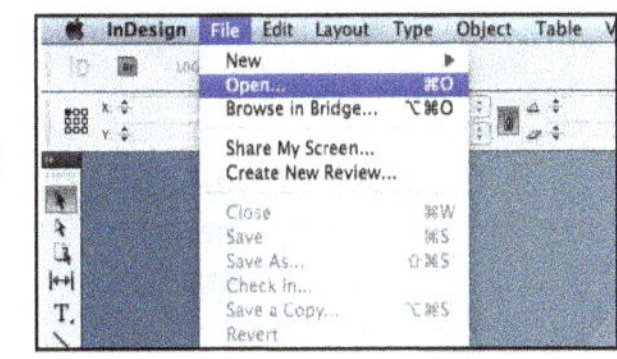

2. Go to top pull-down tabs and select "File" / "Open" and locate your lesson template on your computer desktop.

Creating the text

1. Creating the text box: Go to the "Tool Palette" and select the "Type Tool." Next, click and drag to create a text box in the upper left-hand corner of the template. Make it a medium-size square box for now (visually about 2–2.5 inches). If you created a text box, it will have a blinking line in the upper left corner.

Note: The blinking line indicates it is ready for you to type or insert text into the box.

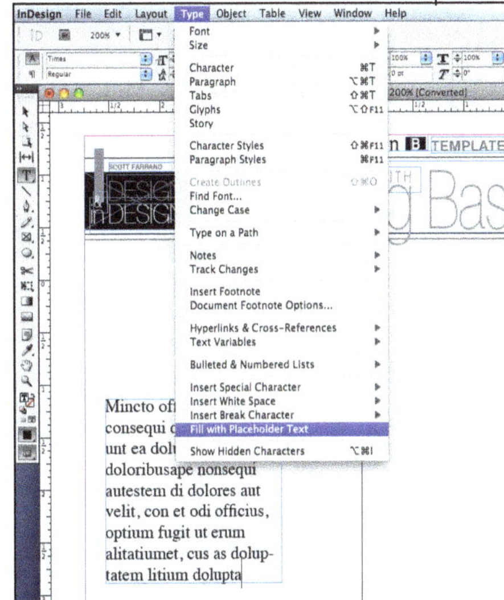

2. Placeholder text: Next go to the "Control Strip" at the top and select "Type" / "Fill with Placeholder Text."

TIP frame edges »

InDesign creates color frames around all content you create to help you place and align them within your design.

*– **Show or hide frames:** Usually the frames are viewable, but if they are not or if you want to turn them off to see your design more clearly, it is easy to change.*
Go to the "Control Strip," and select "View" / "Extras" / "Show Frame Edges."

3. Story to come: With your "Type Tool," highlight the first two words by clicking and dragging over them. Now type "Story to come."

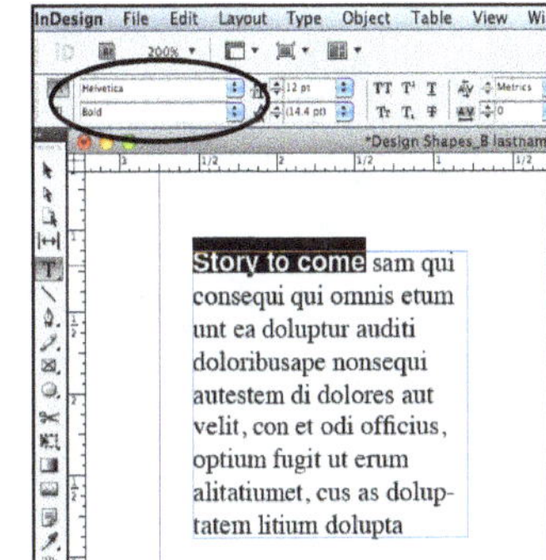

– **Next, using the "Type Tool"** again, highlight the words you just created and

Your notes

SAVE

– ***Reminder:*** *All you have to do is lose all your work once because of a software glitch, power interruption, or any other unforeseen disaster and you will know how important it is to save your work.*

Since you are new to design, I will remind you occasionally as you proceed along the lessons.

Methods:
– "File" / "Save"
– Keyboard "command" "S"

go to the "Control Strip" and click on the "Type" drop-down tab (blue tab) and change the typeface to "Helvetica Bold."

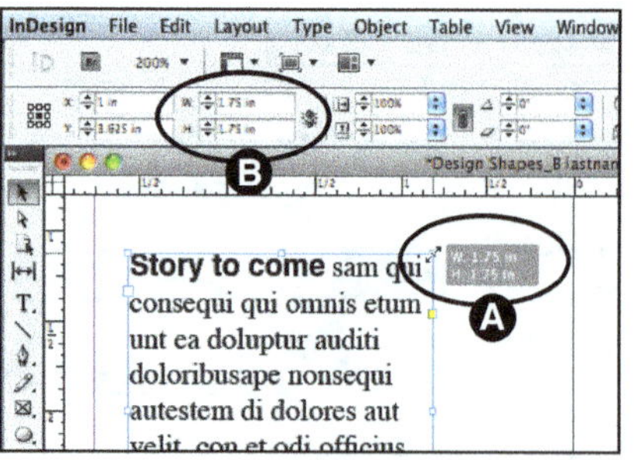

4. Size the text box: Using your mouse, go to the "Tool Palette" and click on the "Selection Tool." Next click on the frame of the text box and handles should appear (small white boxes at the corners and center edges).

– **Select the corner handles** and click and drag until the size is 1.75" X 1.75" (see A).

NOTE: With the box selected, you also can just type in the desired size using the control strip's width and height boxes (see B).

5. Move the text box into position: The instructions ask us to place the text 0.25 inch from first vertical rule on the template page. To be very accurate doing this, we are going to use the rulers and guides to help us align the text to its proper location.

NOTE: Make sure rulers are visible by going to the "Control Strip" at the top, and selecting "View" / "Show Rulers."

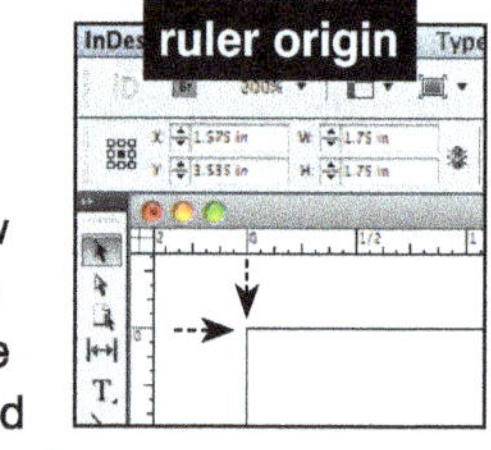

– **Move the ruler origin (zero point).** Normally, the ruler origins (zero) begin at the corner of the document. However, now we want to move them. Get the "Selection Tool" and click at the intersection of the horizontal and vertical rulers. From that point, click and drag to move the ruler origin so it aligns with the first vertical line on the template. We have moved the ruler starting point so we can easily measure .25 inch from that line

Move ruler origin

Guide

Guide

to determine the placement of our text box.

– **Create a guide** by using your "Selection Tool" and clicking and dragging anywhere in the middle section of the vertical ruler to .25 inch from the left of the vertical rule (or -.25). This is the left-hand edge we want our text box to align (C).

– **Create a second guide** by using your "Selection Tool" again and clicking and dragging anywhere in the middle section of the horizontal ruler and dragging the guide so it aligns with the bottom point of the vertical rule on the template (D).

ore info »
To learn more about ***using guides*** */ Pg. 25*

– **Move the text box** into postion by clicking (on any point except the handles) and dragging the text box so it is aligned with both guides .

Creating the rectangle

1. Select the "Rectangle Tool" from the "Tool" palette and go to the top of the middle section of the template and click and drag to create a rectangular shape.

2. Size: Click and drag on one of the corner handles of the rectangle to adjust to the desired size (2.4 inches wide and 1.1 inches in height). The size will be changing in the control strip (see E).

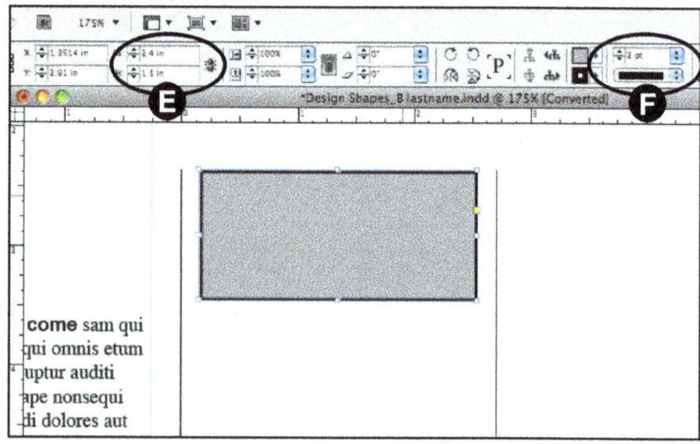

NOTE: An easier way to get an exact size of an object is to type the size (width and height) in the "Control Strip."

3. Location: To get the rectangle in the correct location on the page, click on the rectangle's frame (not the handles) using the "Selection Tool" (black arrow) and drag it. Match the position seen on the lesson sheet.

4. Frame: With the rectangle selected, go to the "Control Strip" (located at the top) and locate the stroke weight and stroke type boxes. Type in the correct weight (2 pts.) and hit the "Return" key on the keyboard (see F).

5. Fill tone: With the rectangle still selected (use the "Selection Tool"), double-click on the "Fill" box at the bottom of the "Tool Palette." The "Color Picker" palette will appear. Type 0% for the C, M, Y, and 30% in the "K" (black) box at the bottom and click

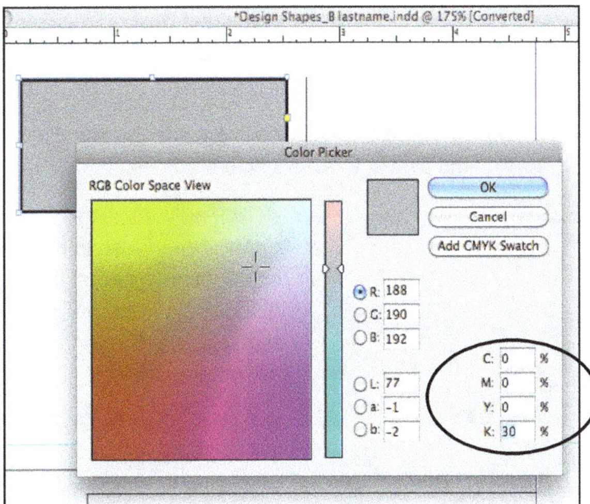

the "OK" button.

To learn more about the **fill and stroke** */ Pg. 27*

Creating the circle

1. Locate ellipse Tool: Find the "Rectangle Tool" in the "Tool Palette" and you will see a small black triangle in the lower right corner of that tool. This indicates there are more tools hidden here.

– Using your mouse, click and hold down on the "Rectangle Tool" and a drop-down palette will appear, which will enable you to select the "Ellipse Tool."

2. Make the circle: Using the "Ellipse Tool," click and drag on any open area of the template. Keep dragging until you have created a circle that is 1.5 inches deep and wide. You can see the size next to your mouse-pointer and in the "Control Strip."

NOTE: If you hold the shift key while using the "Ellipse Tool," you can make a perfect circle.

3. Give it a stroke and fill: With the circle still selected go to the top "Control Strip" and give the circle a frame of 1 pt. (much like you did on the rectangle).

– With the circle still selected, go to the "Fill and Stroke" tools in the "Tool Palette" and click on the "Fill." This will bring up the "Color Picker" palette. Locate the C, M, Y, K controls and type in 0% for each of the colors C, M, Y, & K, which will give you white.

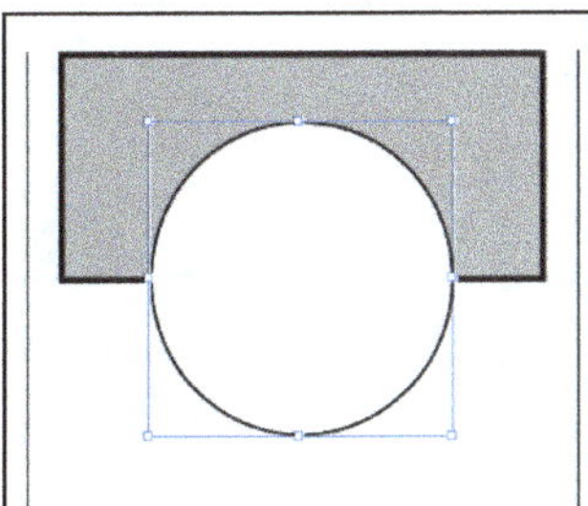

4. Placing the circle: The last step here is to move the circle created into position so it matches what is seen on the lesson page.

– Using the "Selection Tool," click on the frame (but not the handles) and drag the circle so that it is centered horizontally between the rectangle's bottom edge.

– Now make sure the circle's middle handles align with the rectangle's frame to properly center the circle vertically in relation to the rectangle.

Creating the lines

1. Use guides to help: The instructions ask for five lines to be created in the third column on the top of the template. The last line should be aligned with the bottom of the vertical rule. The easiest way to do this is to create a guide.

– **Good news!** You should already have a guide here from when you created the placeholder text (both vertical lines are aligned).

2. Create another guide: The instructions indicate all the lines should be aligned 0.16 inches from the vertical rule on the template. We could use the rulers to determine this location . . . but my math has been questionable at times, so I often use a simple method. I often will create a specific-sized shape to help me with placement and to create guide locations. I know this sounds difficult, but let me show you:

– **Select the "Rectangle Tool"** in the tool bar. Click and drag using this tool anywhere on the page and create a rectangle that is 0.16 inch wide. If you have trouble getting the exact width, go to the "Control Strip" (at the top) and enter 0.16 in the "W" box (width). Now give the rectangle a stroke of .25 pts. (makes alignment more accurate).

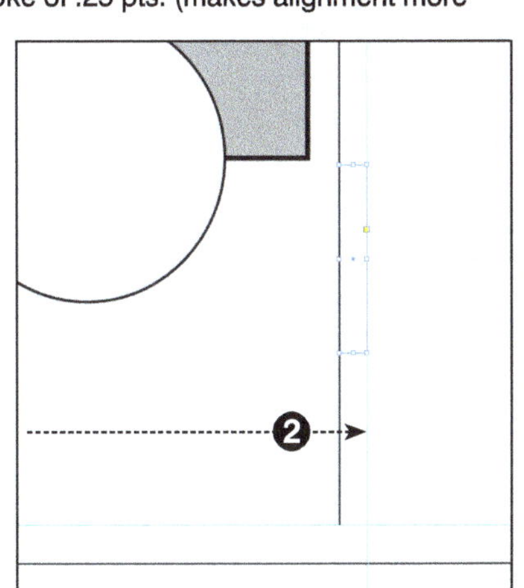

– Next, click (on a side of the box, not the handles) and drag the box so one side aligns with the vertical line on the template.

– Using the "Selection Tool," click within the rulers to the left and drag a guide and align it with the right side of the box you created. Now you have determined the left-hand starting for each of the lines! When the guide is correctly in place, click on the box and delete using the delete key.

3. Create the first line: Click on the "Line Tool" from the "Tool Palette" and start your line by clicking and dragging from the intersection of the two guides you created.

NOTE: Holding down the "Shift" key while creating the line will ensure you make a straight line.

– **Make the line 1.4 inches wide** by dragging until you get the desired length (indicated as you drag in the box that appears). A simple way to get an exact size is to create a line (any length) and then go to the "Control Strip" and locate the "Line Length" box and type in the desired size.

4. Create another guide: To ensure all your lines are the correct length, let's create another guide that aligns with the right side of the line. Remember, use the

Your notes

Your notes

"Selection Tool," click, and drag within the left ruler to create the guide.

5. Space lines evenly: The instructions indicate each line should be 3/8 inch apart from each other. To do this accurately, you will need to create more guides.

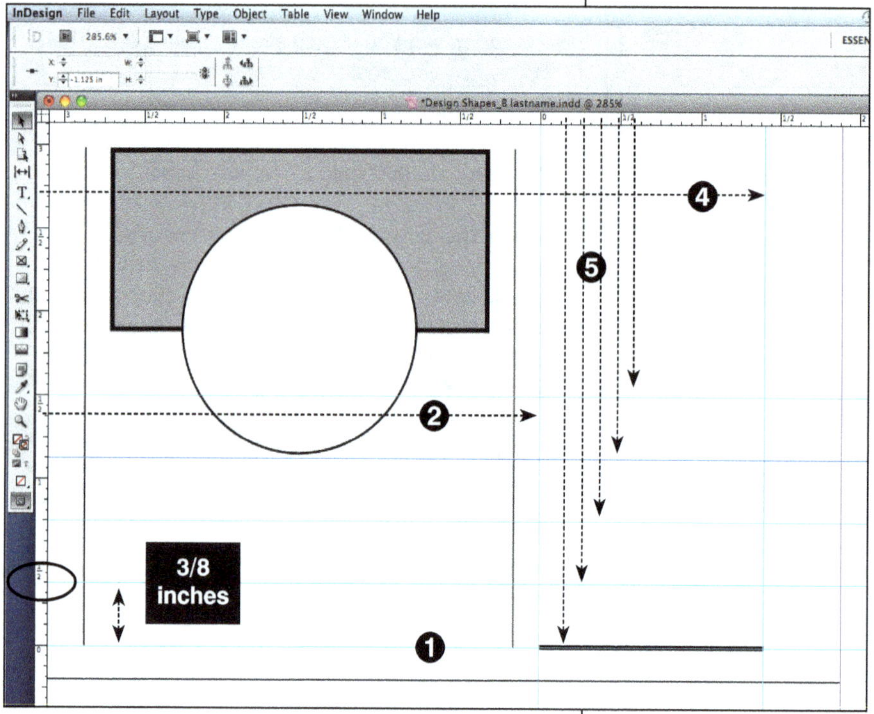

3/8 inches

– **Move ruler origin:** To make measurement easier and accurate, we will move the ruler measurements. This is done by moving the "0" origin form its current location with zero at the corner of the document.

– Using your "Selection Tool," put your arrow in the upper left-hand corner where both rulers meet. Now click and drag the ruler's "0" point to the left end point of the first line created. Now you can easily see 3/8 inch increments in the ruler that reflect your line.

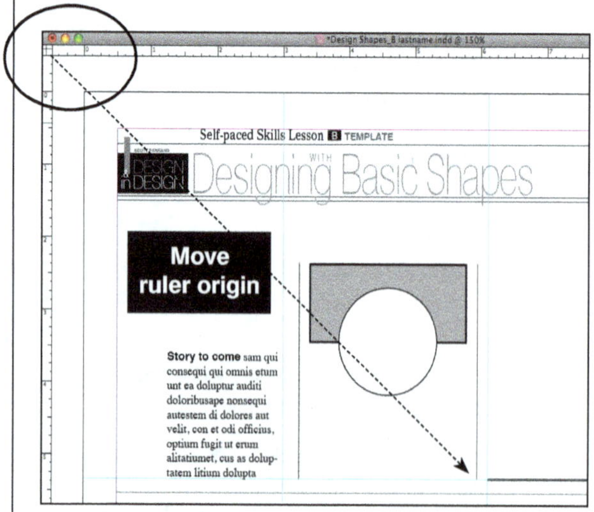

Move ruler origin

– **Go to the top ruler and drag a guide** and place it 3/8 inch above the first line (when doing this you will see your guide location indicated in the ruler to the left. Now create three more guides, one for each line.

– When all guides are created, you will need to move the ruler origin back to the corner of the document.

Place your selection arrow back at the "0" origin (corner where both arrows meet) and click and drag to the corner of the document.

6. Creating the lines: With the line locations identified, it is now time to create all the different lines.

– Click on the line tool and move your mouse to the intersection of two of the guides. Click and drag to create a line to extend to the other guide.

■ **Note: "Snap to Guide."** You will notice that whenever you are close to an edge or line, InDesign assumes you want to align that object and will snap to the point. This is because of a feature called "Snap to Guide."

– You can turn this feature on or off by going to the pull-down tabs at the top and clicking on "View" / "Grids & Guides" / "Snap to Guides."

7. Creating the correct type lines: With the line selected, go to the "Working Palettes" to the right and click on the "Stroke" palette. If you do not see this selection, go to the "Control Strip" at the top of the page and select "Window" / "Stroke."

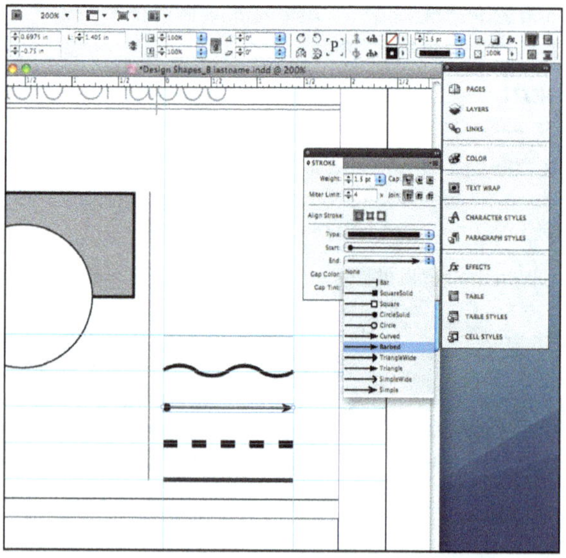

– With the "Stroke" palette open, select the correct line weight (or just type the desired weight and hit the "Return" key on the keyboard).

– Next, select the "Type" of line (solid, dashed, etc.)

– Select the correct "Start" and "End" when creating the line with arrow.

8. More lines: Repeat the above process to create all the lines (steps 6 & 7). Look closely at the size and the types of lines to create the correct ones.

Creating the triangle

To create this shape, you will be introduced to a new tool – **"Pen Tool."** This powerful tool is used in Adobe Illustrator and Photoshop to create any shape imaginable. The tool can be simple or complex depending on how it is used–for this lesson it will be kept simple.

NOTE: It will be much easier to use the "Zoom Tool" (magnifying glass) and enlarge the view to be more accurate when working with the shapes, guides, and using the pen tool.

To learn more about the **Zoom Tool** */ Pg. 28*

1. Creating guide shapes: To make drawing the shape easier, let's create some guides using basic shapes.

– **Create a rectangle** 1.3 inches wide by 2.25 inches tall with a stroke of 0.5 pts (same dimensions of finished arrow). Place the rectangle in the lower left corner of the template. The arrow will be moved to the correct location later.

– If you were to measure the bottom of the triangle, you would discover it is a square that measures 0.49 inch. **Make a 0.49 inch square** with a stoke of 0.5 pts. and center it at the bottom of the rectangle.

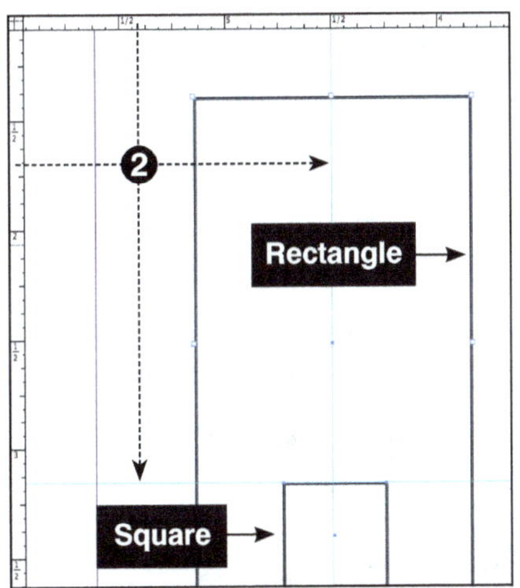

2. Creating ruler guides: Using the "Selection Tool," click on the rectangle created and go to the left-hand rulers. Click in the middle and drag a guide and align it so it runs through the center of the rectangle. This will be the position of the arrow point later.

– Select the square and go to the top rulers and drag a guide so it is aligned with the top of the square. This will become the arrow points later.

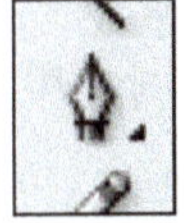

3. Setting up the "Pen Tool." Now the easy part of drawing the arrow, using the "Pen Tool." We will be using the tool much like the early childhood games of dot-to-dot drawing.

– **Set, fill, and stroke:** First select the "Pen Tool" from the "Tool Palette." Next, go to the top "Control Strip" and select "Windows" / "Color" / "Swatches," where you will also find the "Fill" and "Stroke" tools.

– **Click on the "Stroke"** and make it black by clicking on the black square.

– **Click on the "Fill"** and make no color by clicking on the white square with the red diagonal line. Now when you use the pen you will get a line, but no fill. This makes it easier to create the arrow shape.

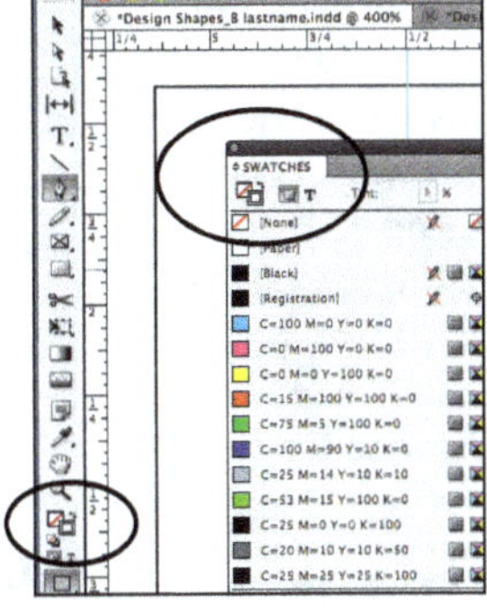

4. Drawing the arrow: Select the "Pen Tool" and move to the top of the rectangle, where the guide intersects with the middle of the shape. **Click once and release** at what will be the tip of the triangle **(position "A")**.

– Now move your mouse to **position "B"** (another corner of the triangle) and click and release.

– Now move your mouse to **position "C"** and click and release.

– Do the same to all the other positions shown below. To finish the arrow, end by moving and clicking on the starting point **(position "A")**.

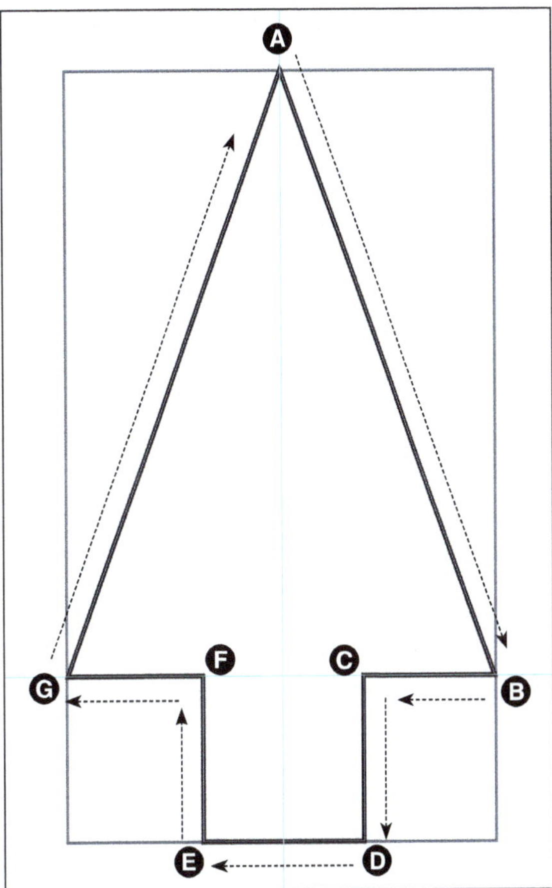

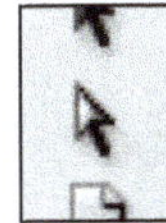

3. Edit shape: If you are like me, it is very likely the triangle is not perfect with the first try. To adjust the shape, use the "Direct Select Tool" in the "Tool Palette." Use this tool to click on any point (not the line), which should turn it white to allow editing. Click on the point and drag to the preferred position.

4. Adjusting arrow points: You most likely have discovered your arrow points do not match the lesson's. This is easy to adjust.

– **Using the "Direct Selection Tool," click on one of**

Your notes

Your notes

the arrow's two lower points (make sure the handles turn white) and using your down arrow key on your keyboard, go down about nine times. Now do the same for the other side.

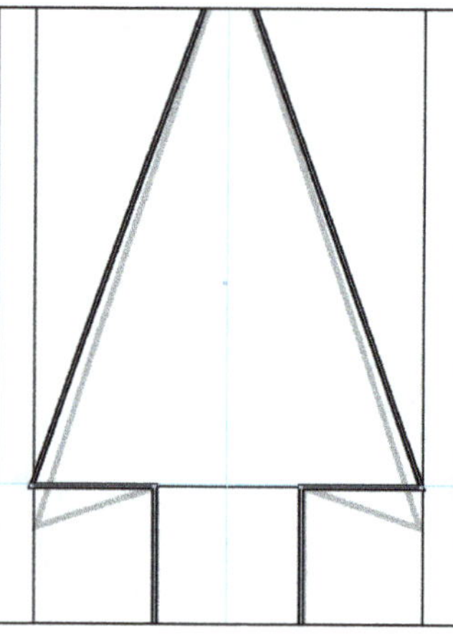

NOTE: I like this method because it is quick and I can move both sides the same amount easily.

– **Rather than using your arrow keys,** you could use your mouse and move the two bottom arrow points down visually. If doing this, I would suggest creating a guide to make sure both points are even when you are finished.

5. Delete guide shapes: Now that your arrow looks like the one on the lesson, you can delete the rectangle and square you created to act as a guide to drawing.

6. Check size: Using the "Direct Selection Tool," click on the arrow and check the size seen in the "Control Strip." If the size is off, select one of the appropriate handles and adjust the shape or . . . the easy way is to select the arrow and just type in the exact size in the appropriate width and height boxes in the "Control Strip."

SAVE

– Reminder: *You may want to save your work.* ***Save soon!***

7. Fill and stroke: To give the arrow its accurate look, use the "Fill" and "Stroke" Tools much like what we did with the previous shapes in this exercise.

– **Fill:** Select the arrow and double-click the "Fill Tool" and type in 15 for the K (black) percent. All other colors should be 0%.

– **Stroke:** With the arrow selected, double-click the "Stroke Tool" and type in 50 for the K (black) percent. Next, go to the top "Control Strip," and make sure you give the arrow a 4 pt. stroke size.

8. Move arrow into place: Using your arrow keys or the mouse, move the arrow into place to look exactly like the arrow on the lesson page.

– You will notice the bottom of the arrow should align with the template vertical rule (I suggest creating a guide to be very accurate).

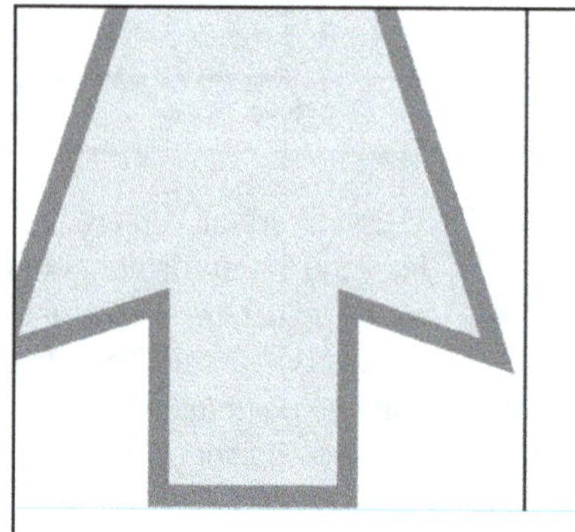

– Also, the right side of the arrow should almost be touching the same template vertical (if using the arrow keys, make the arrow just touch the rule and then move one space to the left).

Creating an illustration

The object is to create an illustration with the tools that you have just learned. Pick one of the illustrations from the lesson, and recreate it in the 4-inch box at the bottom of the page.

IMPORTANT: A portion of the lesson is also about learning to see. Can you reproduce the illustration EXACTLY as seen? Pay attention to spacing, shading, and size of lines and remember that you are enlarging the illustration over three times the size as the original seen on the lesson page (lines must be thicker to match).

■ **There are several more skills** that you will be introduced to in this exercise. All of the illustrations require you to know how to move elements to different layers. Often, you will create elements that you may want to move in front or back of other elements.

More info »

To learn more about **Working with layers** / *Pg. 28*

Creating the newspaper icon

To make this illustration, you will use the same basic shapes you previously have learned in this lesson. Notice how the illustrations use thin rectangles to symbolize words and larger rectangles to symbolize images to create a newspaper look.

1. Newspaper: Create a large rectangle and place it in the center of the 4-inch frame on the template. Try to size it correctly, and notice how it has even borders on all sides (as seen in illustration).

– **Give the box a fill of white and stroke of .5 pts.** I do much of my early creating in white with black frames so I can more accurately see the shapes and spaces. I will add tone later.

2. Newspaper text: Create a thin rectangle that has a width that is about half of the newspaper shape you created. Give this rectangle a fill of medium black (40%) and no stroke.

– **Create a guide** that aligns with the left-hand side of the rectangle.

– **Duplicate the shape** by using your "Selection Tool" and clicking on the rectangle. Next, go to the "Control Strip" and select "Edit" / "Duplicate."

– **Move this new rectangle** so its left edge aligns with the first rectangle, using the guide. Make sure you have turned on the "Snap To Guide" feature to help align the rectangle. To do this, go to "View" / "Grids & Guides" / "Snap to Guides."

NOTE: Looking at the illustration, you will notice the space between the rectangles is slightly less than the depth of one rectangle.

– **Create remaining text rectangle:** Repeat the steps of duplicating the rectangles and aligning them until you have created the desired number of rectangles. Use ruler guides or shape guides (learned previously) to make sure all the rectangles are evenly spaced.

– **Group rectangles:** To make the task of creating more gray rectangles and moving them easier, it will be best if we group them into one element. Using your "Selection Tool," click on the first rectangle. Now hold down the "Shift" key on your compter's keyboard and click on all the remaining rectangles. With them all selected, go to the "Control Strip" and select "Object" / "Group."

– **Duplicate group of rectangles:** The design requires more text rectangles, so click on the group of rectangles and duplicate them. Align both groups and space them apart to match illustration.

– **Resizing rectangles:** Once you have the two groups of rectangle, you may need to adjust the sizes. Click and drag on one of the middle handles of the grouped elements to adjust the width or height.

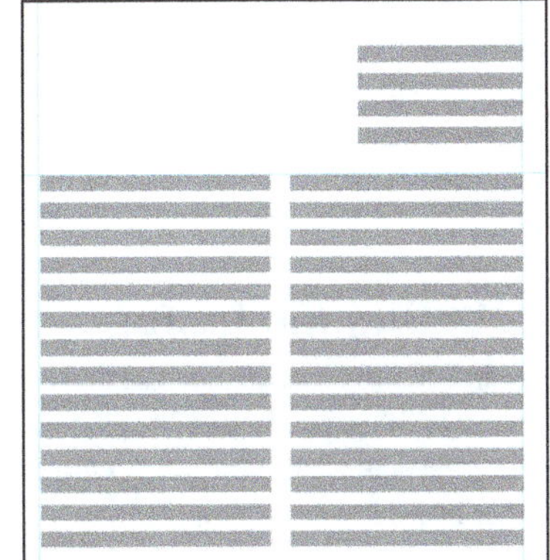

– **Creating the third rectangle group:** Duplicate one of the retangle groups and ungroup them. Select and delete all but four rectangles. Next, group the remaining four bars and change the width to match.

3. Image shapes: You need to create three differently shaped rectangles to represent images.

– **Size and tone:** Create to match size in illustration. Notice their color is a gray and is significantly darker than the text rectangles.

– **Location:** Notice how they align to text rectangles.

4. Newspaper tone: Put the tone in the large n ewspaper shape and put a stroke of none.

5. Newspaper shadow: On the left side of the newspa-per, you will notice a shadow. To create this shape, use the "Pen Tool," much like creating the previous arrow.

– **Hint:** I found it best to create this shape and then send it to the back.

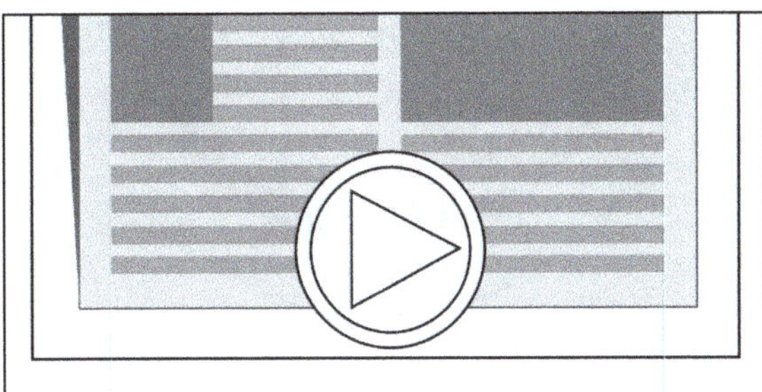

6. Newspaper button: The final step is to create the newspaper button. Make this using two circles and a triangle that are all centered together.

– **Tone:** Select each and try to match the tone seen in the lesson illustration.

– **Group all three button elements** and move into the correct location.

Creating the smile illustration

To make this illustration, you will use the same basic shapes you previously have learned in this lesson. You will discover the simple and complex uses of circles used in the illustration.

1. Smiling face: This portion is made of three circles and two ovals. First, using the "Ellipse Tool," create a circle that measures about 2.34 inches.

Your notes

Your notes

Remember, to make a perfect circle, hold down the shift key while making the circle.

– **Fill this circle** with light gray tone.

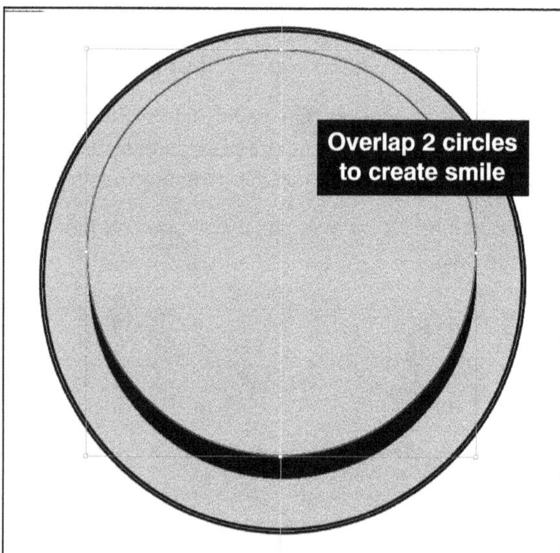

2. Smile: Make another perfect circle that is smaller than the circle used in the face. Fill this circle with black.

– **Duplicate the black circle** and fill this circle with the same gray tone used in the face.

– **The smile is made by offsetting the second gray** circle so the top covers the top portion of the black circle, yet the black is seen at the bottom.

– **Align and group smile:** When both circles are aligned to create the perfect smile, select both and group them. Now place these correctly on the face circle.

3. Eyes: Create two black ovals the same size that are evenly spaced. Place these at the upper portion of the face circle.

HINT: I would suggest creating a vertical guide that runs through the center of the face circle to help.

4. Headphone earpiece: This part of the illustration is made out of four shapes that are overlapped to give the appearance of a music headphone earpiece.

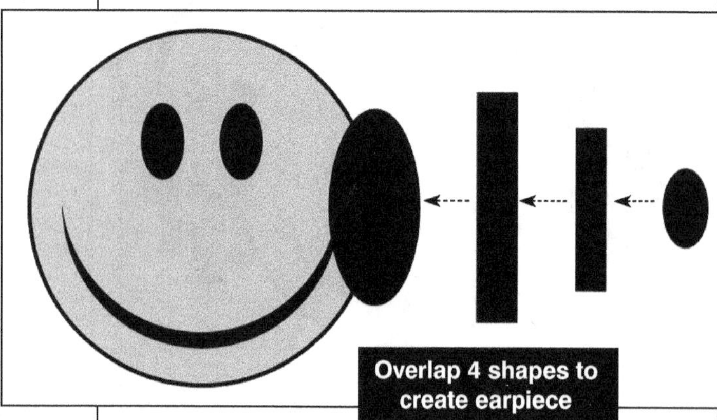

– **First, create an oval** with a fill of black.

– **Second, create a large rectangle** with a fill of black and a 2 pt. white frame.

– **Next, create a second black rectangle** that is smaller than the first, with no stroke.

– **Finally, create a small black oval.**

– **Combine shapes:** Overlap all four elements to make one element that appears like the illustration. Select all four elements and group them.

– **Remember,** do this by selecting each element while holding the "Shift" key down and then go to "Object" / "Arrange" / "Group."

5. Second headphone earpiece: Take the grouped earpieces created and duplicate them ("Edit" / "Duplicate").

– **Flip the earpiece** so it will work for the opposite ear. Select the element and go to the top "Control Strip" and locate and click on the "Flip Horizontal" tool.

– **Move second earpiece** into place.

6. Move face: Select the smiling face and move it to the forefront by selecting "Object" / "Arrange" / "Bring to Front" at the top in the "Control Strip."

7. Group parts: Select all the items created so far and group them together.

8. Headphone band: This is made of one large circle!

– **Create a large circle** with a fill of none and a heavy stroke.

– **Now the secret!** Create a large white rectangle with no stroke and place it on the lower portion of the circle just created. Send both of these elements to the back, and you have the top of the headphones.

Creating the guitar

At first glance it appears that this illustration cannot be made with basic shapes, but it can. While this one illustration is a bit harder than the others, it will improve your InDesign skills significantly.

Take the challenge and along the way you will begin to discover the power of working with basic design tools.

1. Guitar neck basics: This portion is made of three shapes that overlap each other. I would suggest making them all with a fill of none and stroke of black at first to make it easier.

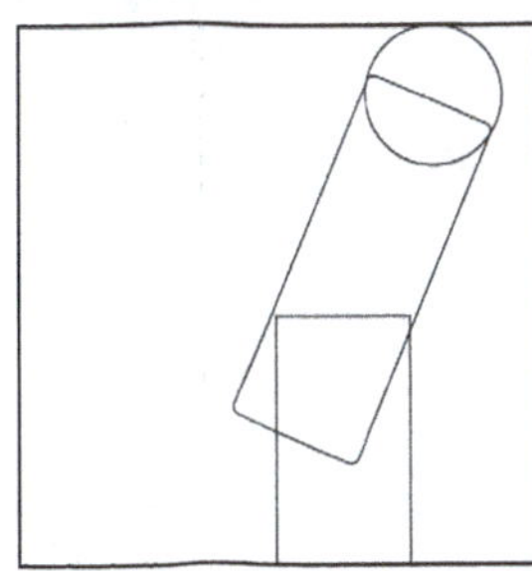

– **Bottom rectangle:** Make this shape 1.03 inches wide by 1.8 inches tall.

– **Rounded corner rectangle:** This should be the second shape created. This rectangle will require three seperate steps to make. First, create a basic rectangle that is 1.03 inches wide by 2.7 inches tall.

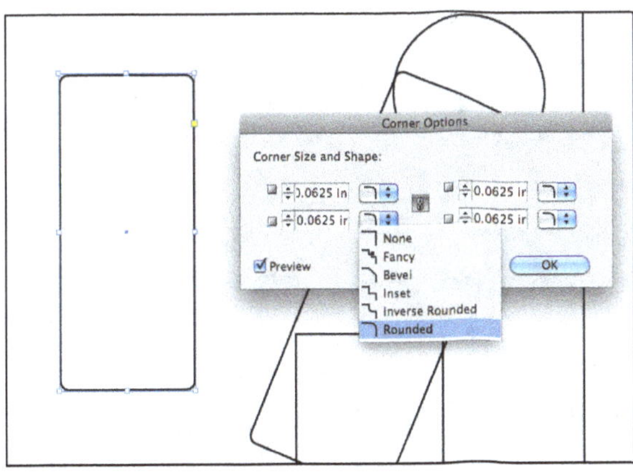

– **Create rounded corners:** With the shape selected, go to the "Control Strip" and select "Object" / "Corner Options," and select "Rounded" with 0.625 (all corners). Click on the "Preview" button in lower left corner to make it easier to see your settings.

– **Next, rotate:** Select the shape and go to the "Control Strip" and select "Object" / "Transform" / "Rotate" and set the angle at -23 degrees (click preview to see your settings)

2. Guitar neck addition: The guitar needs the addition of one more rectangle that is 0.7 inch wide by 1.67 inches deep.

– **This shape should overlap** the others with the left corner overlapping the first rectangle and the top right corner overlapping the circle.

– **Rotate** this shape 15 degrees.

3. Color shapes: Select all the shapes created and fill with black. While this still may not look like a typical electric guitar, just wait until the next step.

4. Take away some black: The final step to making the guitar neck shape is to create two white circles that overlap the previously created black shapes.
– Fill the circles with white and stroke of none.

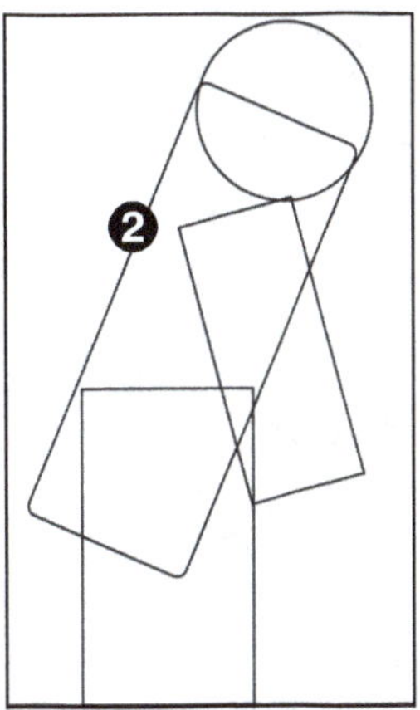

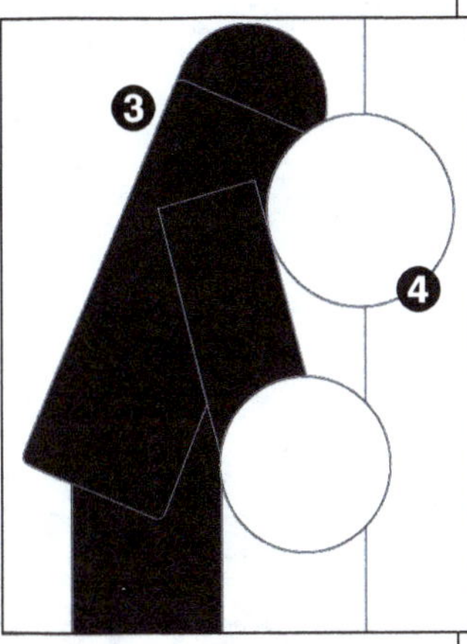

5. Guitar strings: The first step is to make the strings, which are six white lines, evenly spaced.

6. Guitar tuning posts: These are made of two circles with one circle that has a gray stroke. These should be evenly spaced and touch the guitar strings created.

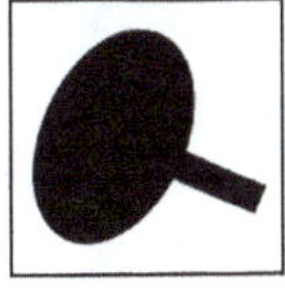

7. Guitar's tuning pegs: The pegs that reside outside the guitar neck are made of thick black lines and small black ovals that have been rotated to be perpendicular with the neck.

Hint: To make things easier and faster, make one each of the tuning posts and the tuning pegs and group each. Now duplicate each and place as needed.

6. Background: Look closely and you will see that the background is made up of rectangles that get smaller in size and lighter gray as they proceed to the top of the illustration border.

– **Spacing:** All background rectangles are evenly spaced.

7. Template border: To complete your illustration, you will need to select the outside frame (as part of the template) and make sure it has a fill of none. You also will need to move it to the front to hide all the shapes used and imperfect edges.

Congratulations

You made it!

Completing the first lesson is the hardest, because you are so unfamiliar with all the InDesign tools.

I promise it will get much easier as you progess.

Your notes

SAVE

– ***Reminder:***
You may want to save your work.
Save often!

DESIGNING with type

"**In design** there are infinite possibilities, but only a few that will work."

Much of learning about typography is unlearning what you have already been taught. You spent 12 years in school as a youth learning how to write, but little to none about how to present that content. This is why I see so much poor communication, which often can be attributed to poor use of type.

During my 20 years working in newspapers, I got the reputation as the "Type Guy" because of my passion for using and designing type well. I had learned during that time that words are powerful yet the display of those words can be significantly diminished or given great power if designed well–and it all starts with typography.

During this chapter, I want you to learn to see design. Recognize the difference between serif and san serif type and other typefaces. See the differences of type in italic, all caps, light, and bold.

This lesson will make you more knowledgeable about typography and the type tools in InDesign so you will have the skills to give your work the clarity and impact it deserves.

Your notes

Understanding type

You never know enough

Even during the early years of my career I had become well versed in the principles of design and the use of typography , and had a good number of awards that validated those skills. However, that was soon to change as I was introduced to Rob Covey, a gifted designer and former art director of *U.S. News & World Report* magazine, who was hired to assist me with a redesign of our newspaper . . . I thought (but soon discovered he was to become my mentor).

Well into the redesign, after many 14-hour days, Rob told me he thought I often used the wrong typeface on the story's headlines. How could that be! I argued that I always picked the appropriate typeface that expressed the tone and emotion of that story, and won awards for my work. To prove his point, he took away all my fonts, except Times (serif type) and Franklin Gothic (san serif type) for a year and challenged me to become creative in the use of type.

For the next six months I experienced the agony of typeface withdrawal. I discovered I had indeed developed the deadly disease of "Pick a Type." However, during that year I must have discovered thousands of different ways to use these two typefaces separately and together. I was reminded that design

is not only about selecting the correct typeface, but it is also about how you use the type.

Great type use is about the integration of the content (words), typography, and media to create an efficient design that speaks to the audience.

Extension of the spoken word

The next time you select a typeface, remember what it is like at a great party when someone from Texas begins talking to you and then is joined by two others, one from Boston and the other from Minnesota and five minutes into this conversation your good friend from the low country of South Carolina walks up. While each one's conversation is genuine and enjoyable, together your mind is going crazy trying to understand all the different dialects.

The written word is an extension of the spoken language. However, the written word typically bypasses tonal and facial expressions that are an important part of our society's communication. The good news is that one of the primary functions of typography is to bring the extension of the spoken word to the content. A well-chosen typeface, paired with the correct words, can strengthen the volume, tone, and texture of those words.

Remember the trap I fell into; just picking a typeface is often not the answer, using too many typefaces at one time in a project can be dizzying to the audience, much like that great party mentioned above.

Typography basic: How do you start?

In the past 30 years designers have gone from hundreds to what seems an unlimited number of typefaces to choose from. Why? The advancements of the digital technologies has had a great impact. It is now significantly easier and quicker to create new typefaces. If you do not find the correct typeface for your use, you can even create your own custom typeface in a short period of time.

So, with all these choices how do you begin? I suggest that you first start by narrowing your choices. While type can be divided into many different groups, I like to use these five simple groupings that are based on historical development and structural form.

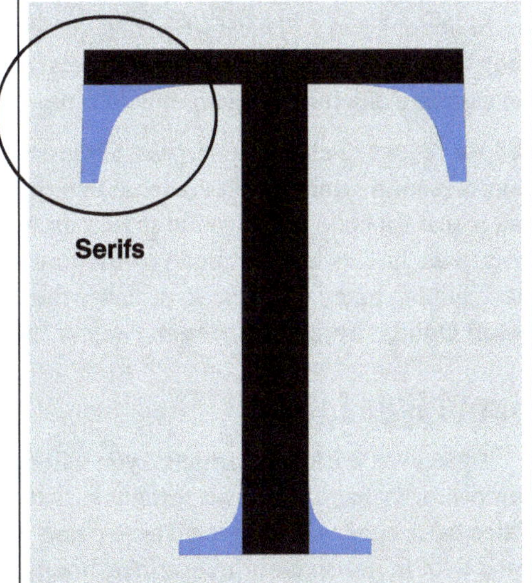

Serif typefaces: This is the typography that contains decorative structures at the ends of letters that are thought to have originated with the Romans. The serifs can be square or pointed, thick or thin, depending on the serif style. These typefaces are one of the most common, found in newspapers, books, magazines, early typewriters, and many other forms because of the high legibility of the letters in print. These typefaces are often thought of as more traditional, authoritative, and powerful.

Examples: Times, Garamond, Bodoni, Rockwell

Sans serif typefaces (also called san serif): These are typefaces that have no (sans – French for "without") serifs. While many of these typefaces go back many years, they were mainly used in headlines and large type except in Europe where they have been commonly used in text also. Some of these typefaces are among the most legible typefaces in most media because of their simple functional form. These typefaces are often perceived as contemporary, bold, simple, and functional.

Examples: Helvetica, Avant Garde, Gothic

Blackletter typefaces: These tend to be very ornate old typefaces with elaborate thick to thin strokes and serifs. Often they appear dark and complex and were popular in Europe from the 11th to 18th centuries. Many audiences now have difficulty reading words done in these typefaces because of how long ago they were used and letter shapes have significantly changed since that period of time. You see these typefaces commonly used in diplomas, monograms, college Greek organizations, tattoos, and most recently adopted by many skateboarder designs. Be careful using large amounts of these typefaces because of their complexity and difficulty to read quickly.

Your notes

Your notes

Examples: Old English, Fraktur, Goudy

Script or cursive typefaces: All these typefaces attempt to imitate the handwritten forms of communication. You will find these letters commonly used on invitations and certificates. They can vary in styles from fluid brush strokes to very ornate italic scripts of the 17th and 18th centuries. When using these typefaces, they often denote a tone of femininity, formality, caring, and peronal touch. But be careful because these typefaces require using proper size, letters pacing and leading and often are not read quickly.

Examples: Brush script, Snell Roundhand, Pablo

Decorative or novelty typefaces: Most often these are the crazy, fun specialty typefaces. They are the ones that do not fit in the other categories and are often used large and can be some of the hardest to read because of their unfamiliar letter shapes. The 20th century saw the growth of these typefaces because of the creation of digital type, making them easier to make and use. While they are unique, many of them have distinctive symbolism attached to the typeface because of their original use, thus making them hard to use for other needs.

Examples: Shatter, Shotgun Blanks, Crazy Creature

Family & fonts

Once you have a type group that might meet your communication needs, you need to consider the type family. Like your family, these are typefaces that are of the same origin but like human families, each member is slightly different. There are many different size families and the larger the type family the more options you will have when designing. The good news is they work well together. The Swiss typeface (to the right), is an example of a fairly large family of type.

Swiss
Swiss Thin
Swiss Bold
Swiss Italic
Swiss Condensed
Swiss Condensed
Swiss Extended
Swiss Extended
Swiss Outline

A font refers to all the uppercase, lowercase, punctuation, numbers, and symbols that make up one typeface. Worth noting is that fonts do not have the same number or kind of symbols in each. This is determined by the font creator and they have hidden many of them. To discover the unique characters or symbols, press the "Shift" or "Option" or "Shift Option" keys while pressing any of the computer keyboard keys.

Some type terms

If you ever work with printers, you will quickly discover they have their own terminology that dates back hundreds of years. These terms are used a lot in newspapers, magazines, books, and all types of desktop publishing projects when using QuarkXPress or InDesign. My suggestion is to stop trying to avoid them but jump in and learn them so you can effectively publish your work in the future.

What is a point? A point is the smallest unit of measure in printing and is often abbreviated as "pt." Most sizes of type are given in points; for instance, the standard word/letter size in Microsoft Word is 12 pts.

What is a pica? This unit of measurement is larger than a point and is often used to describe text widths in printing. I tell those just learning these terms, this measurement is about an 1/8 of an inch.

12 points = 1 pica   6 picas = 1 inch   72 points = 1 inch

Leading

Since the times of Gutenberg, the creator of the first printing press, spacers have been used in between lines of type to control the alignment of letters. These wood (and later lead) spacers were referred to as leading, which is measured in points.

– **No leading means** the letters might often touch each other, thus reducing legibility of the words.

– **Standard leading** is usually about 20 percent larger than the type size. This translates to adding 1.5 to 2 pts. for standard body text type (8-14 pt. type). InDesign will automatically set the leading and sets 10.8 pts. leading for 9 pt. type.

– **Additional leading** is used to make text more legible for early readers and senior citizens. Larger amounts of leading is also seen in poems and invitations when you want to create a slower reading pace.

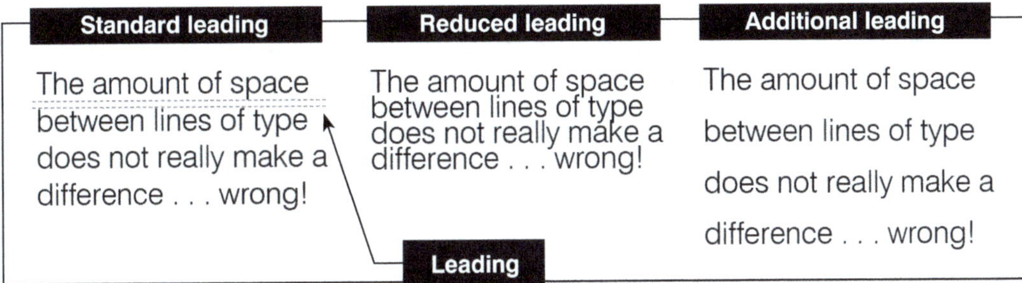

Letter spacing

Letter spacing, also commonly called tracking, is the consistent amount of space between a group of letters. Originally, most typefaces had the same amount of space between each letter, because that is what was necessary when creating wood and metal letters used in impression printing.

If you look closely at display type used in advertising, you will discover that many have had the spacing between letters reduced. The reason is that many typefaces were created for smaller use and the standard letter spacing is good for that use, but will appear too much when used for large display headlines.

Default letterspacing

Display Headline

Reduced letterspacing (-30)

Display Headline

How much letter spacing is needed?

– **Body text:** I would most often use the default letter spacing. Too little letter spacing in small type will diminish legibility.

– **Headlines:** For the best legibility, I would suggest reducing the letter spacing until the letters are just touching each other in most cases.

– **InDesign letter spacing:** When adjusting the letter spacing, use the "Tracking Tool" in the "Control Strip." There are three methods to adjust the letter spacing:

■ **Blue buttons with arrows:** Click down to a pull-down tab that gives specific standard amounts.

Your notes

Your notes

■ **White buttons with arrows:** Clicking on these will adjust the kerning up or down in increments of 10.

■ **Center area:** You can fine tune your letter spacing by typing specific amounts.

Kerning

While letter spacing involves the same spacing between all letters, kerning is the spacing between specific pairs of letters. I use kerning a lot when dealing with display typography. After using letter spacing you will often notice that some of the letters do not appear to be as evenly spaced as others. This is when you will need to address kerning pairs of letters to visually improve the legibility of the word.

Kerning pairs?

There are many different pairs of letters that need to be kerned when you consider the thousands of typefaces and the many different languages in the world. However, when dealing with the English language and the most common typefaces, I have learned that there are about 30 common kerning pairs that often need to be addressed. Here are a few:

Letters like T and Y, which have overhanging tops combined with lowercase letters.

Letter pairs like H, N, M, and L where both letters have vertical sides.

Any rounded lowercase letters paired with a lowercase y.

Capital letters like A and R that have wide bottoms, combined with round lowercase letters like o, a, and e.

Kerning uses

– **Body text:** Very seldom is kerning an issue for small typography or body text.

– **Headlines:** Most type faces will need some kerning. However, the amount will vary greatly from one typeface to another.

– **InDesign kerning:** Using the "Type Tool," you will need to click between two specific letters that need the spacing adjusted. This is referred to as a kerning pair. Next, go to the top "Control Strip" and locate the "Kerning" tool. Now kern the letters using one of three methods like the letter spacing previously detailed.

Type composition

How you set the text block composition will influence the tone of the design and the legibility. Two of the most commonly used type compositions are "justified," which you see in most newspapers, and "ragged right," which you see in many advertisements and some publications.

Ragged right

This method is also often called justified left or flush left.

■ **Pros:** Readership research has indicated this type of text composition is one of the easiest and quickest for American and most western civilization audiences to read. This is because most people in this region are used to reading from left to right and this method also offers fewer hyphenations of words. Also the perception of text in this format is that it is has a feeling of being more contemporary and relaxed.

■ **Cons:** Not many. This is not the best when using a lot of small text. Also, ragged right composition is not the most efficient in getting the most words in the smallest space.

Centered

■ **Pros:** You will see this type often used in invitations and some advertisements because it is unusual and

Ragged right alisqui aeperum autation restinc tionsequia sit autemquae laut eni alibusam quossi dolo iumquodist, sin resequis voluptur rempore ritasperum harchictum re sinis il maxim aut liqui omnit aute est, omniscient unt aborita sperit, simentio eniendam que dis dolupta voloruptat eiur, optat occate sam, to et remo	**Centered** alisqui aeperum autation restinc tionsequia sit autemquae laut eni alibusam quossi dolo iumquodist, sin resequis voluptur rempore ritasperum harchictum re sinis il maxim aut liqui omnit aute est, omniscient unt aborita sperit, simentio eniendam que dis dolupta voloruptat eiur, optat occate sam, to et remo	**Flush right** alisqui aeperum autation restinc tionsequia sit autemquae laut eni alibusam quossi dolo iumquodist, sin resequis voluptur rempore ritasperum harchictum re sinis il maxim aut liqui omnit aute est, omniscient unt aborita sperit, simentio eniendam que dis dolupta voloruptat eiur, optat occate sam, to et remo	**Justified** alisqui aeperum autation restinc tionsequia sit autemquae laut eni alibusam quossi dolo iumquodist, sin resequis voluptur rempore ritasperum harchictum re sinis il maxim aut liqui omnit aute est, omniscient unt aborita sperit, simentio eniendam que dis dolupta voloruptat eiur, optat occate sam, to et remo om-

makes the small amount of copy special.

- **Cons:** This is one of the hardest and slowest text compositions to read with large quantities of type.

Flush right

This method is also called justified right or ragged left.

- **Pros:** This is used often with a small amount of copy, like captions, which allows the designer to align the words with the photograph for a more harmonious design.
- **Cons:** Flush right is one of the least used because it opposite of how we read, thus making copy in this form some of the hardest to read.

Justified

- **Pros:** Commonly used. It is steeped in tradition and gets the most copy in the smallest space.
- **Cons:** If the type size or column width is too small it will hyphenate a lot of words and cause uncomfortable word and letter spacing problems.

Type weight

We started off this section stating that one of the functions of typography is to give the words human expression. But type can also express tone and volume, which you most likely recognize as regular, bold, and italic from your use of basic word programs. However, when you select a word and click on the bold selection, it simply adds a small stroke on all edges of the text. This gives the word a heavier weight, which symbolizes a louder volume. A better option is to select a bolder typeface from a larger family of type, because the type designer created these by using varied strokes so they become bolder but retain greater legibility.

Also using varied weight typefaces layers the information. What this means is it emphasizes the content so the viewer notices one portion before another, thus delivering a clearer and more powerful message.

Type adds volume
Type adds volume
Type adds volume
Type adds volume
Type adds volume
Type adds volume

Summary

You have been taught that using different headline typefaces is good, so you use many in your project . . . wrong!

You have been taught if you write too much, just make the words smaller to fit . . . wrong!

Need I go on?

What has been covered so far in this section is just the beginning of learning to use type. As you go on you will discover more things that you learned are not correct.

What I want you to do in the next InDesign lesson is to become good using the type tools and learn to see the design:

– Bold vs. light type
– Alignment of elements
– Differences in sizes

This lesson is hard, but when you finish you will be much better at InDesign.

Your notes

DESIGNING with type

LESSON . . .

A

What InDesign skills will you learn?

- To adjust letter spacing and kern type
- How to create reverse type
- To create justified text in multiple columns
- How to change the shape of typography using the horizontal scale tool
- How to rotate typography
- Methods to scale type

SCOTT FARRAND

DESIGN & DESIGN in DESIGN

Designing WITH Typography

Creating an ad

BowWow! Magazine

SAVE 47% OFF THE COVER PRICE

12 ISSUES FOR JUST $21.99

☐ Start my BowWow! subscription ☐ Start one for my friend

MY SUBSCRIPTION:

Name

Address City

State Zip E-mail

SEND MY GIFT TO:

Name

Address City

State Zip E-mail

☐ Bill me ☐ Payment enclosed

This is the guaranteed lowest rate at these terms, excluding special business rates. All prices in U.S. funds. For Canada, $21. For all other countries, $29. Sales tax required for magazines sent to D.C., 5.75%; and S.C., 7% Canadian price includes GST. If you prefer to send payment now, please place this reply card and your check in an envelope and mail to *BowWow! Magazine*, P.O. Box 33031, Atlanta, GA 33660. Please allow 2 - 4 weeks for delivery, of your first issue.

LSABQ11

Well, the advertising department lost the artwork for this magazine ad, so we need your help. Like always, the publication is going to press in a couple of days, so we need that ad ASAP. The goal is to make your work look EXACTLY like the current ad. This lesson will require you to learn new InDesign tools, so you will need to get started soon to meet the pending deadline.

Specifications

■ **Size:** The ad must be 6.6 inches wide by 4.9 inches deep. Ad shown is correct depth, but the width is off about .25 inch.

– You will need to adjust / align this content visually.

■ **Template:** You need to start the lesson using the template provided. On the template are two images. You will need to create the outside frame and center it on the page.

NOTE: This lesson's template includes images. It is important that this file and images be kept within the same folder to print correctly. When images are used, a link is created and if you move or rename any of the files the link will be broken.

■ **Content:** The ad must contain all the information and elements shown below.

■ The ad elements and typography should look exactly like the ad (as close as possible with the typefaces available on your computer).

■ Pay special attention to letter spacing, kerning, leading, and if the typeface is plain, bold, italic, condensed, or has additional letter spacing added.

Hint: To match the rules within the ad, use lines that are 0.5 pts. in size.

The final product

■ The final printout will need to be on a standard 8.5" X 11" paper with the ad centered on the paper.

■ Include your name on the lower left corner of the paper.

Assessment criteria

■ Does the ad contain all the information and elements?

■ Is the ad the correct size and centered on the page?

■ Does the ad look exactly like the example?
Are the typefaces (serif and san serif), type sizes, borders, leading, body and spacing correct?

– Remember, one of the dimensions has been changed slightly, requiring you to visually adjust the placement of elements.

■ Are the lines straight and evenly spaced?

■ Ready to publish? Is it clean, precise, and free of signs of struggle, such as uneven borders and inconsistent type?

Instructions Designing with Type

Locating lesson template

For this lesson you will need to locate the lesson, which is inside a folder named "Design Type_A template." Within this folder you will find two things, an InDesign template named "Design Type_A template" and photo illustrations (Dog1.tif and Dogbowl1.tif) that will be used in the lesson.

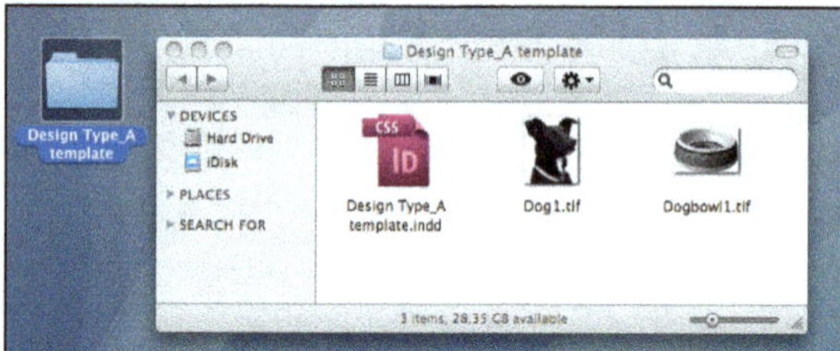

Getting organized

Locate the template folder and place it on the desktop of your computer.

■ **REMEMBER:** Always drag a copy of the InDesign lesson to your computer desktop first. Never open and work on a file that is located on a server or your thumb drive. Failure to remember this could result in a file that goes bad and will not open or print later.

Next highlight the word "template" on part of the folder name and replace it with your last name. This will ensure you are always working on your copy and can find the file later if needed.

– Open the folder and **locate the InDesign file** and replace the word "template" with your name here also.

■ **IMPORTANT: Keep the InDesign lesson file, "Dog1.tif" and "Dogbowl1.tif" files inside this folder at all times.** If you do not, the link between the image and the lesson will be broken and the file will not print correctly. You will learn more about how this works in a later lesson.

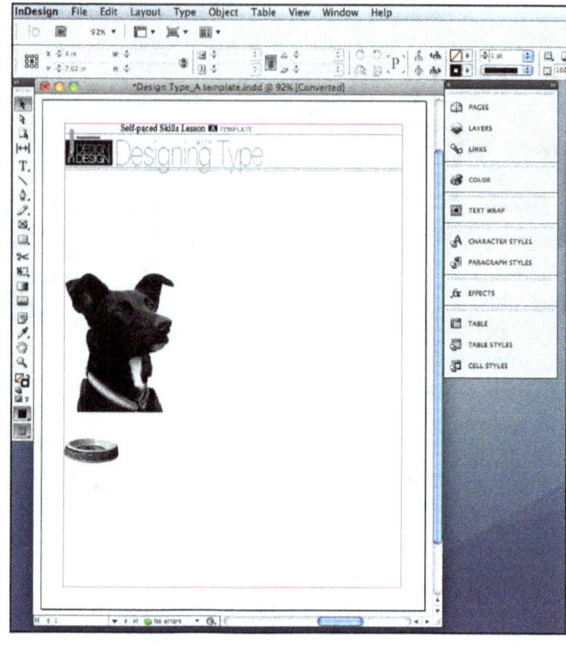

Starting the lesson

1. Move the images: Using the "Selection Tool" from the "Tool Palette" click on the middle of each of the two images on the palette (dog and bowl) and drag them separately to the left side (off the page) for later use.

2. Select the "Rectangle Tool" in the "Tool Palette." Next, click and drag to create a 6.6 inches wide by 4.9 inches deep rectangle. If you are having trouble getting the exact size just go to the top "Control Strip" and type in the exact size in the "Width" and "Height" settings.

3. Create the border: With the rectangle selected, locate the InDesign "Palettes" located to the right and click on "Stroke." If this palette is not visible go to the top and click on "Window" / "Stoke."

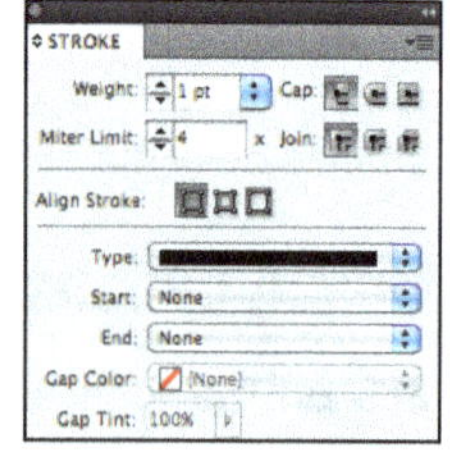

Type control strip

The "Control Strip" is constantly changing depending on the tools you are using from the "Tool Palette." This is what you will see if you are using the "Type Tool."

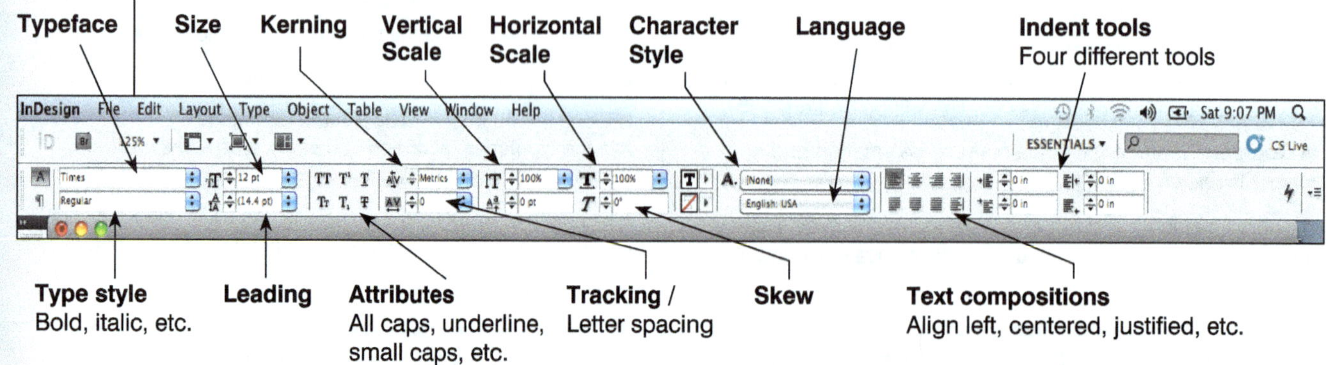

– Match the stroke weight and type seen in ad.

4. Center the ad frame: Use guides to make it easy.

– **First make sure your page rulers are visible.** If yours are not, go to the top and click on "View" / "Show Ruler." If they are not in inches, go to program settings.

To learn more about **program settings** */ Pg. 60*

– **Set vertical guide:** Get your "Selection Tool" from the "Tool Palette." Next, find the middle of the left-side ruler and click and drag from this point to the middle of the page (4 1/4 inches).

– **Set horizontal guide:** Use the "Selection Tool" and find the middle of the top ruler; click and drag from this point to the middle of the page (5 1/2 inches).

5. Move the ad frame to center: Using the "Selection Tool," click and drag the ad frame to the center of the page. If you align the middle handles on the ad to the guides, you will have the advertisement in the middle of the page.

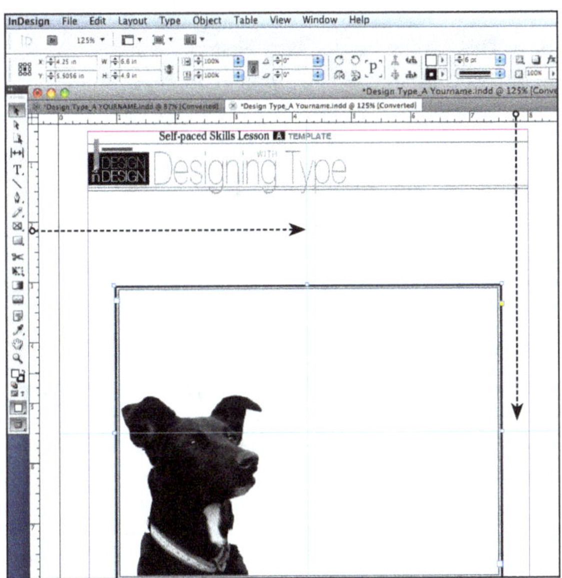

The dog image

1. Move the image: Using the "Selection Tool," click on the middle of the dog image and drag to the lower-left corner of the ad to match the lesson example location.

IMPORTANT: If you did not get the image to the correct location on the first attempt, you may find selecting the image impossible. The reason is that InDesign assigns each element you create to a different layer based on when it was created. Since I created the dog image on the page before you created the frame, it is underneath.

To learn more about the **InDesign layers** */ Pg. 28*

Easy solution: Click on the ad frame and go to the top "Control Strip" and select "Object" / "Arrange" / "Send To Back." Now click on the dog image and move to the correct location.

– **Bring the ad frame back to top** by selecting the ad frame edge and go to the top and select "Object" / "Arrange" / "Send To Front."

Creating guides

There is nothing worse than finishing a project and discovering it is the wrong size. It is so easy to accidentally click on the outside frame and change the shape when you are creating so many small elements.

1. Create guides: Click and drag from the middle of the document's rulers to create guides to align with all edges of the ad frame.

Make yours match (quickly)

Here are a few hints to help make your InDesign lesson match the lesson example and save you time.

– **Get a ruler and measure** some of the elements' vertical positions. The ad seen on the lesson is the same depth as yours; however, you will need to do some visual adjustments because the ad seen is not as wide as the required width of your ad.

– **You will make mistakes:** Try not to be perfect the first try. You will make mistakes, but InDesign has an undo.

 **ore info »**

To learn more about **undoing mistakes** */ Pg. 60*

First try to get all elements on the ad the best you can. Next, go back and make adjustments to each item's size, location, and stroke.

– **Print:** After getting most of the elements on the ad, save the file and print. Examine each element and make notes to what you need to do to get a closer match. Make corrections and print again. Repeat until yours is a match.

– **Type match:** I know identifying the exact font takes some experience and time. The goal should be to find a typeface, weight, and size that is very close. I designed this lesson so that there is at least one serif and san serif typeface that will be a close match for either basic Apple or Window computers.

Create display type

1. Create the "47%:" Using the "Type Tool" located in the "Tool Palette," click and drag outside the ad area to create a type container. Now type in "47."

NOTE: It is wise to make the type container bigger than needed to make sure all the content will fit. After you have typed all the content, click on the text box handles and reduce the container size. Doing this will make it easier for you to edit or move the type later.

2. Type attributes: With the type highlighted, select the font and size to match the example.

Hint: The font is a san serif and will match either Gill Sans, Helvetica Black, Arial Black, or Franklin Gothic Demi.

Your notes

– ***Reminder:***
You may want to save your work.
Save often!

3. Move type: Click and drag the "47" into position.

4. Create percentage: You will need to create the "%" as a separate element in order to align it correctly. Using the "Type Tool," create a text box outside the ad frame area and type the "%."

– You will notice that the "%" is the same typeface (but smaller) as the "47" already created.

– Using the "Selection Tool," click on the element and move this into place. Look how it relates to the "47."

5. Create "SAVE": Get the "Type Tool" and create a type box outside the ad frame area. Type in the word "SAVE."

– Notice that the "SAVE" is the same typeface as the type already created. It is common for designers to use the same typeface often, just in different ways.

– Using the "Selection Tool," click on the element and move this item into place.

Condensing type

When you study print design, you will realize a lot of typography has been manipulated for specific uses. One method is to horizontally scale type to give a more condensed look. The words "OFF THE COVER PRICE" have been scaled horizontally.

1. Create "OFF THE COVER PRICE:" Get the "Type Tool" and create a type box outside the ad frame area.

– Type in the words.

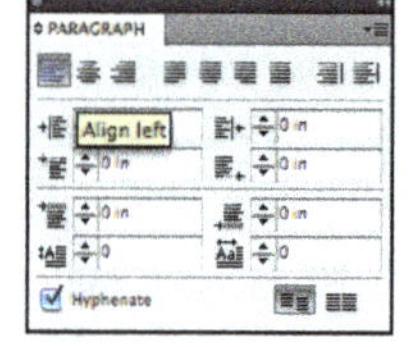

2. Setting alignment: To align the word to the left, we will be using the "Paragraph" palette.

– With the word selected, go to the "Control Strip" and select "Window" / "Type and Tables" / "Paragraph." Now click on the "Align Left" symbol at the top.

TIP using palettes »

You will be using palettes often to set attributes for many elements you create, so understanding them will be helpful.

– ***Location:*** *The palettes will be located to the right of the document or you will find them within the "Window" pull-down menu in the top "Control Strip." Remember, black arrows indicate more palette choices.*

Open visible palettes: *Click on the word and the palette will open.*

Moving palettes: *Click on the palette name and drag to preferred position. Clicking on the dark top gray bar also works.*

Closing palettes: *Click on the small circle in top gray bar to close. Click on palette name and drag to all palettes to right, docks your palette with others.*

---

3. Typeface and size: Using the "Control Strip," select the typeface (same as other type created) and set the size to closely match the example.

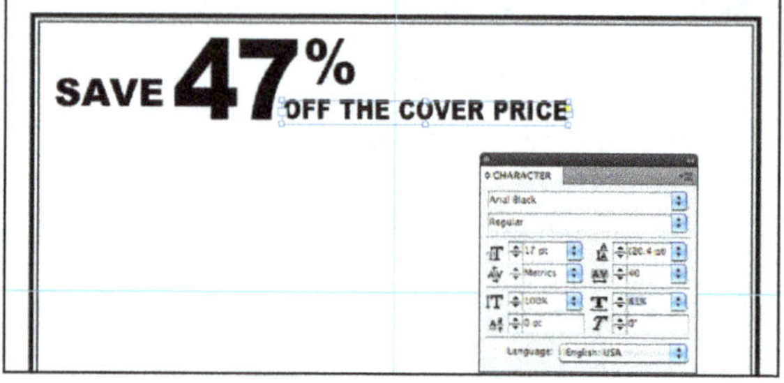

– Using the "Selection Tool," click and move the type.

4. Move the element: Using the "Selection Tool," click and drag the words in the proper position. Notice how they align with the bottom of the "47."

5. Condense type: By now you have noticed the type is too wide. Using the "Type Tool," highlight all the words.

Hint: This can be hard at first. First, use the magnifying glass tool and zoom in on the type. Next, align the tool with the baseline of the type and click and drag to highlight all the letters.

– **Using the "Horizontal Scale Tool"** in the "Control Strip" reduce the scaling (squeezing the letters) until it fits properly to match the example.

Creating reversed type

1. Black bar: Using the "Rectangle Tool" create a thin rectangle approximately the width and height seen in the lesson example. Pay attention to space at both ends of the bar.

2. Make black: Go to the "Tool Palette" and double-click on the "Fill Tool" and make the "K" 100% (0% on the C, M, Y).

3. Create another type box and type "12 ISSUES FOR JUST $21.99." Select the correct typeface and the correct size, trying to match the lesson. Place this type directly below the black bar created earlier.

4. Center type: Highlight the text and go to the top ("Control Strip") and select the "Align Center" type composition setting. Next, make the text box about the same width as the black bar.

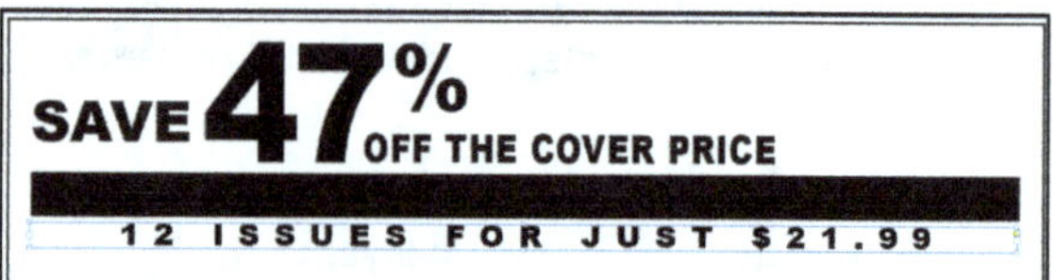

5. Add letter spacing: With the type still highlighted, go to the "Control Strip" and locate the "Tracking" and add space between the letters until it matches.

– **HINT:** First use the blue arrow drop-down tabs in the tracking setting and select a large amount of letter spacing to get close and then add small amounts with the black arrows to get a perfect match.

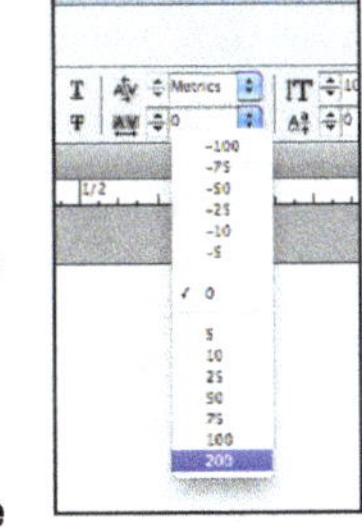

6. Make letters white: Using the "Type Tool," highlight the "12 ISSUES FOR JUST $21.99" and make white by double-clicking on (Type) "Fill" tool. This brings up the "Color Picker" palette, which you need to make the color white (C: 0%, M: 0%, Y: 0%, and K: 0%).

– **Move type:** Using the "Selection Tool" (black arrow), click on the type and move into place.

– **HINT:** I often do use the arrow keys on the keyboard to move elements because it allows me to be more accurate at times. Try it and discover what works the fastest and easiest for you!

Creating box and type

1. Square: Select the "Rectangle Tool" in the "Tool Palette" and click and drag to create a box. Use the handles to adjust the shape and size.

NOTE: Holding down the "Shift" key while making a box will **create a perfect square box** (needed in this lesson). This also works to make a perfect circle. Entering the exact sizes in the width (W) and height (H) boxes in the "Control Strip" will also work.

2. Putting a frame on the box: With the box selected, go to "Stroke" in the "Tool Palette" to select the color (black). Next, go to the "Control Strip" and select the stroke size (.5 pts.), and type of line (solid and plain).

NOTE: The stroke can also be adjusted in the "Control Strip."

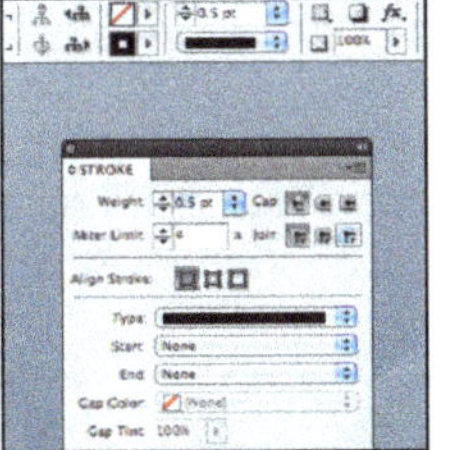

3. Move box: Select the box and move to correct position. Notice how the left edge of the box should align with the black bar's left edge above.

NOTE: Moving small items can be frustrating, because, often the handles are selected and moved while attempting to move the element. Often it is best to select the element and move it with the arrow keys.

4. Creating another box: The ad calls for another subscription box. Rather than create another, there is an easier way. With the box selected, go to the "Control Strip" and click on "Edit" / "Duplicate." Now you have a second box the correct size and with the correct stroke.

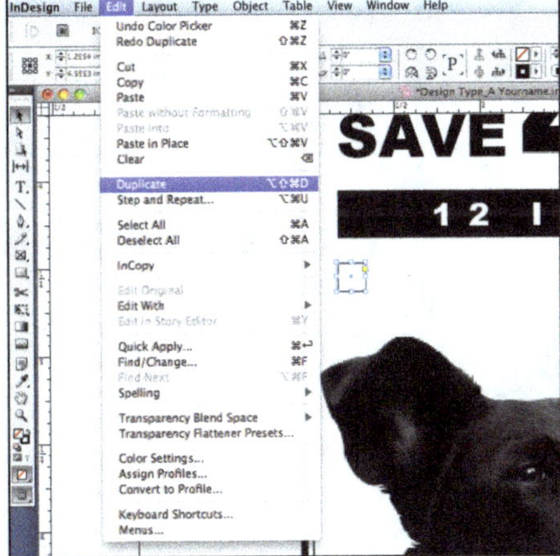

– **Now move the box** to the correct location.

4. Start my BowWow! Subscription: Using the "Type Tool," create a wide text box (I suggest outside the ad and move later) and type the words. Now select the correct typeface, size in the "Control Strip" to match the lesson example.

– **Duplicate the type** just created (just like the previously created box) and move to the correct location. Now, using the "Type Tool," highlight the text and change the words to "Start one for my friend."

My subscription

1. Text: Just like all the other text, use the "Type Tool" and create a text box and type in the correct words. Now match the typeface and size.

– **HINT:** This is very common serif typeface found on all Macs and PCs.

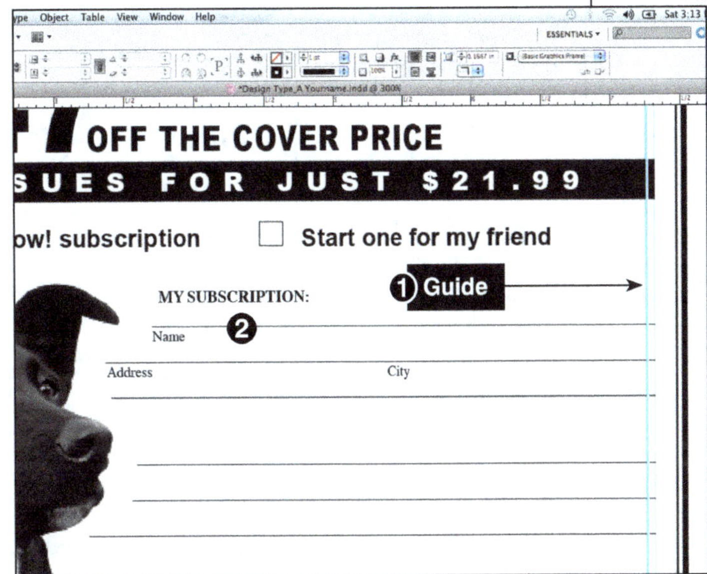

Creating lines and type

1. First, create a guide: Did you notice how all the lines are aligned with the top black bar? Creating a guide will help you align all the lines you create.

– **Click within the left ruler** and drag a guide to the right side so all the lines will align up consistently.

– **Set snap to guide:** This feature in InDesign will make the lines you create snap to the guide when you are close. Go to the top and select "View" / "Grids & Guides" / "Snap to Guide."

2. Select the "Line Tool" from the "Tool Palette." Starting to the left, click and drag across to the right-hand guide. However, it is best to do this while holding down the "Shift" key. Holding down this key makes a perfect straight line.

– **Now select the line type and line weight** in the "Control Strip" above or "Stroke" palette.

3. Create text boxes for the words needed under each line (match the typeface, size, and placement).

Your notes

SAVE

*– **Reminder:** You may want to save your work. **Save often!***

Your notes

SAVE

– Reminder: You may want to save your work. ***Save often!***

HINT: Create one of the words first and print out your ad design and check font and size. If it is a match, duplicate the text box, highlight and change words, and then move to a specific location. This will save you time!

4. Repeat this process to create all the lines and text under each line.

Payment content

1. Boxes: These boxes are created like the first boxes. Pay attention to the stroke and the shape.

2. Text: These are created like all the other text. Match the typeface and size to the lesson example.

Guarantee content

1. Text: Using the “Type Tool,” Create one large text box outside the ad and type in all the words seen at the bottom of the ad.

– **Often all the type will not fit** in the text box you created. When this occurs, InDesign will let you know with an icon in the lower-right side of the text box that is a small red box with a plus in the middle.

2. Text columns: Now the copy needs to be put into two text columns. With the text block selected, go to the “Control Strip” and select “Object” / “Text Frame Options.”

3. The “Text Frame Options” palette appears. This palette puts many text options at your fingertips. Look for the columns and enter two for the number. This takes the current type box and divides it into two columns.

NOTE: When the text width is changed, the columns adjust automatically to accommodate the new size.

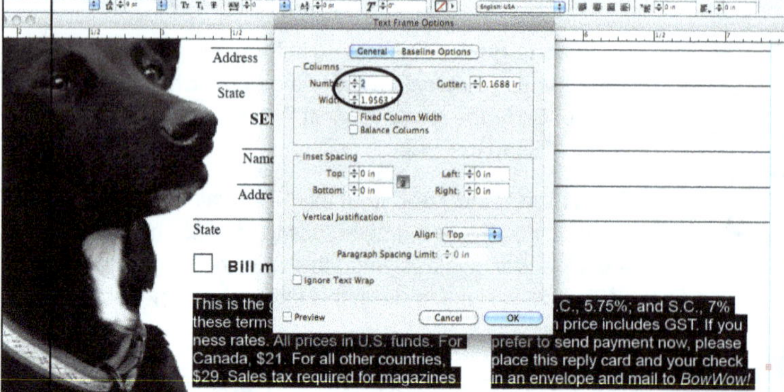

4. Size: With the text still selected, adjust the size (smaller).

5. Adjust the leading: This is the amount of space between two lines of type. When type is created, the computer sets a default amount based on the type size. Often you will need to adjust this because of the typeface used, increasing legibility, or many other reasons. To create this text correctly, it will need additional leading.

– **Go to the “Control Strip”** and change the “Leading” by clicking on the arrows or typing an exact amount.

6. Text composition: Looking closely, it is obvious that the sides of the two columns of type are aligned. This is achieved by selecting the correct text composition.

– **Using the “Type Tool,” click and drag** over all the text to highlight the text.

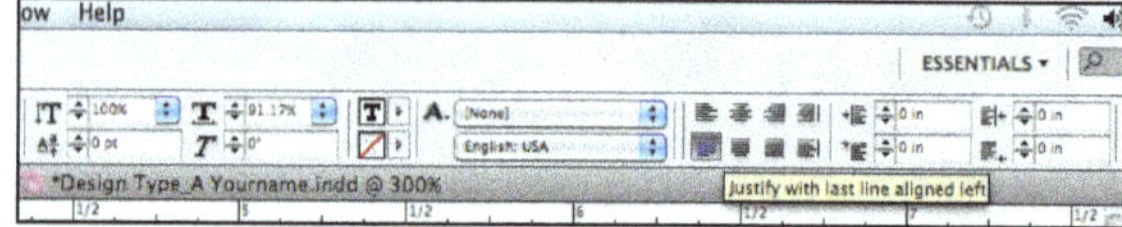

– Now go to the “Control Strip” and locate the type composition settings and choose the **“Justified with last line aligned left.”**

Ad identification

While this is small, it is an important element that gets your ad in the correct publication, correct date, and on the correct page.

1. Create a text box and type the ad identification info.

– **Match** the typeface and size.

2. To rotate this type as seen in the lesson example, click on the text box with the “Selection Tool.” Now rotate the text using the rotation tool in the “Control Strip.”

Dog Bowl

Now it is time to add the last elements–the dog bowl and type.

1. Locate the dog bowl on the template and using the “Selection Tool,” click on the image and drag it into place (try not to click on the handles).

2. Create a text box and type the words “BowWow! Magazine.” Match the typeface, size, and leading. Next, move it into position.

You are almost finished

Go back and edit your work to perfection!

– Edit content (is it all there)

– Edit sizes and placements (watch for borders)

– Edit attribute (bold, italic, etc.)

– Now print out a finished lesson and be proud you have learned a lot about InDesign.

DESIGNING with type

LESSON . . .

What InDesign skills will you learn?

- How to scale and rotate typography
- Adjust letter spacing and kerning type
- How to create reverse type
- To create justified text in multiple columns
- Change the shape of typography using the horizontal scale tool

Designing WITH Type

Creating a page

Overview

The editor lost one page of the upcoming magazine, so we need your help. Like always, the publication is going to press in a couple of days, so we need the design ASAP. The goal is to make your work look EXACTLY like the design shown. This assignment will require you to use new InDesign tools and learn to see type sizes, spacing and alignment.

Specifications

■ **Size:** The design must be 4.9 inches wide by 6.6 inches deep.

– Design shown is correct depth, but the width is off about .25 inch. You will need to adjust width visually.

■ **Template:** You need to start the lesson using the template provided. On the template is the doorbell image. You will need to create the outside frame and center the page design on the template page.

NOTE: This lesson template includes one image. It is important that this file and images be kept within the same folder to print correctly. When images are used, a link is created and if you move or rename any of the files the link will be broken.

■ **Content:** Must contain all the information and elements shown. You will need to create all the text.

■ **The page elements** and type should look exactly as that shown (as close as possible with your computer typefaces available).

■ **Pay attention to letter spacing,** kerning, leading, and if the typeface is plain, bold, italic, condensed, or has additional letter spacing.

HINT: To match the rules within the design, use lines that are 0.5 pt. in size.

The final product

■ The lesson will need to be printed in black and white on a standard 8.5" X 11" paper.

■ Include your first and last name at the lower left corner of the paper.

First dates GONE WRONG

Just getting someone to say yes is stressful, but this is only the beginning. To relieve sweaty palms and awkward silences, know this before the doorbell rings.

By Stanley Missonfolk

LAST-MINUTE ADVICE

For males	Awkward locations	Questionable activites
Please pay	Family events	Shopping
No pawing	Strip bars	Tanning
For females	Weddings	Confession
No primping	Funerals	Paintball
Smile	Libraries	Sky diving

Please say you didn't do that

Check out others

■ So you thought no one would notice when you gave the server a quick look (you know the look). Both males and females are tempted to flirt with waitresses or other patrons when out. What a bad move.

Fashionably late

■ Even five minutes is inexcusable on the first date. That someone special you found is already anxious thinking they might become the next horror story of being stood up. What were you thinking?

Answer a text

■ So you had to whip out the new phone and text your friend. Unless you are a heart surgeon or a superhero incognito, it is rude to use your phone when you are supposed to be giving someone special your full attention. Tell me you did not do this.

Food dribble

■ Well the spaghetti at the fine Italian restaurant proved to be a bad choice. Embarrassment from spilled food is the last thing you needed. I can't look.

Assessment criteria

■ Is the design the correct size and centered on the page?

■ Does the design contain all the information and elements?

■ Does the content look exactly like the example?
Are the typefaces (serif and san serif), type sizes, borders, leading, body, and spacing correct?

– Remember, one of the dimensions have been changed slightly, requiring you to visually adjust the placement of elements.

■ Are the lines straight and evenly spaced?

■ Ready to publish? Is it clean, precise, and free of signs of struggle such as uneven borders and inconsistent type?

Locating lesson template

For this lesson you will need to locate the lesson, which is inside a folder named "Design Type_B template." Within this folder you will find two things, an InDesign template named "Design Type_B template" and a photo illustration (Type_doorbell1.tif) that will be used in the lesson.

Getting organized

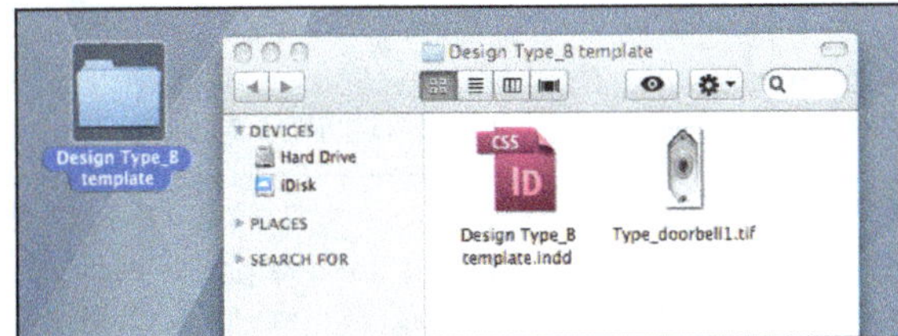

Locate the template folder and place it on the desktop of your computer.

■ **REMEMBER:** Always drag a copy of the InDesign lesson to your computer desktop first. Never open and work on a file that is located on a server or your thumb drive. Failure to remember this could result in a file that goes bad and will not open or print later.

Next, highlight the word "template" on part of the folder name and replace it with you last name. This will ensure you are always working on your copy and can find the file later if needed.

– Now open the folder and **locate the InDesign file** and replace the word "template" with your name here also.

■ **IMPORTANT: Keep the InDesign lesson file and the "Type_doorbell1.tif" file inside this folder at all times.** If you do not, the link between the image and the lesson will be broken and the file will not print correctly. You will learn more about working with photographs in a later lesson.

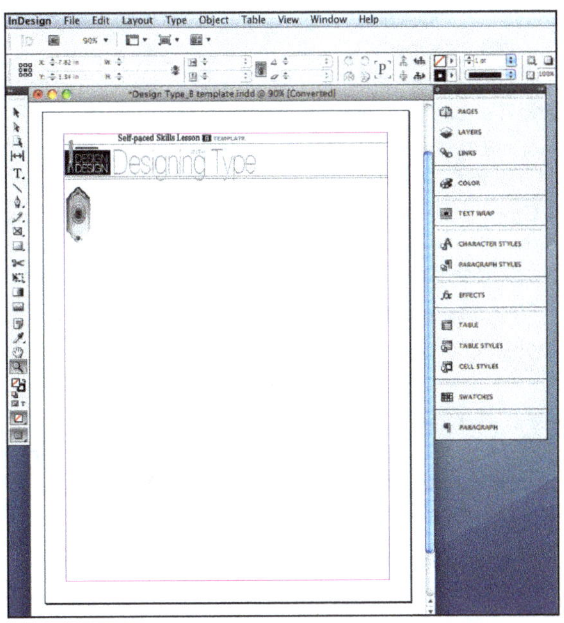

Beginning the lesson

1. Select the "Rectangle Tool" in the "Tool Palette." Next, click and drag to create a 4.9 inch wide by 6.6 inch deep rectangle. If you are having trouble getting the exact size just go to the top "Control Strip" and type in the exact size in the "Width" and "Height" settings.

2. Create the border: With the rectangle selected, locate the InDesign "Palettes" located to the right and click on the "Stroke." If this palette is not visible go to the top and click on "Window" / "Stoke."

– Match the stroke weight and type to the design seen on the lesson.

3. Center the magazine article frame: To center the frame correctly it is easiest to create guides.

Type control strip

The "Control Strip" is constantly changing depending on the tools you are using from the "Tool Palette". This is what you will see if you are using the "Type Tool."

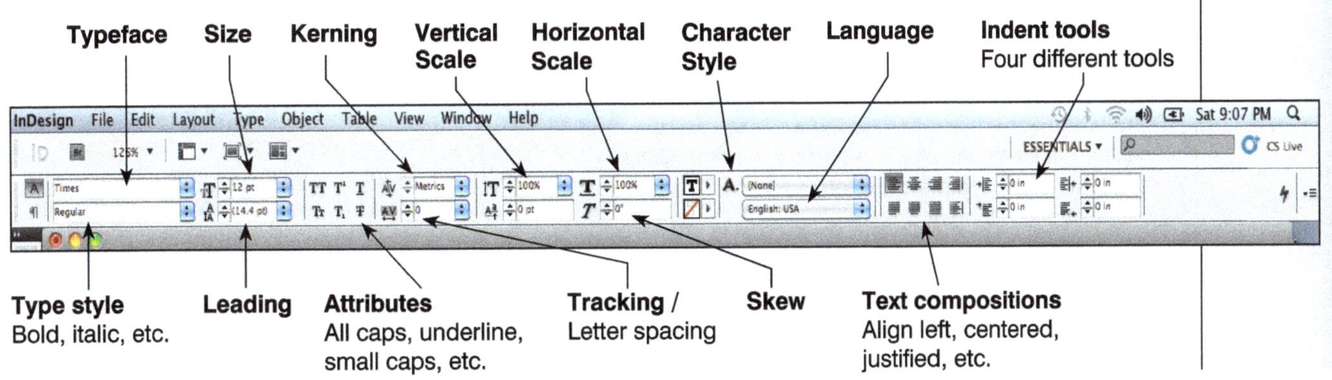

Your notes

TIP program settings »

If you find that your object sizes, rulers, or other settings are not correct for you or the lessons, you will need to adjust the InDesign preferences.

*– **Location:** Go to the top of the computer screen and locate "InDesign" click / hold and select "Preferences" / "Units & Increments."*

*– **Changes:** Locate "Ruler Units" and change "Horizontal" and "Vertical" to inches.*

*– **Other Units:** Set "Text Size" to "Points." Also set "Stroke" to "Points."*

*– **Other options:** The preferences allow you to make many other changes to suit your needs.*

– **First, make sure your page rulers are visible.** If yours are not, go to the top and click on "View" / "Show Ruler."

– **Set vertical guide:** Get your "Selection Tool" from the "Tool Palette." Find the middle of the left-side ruler and click and drag from this point to the middle of the page (4 1/4 inches on the top ruler).

– **Set horizontal guide:** Use the "Selection Tool" and find the middle of the top ruler and click and drag from this point to the middle of the page (at 5 1/2 inches).

5. Move the frame to center: Using the "Selection Tool," click and drag the frame to the center of the page. If you align the middle handles on the magazine article frame to the guides, you will have it in the middle of the page.

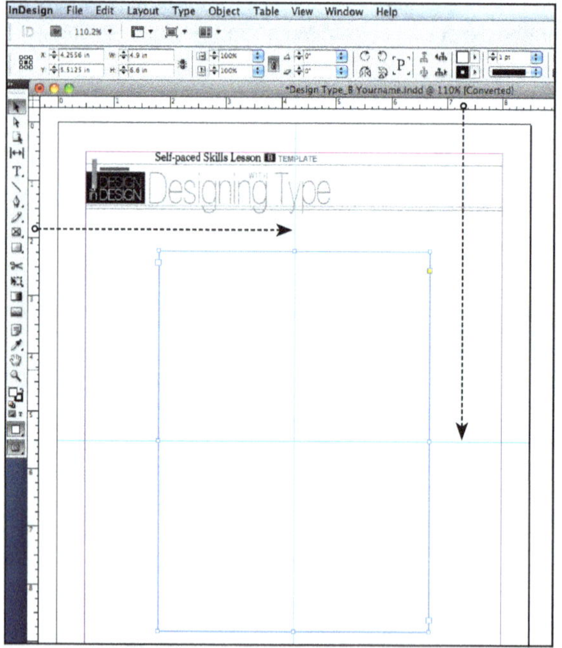

Article design guides

There is nothing worse than finishing a project and discovering it is the wrong size. It is so easy to accidentally click on the outside frame and change the shape when you are creating so many small elements.

1. Create guides: Click and drag from the middle of the document's rulers to create guides to align with all edges of the article frame.

Make yours match (quickly)

Here are a few hints to help make your InDesign lesson match the lesson example and save you time.

– **Get a ruler and measure** some of the elements' vertical positions. The article seen on the lesson is the same depth as yours. However, you will need to do some visual adjustments, because the article seen is not as wide as the required width of your article design.

– **You will make mistakes:** Try not to be perfect the first try. You will make mistakes, but InDesign has an undo.

TIP undoing mistakes »

InDesign knows you will make mistakes so undoing wrong moves is simple.

*– **Method:** Just stop and go to the top and select "Edit" / "Undo" (which is the top selection).*
*– **Keyboard undo:** Press the keys "Command" and "Z" at the same time (can be done multiple times if needed).*

Try first to get all elements on the design the best you can; then go back and make adjustments to each item's size, location, and stroke.

– **Print:** After getting most of the items on the design, save the file and print. Examine each element and make notes to what you need to do to get a closer match. Make corrections and print again. Repeat this process until yours is a perfect match.

– **Type match:** I know identifying the exact font takes some experience and time. The goal should be to find a typeface, weight, and size that is very close. I designed this lesson so that there is at least one serif and san serif typeface that will be a close match for either basic Apple or Window computers.

Creating more guides

How do you figure where to put the headline? Well, it starts by examining the overall article design. Let's start with establishing the vertical line in the design.

1. Create a vertical guide: Let me get you started. Using the rectangle tool, create a box that has a width of 1.8 inches and a depth of .4 inch.

– **Align the right edge of the box** with the right side of the article frame.

– **Create guide:** Using the "Selection Tool," click and drag from the middle of the left side ruler to the left edge of the box to create a guide. With the guide in place, delete the box used to measure the distance.

2. Create other guides: Examine the article design closely and you will see that most of the content is inset about 1/8 of an inch inside the article frame.
Knowing this, let's create guides to help us now and later. We could use the rulers to measure the distance, but an easier way (a trick I have learned) is to use the text frame options.

– **Using text frame options:** Using the "Selection Tool," click on the article frame. Next, go to the top and select

"Object" / "Text Frame Options."

– **Locate the "Inset Spacing"** and enter "0.13 in" for all settings (top, left, bottom, and right) and hit "OK." Now, was this not easy!

3. Create guides: Using the "Selection Tool" (black arrow), click and drag from the middle of the rulers and drag guides to align with insets created on all sides.

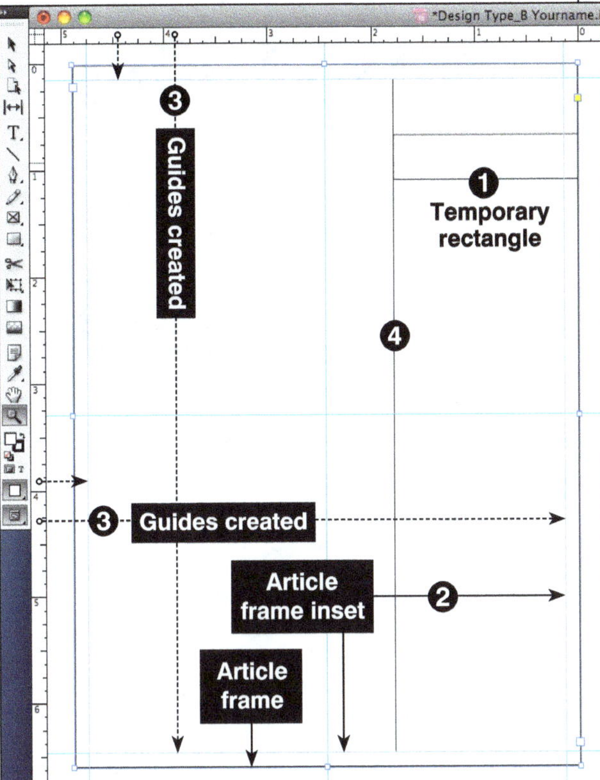

4. Create vertical line: The last step is to get the "Line Tool" and create a line that begins at the top guide and ends at the bottom guide (see above). Using the "Control Strip," make the line .5 pt. black.

Creating headline type

How do you figure where to put this headline? It starts by examining the overall article design. Let's begin with establishing the vertical guide in the design.

1. "First dates" headline: Using the "Type Tool," create a large text box and type the words "First dates."

– Still using the "Type Tool," highlight the words you created and select the correct typeface and size that match the lesson example (It is very bold type).

– **Align:** Grab the handles of the element and reduce the text box size as much as possible so the words are still visible. Now use the "Selection Tool" (black arrow), and click and drag the element into the correct position.

HINT: Looking at the lesson example, notice how the right side of "First dates" aligns about 1/8 inch from the vertical rule created. I would suggest creating another guide to help align this and other elements to be created.

2. Create line: Using the "Line Tool," create a thin line to extend under the headline created.

3. "GONE WRONG" headline: Select the "Type Tool" and create a large text box again and type the words "GONE WRONG." Hit the return key after the first word to force the second word to go to the next line.

– Still using the "Type Tool," highlight the words you created and select the correct typeface and size that match the lesson example. You can use the "Control Strip" in most cases, but sometimes it is easier to use the "Character" palette located at the right.

– **HINT:** It is a bold typeface (same as first headline).

To learn more about ***using palettes*** */ Pg. 54*

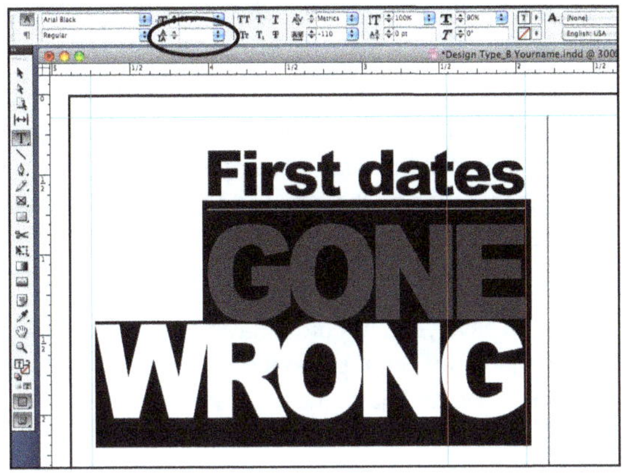

Align words: This part is easy. With the words highlighted, go to the "Control Strip" at the top and locate the text compositions. Click on "Align right" and move the words into the correct position.

– **Adjust leading:** You will see the lesson example does not match yours, because the space between the words (leading) is not the same. Highlight the words, locate the leading in the "Control Strip," and reduce the leading until the lines of type almost meet.

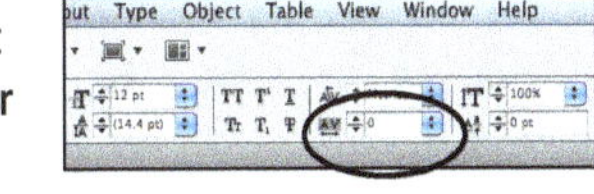

– **Align letter spacing:** At this point you will discover that despite the size the letters are not spaced the same as the lesson example. Highlight all the letters and using the "Tracking" tool in the "Control Strip," reduce the letter spacing to match the lesson example.

4. Shading on GONE: Using the "Type Tool," highlight the word "GONE." Locate the "Fill" in the "Tool Palette." You will notice the "Fill" icon now has a "T" letter indicating the fill of the type.

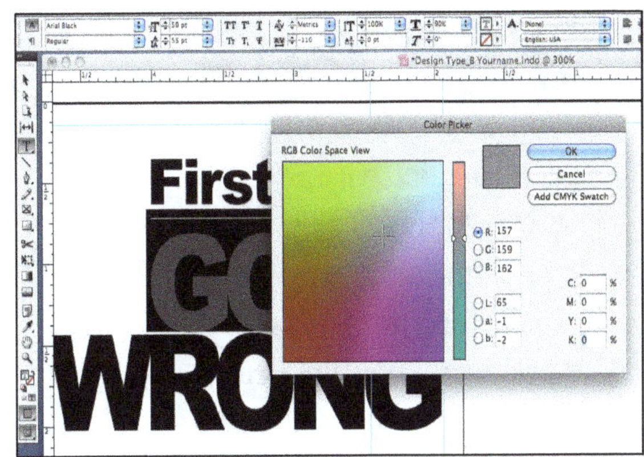

Your notes

– ***Reminder:*** *You may want to save your work.* ***Save often!***

Your notes

– **Make gray:** Double click on "Fill" and the "Color Picker" palette appears. Change the "K" (is the black) percentage to match the gray type indicated in the lesson example.

Headline sentences

The secret to this segment is to pay special attention and match the size and letterspacing of the words.

1. Create first line: Using the "Type Tool" Create a wide text box and type in "Just getting someone to say."

– **Font & size:** With the text still highlighted match the font and size (height). I would suggest printing out your project at this time to check the size, and adjust if needed.

– **Letterspacing:** Highlight all the letters and using the "Tracking" tool in the "Control Strip" reduce the letter-spacing to match the lesson example.
HINT: Keep adjusting the size and tracking/letterspacing until the line matches horizontally.

2. Create lines 2, 3, 4 & 5: Duplicate the first line created to save you time (from having to do the size, font and letterspacing). Using the "Selection Tool" click on the first line and go to the top and select "Edit" / "Duplicate."

– **New words:** Using the "Type Tool" highlight the duplicated text and type in the words for the next four lines (all in one text block). Use the return key to make the text go to the next line.

– **Align text right:** With the text still highlighted go to the "Control Strip" and align the words to the right using the correct body composition tool ("Align right").

3. Create last two lines: Duplicate the text block created above. Type in the correct words and follow the same steps to finish these last two lines.

4. Adjust leading: Now adjust the leading (spacing between all the lines of type created so they all are evenly spaced. Some will have to be done using the mouse or arrow keys and some will need to be adjusted using the "Leading" settings in the "Control Strip."

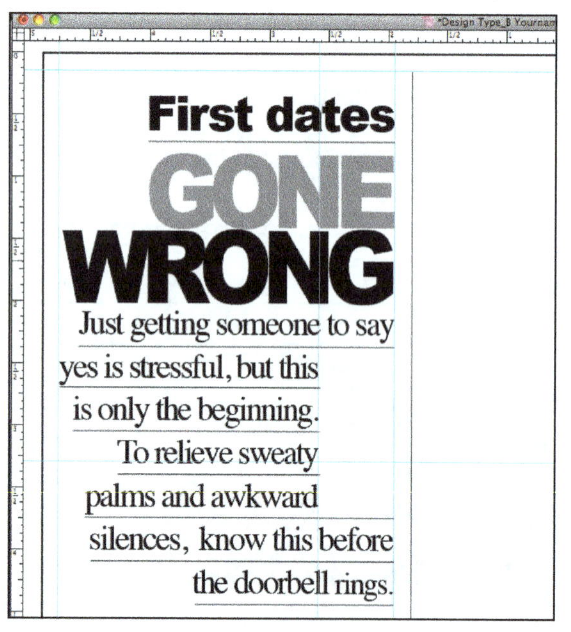

Lines under headline sentences

Using the "Line Tool," create lines with the correct weight, length, and spaced evenly between the lines of type.

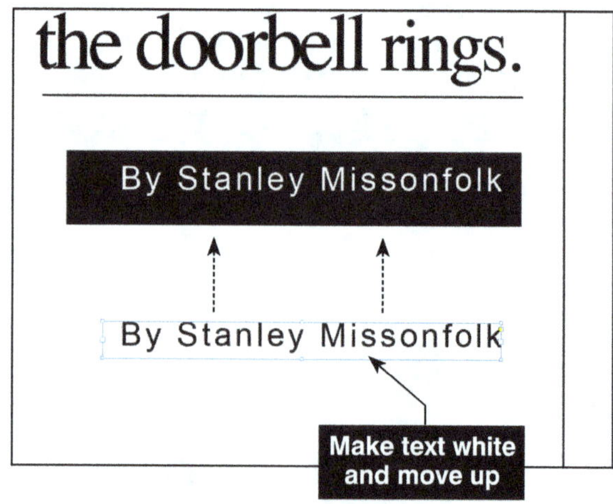

Byline: reversed type

The element is made of two separate items.

1. Create shape: Select the "Rectangle Tool" and create a rectangle the approximate size seen in the lesson example.

– **Rectangle color:** With the rectangle selected, double- click on the "Fill" tool in the "Tool Palette," which will bring up the "Color Picker." Create the color black by making the C: 0%, M: 0%, Y: 0%, K: 100% (K is the black), and clicking "OK."

2. Type: Using the "Type Tool," create a text box under the black rectangle (created in step 1) and type in the credit.

– **Type color:** Highlight the byline text created with the "Type Tool," double-click on the "Fill Tool," and make the type color white by entering 0% on all colors (C, M, Y, and K).

– **Move type:** Select the credit using the "Selection Tool" (black arrow) and move up over the black rectangle created.

HINT: I often find it easier to move small or difficult elements with the arrow keys rather than the computer's mouse.

Last-minute advice headline

This part of the lesson requires you to learn how to put text into multiple columns.

1. Gray box: Select the "Rectangle Tool" in the "Control Strip" and create a large box in the lower-left corner of your design.

– **Fill:** With the rectangle still selected, double-click on the "Fill" tool to bring up the "Color Picker" palette and make a gray to match the lesson example. Remember, gray is made from a percentage of black (K: %).

2. Headline: Using the "Type Tool." create a text box outside the magazine article design and type in the words "LAST-MINUTE ADVICE."

– **Font & size:** Highlight the headline and match the typeface and size to the lesson example.

– **Move the headline** on top of the gray box created to the correct location indicated by lesson example.

3. List information: Select the "Type Tool," and create a rather deep text box outside the magazine article design.

– **Content:** Type in the content as seen on the lesson example.

– **Correct typeface:** Highlight the text and make the content a typeface that matches the lesson design using the top "Control Strip" to match the lesson.

– **Font size:** Change the type size using the "Control Strip."

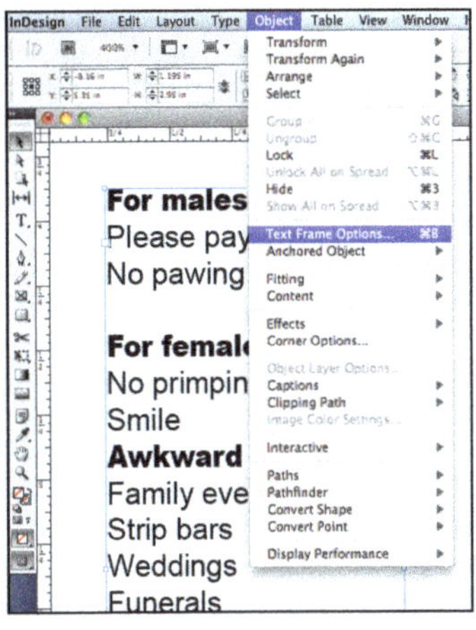

4. List to columns of type: Using the "Selection Tool" (black arrow), select the content type you created and go to the top of your screen and click on "Object" / "Text Frame Options."

– **Columns:** Change the number of columns to 3. You can also adjust the gutter width (amount of space between columns of type), but we will leave this to the default.

– **HINT:** If you want to see your changes as you make them, click on the "Preview" button at the lower left of the window.

5. Move content: Select the content and move onto the gray box created earlier. Adjust the content to match the lesson example:
– Width and depth of text box
– Type size
– Type leading
– Type attributes (regular, bold, etc.)

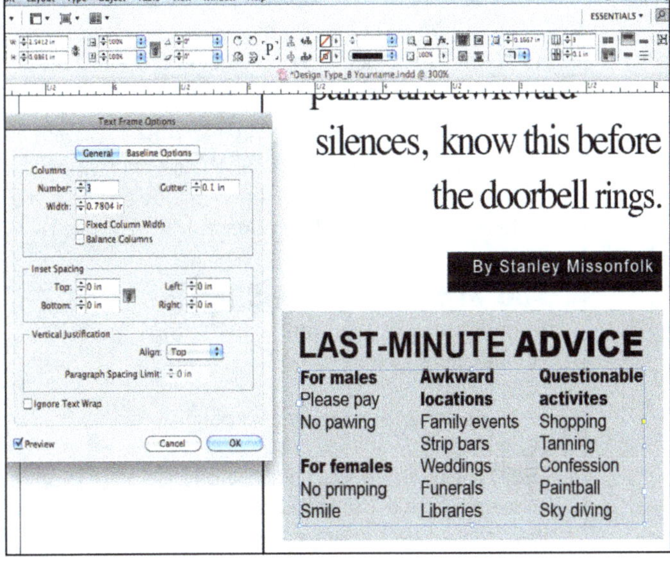

Doorbell image

1. Image layer: If you moved the doorbell to the required location first, you would discover that it would disappear. This is because the image would be behind other elements, since they were created after the doorbell. You will need to move this image to the top layer.

– **Select the doorbell image** using the "Selection Tool" and go to the top and click on "Object" / "Arrange" / "Bring to Front."

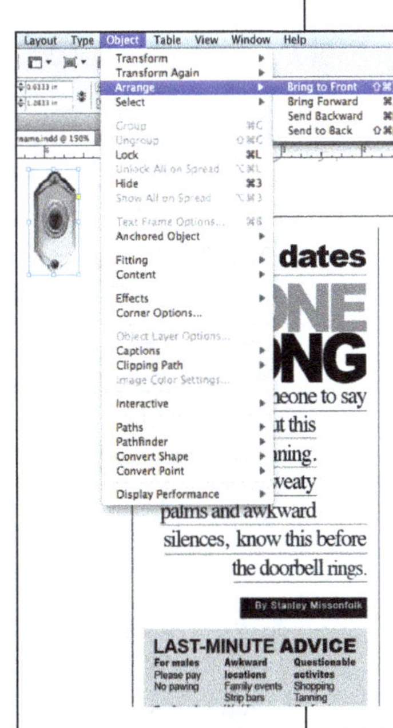

2. Move image: With the image still selected, click and drag photo image to the correct position.

**ore info »**

To learn more about the ***InDesign layers*** */ Pg. 28*

Your notes

Your notes

Magazine sidebar

The last part of this magazine article design is the sidebar package, which includes a headline and four small sections, each with their own small headline.

1. Black bar: The design calls for a small black bar at the top of the package. Use the "Rectangle Tool" to create this bar and move it into the correct position.

– **Fill:** Double-click the "Fill" tool and make the rectangle black (K:100%). No stroke.

2. Text content: The easiest way to create this element is to create all the text within one text box. This will allow for more accurate alignment and spacing of all the items.

– **Create type box:** Using the "Type Tool," create a very tall text box outside the magazine article design (this makes it easier at first).

– **Type in all the words** seen in this sidebar. After each headline, enter a return on the keyboard. Do not worry that it is the correct typeface or font at this stage.

3. Bold headline: Using the "Type Tool," highlight the top headline "Please say you didn't do that" and go to the top "Control Strip" and select the correct typeface and font size.

– Match the leading (space between lines of text).

– Match the text composition (ragged right, centered, justified, etc.).

HINT: Designers often will use the same typefaces or variations of the typefaces in their designs to layer the information and create harmony.

4. Light italic headlines: Using the "Type Tool" Highlight the next headline "Check out others" and go to the top "Control Strip" and select the correct typeface and font size.

– Match the leading (space between lines of text).

– Match the text composition (ragged right, centered, justified, etc.)

REPEAT this for all the other similar headlines in this text box.

5. Body text: Using the "Type Tool," Highlight the top body text that starts with "So you thought no one would . . ." and go to the top "Control Strip" and select the correct typeface and font size.

– Match the leading (space between lines of text).

– Also match the text composition (ragged right, centered, justified, etc.).

– **Indents:** Using the "Type Tool," click at the beginning of each body text block and add spaces (indent) for the black boxes to come.

REPEAT this for all the other similar body text blocks within this text box.

6. Move: Use the "Selection Tool" and move the text box into place on the magazine article design. Using the text box handles, adjust the size according to the lesson example.

7. Adjustment: When the content was moved, you may have discovered it did not fit or look correct, so now is the time to make all the adjustments to each section to make a perfect match.

8. Small black boxes: Using the "Rectangle Tool," create a small square box outside the design.

– Give it a fill of black.

– Move the box to the correct position to see if it is the correct size.

HINT: I have found that moving with the arrow keys is the easiest. My second preferred way is to use the "Zoom Tool" and magnify the view a lot and then use the "Selection Tool," to click on a middle section of the object and click and drag into place using the mouse.

– **Duplicate box:** When you have discovered the correct black square box size, use the "Selection Tool" click on the box and go to "Edit" / "Duplicate." Now move into the next correct location.

Creating the box another way: If you have typeface called "Zapf Dingbats" there is a better way to create the small black box. Using the "Type Tool," click at the beginning of the text block and type a lowercase "n."

– **Next**, highlight this letter using the "Type Tool" and change the typeface to "Zapf Dingbats." This typeface is made up of numerous familiar and unique symbols and the lowercase "n" is a black square.

❶

Please say you didn't do that ❸

Check out others ❹

❽ ■ So you thought no one would notice when you gave the server a quick look ❺ you know the look). Both males and females are tempted to flirt with waitresses or other patrons when out. What a bad move.

Fashionably late

■ Even five minutes is inexcusable on the first date. That someone special you found is already anxious thinking they might become the next horror story of being stood up. What were you thinking?

Answer a text

■ So you had to whip out the new phone and text your friend. Unless you are a heart surgeon or a superhero incognito, it is rude to use your phone when you are supposed to be giving someone special your full attention. Tell me you did not do this.

Food dribble

■ Well the spaghetti at the fine Italian restaurant proved to be a bad choice. Embarrassment from spilled food is the last thing you needed. I can't look.

You are almost finished

Go back and edit your work to perfection!
– Edit content (is it all there)?
– Edit sizes.
– Edit placements (watch for borders).
– Edit leading.
– Edit type attribute (bold, italic, etc.)
– Now print out a finished lesson and be proud that you have learned a lot about InDesign.

SAVE

– Reminder: You may want to save your work. Save often!

DESIGNING with color

"**Bad use of color** is everywhere, but the good use of color is rare."

You most likely can tell by now that I am very passionate about good design. Well, my passion about color might even be more intense. The reason is that I see poor uses of color every day. Many of these uses of bad color even extend well beyond communication design. Color is an integral part of our society and extends to all ages, gender, and groups of our society. The challenge is that almost everyone uses color. All people seem to have strong opinions on color and most display or use color poorly.

My challenge to you is to help me rid our society of bad color usege and help enlighten the many who have been taught that color is solely based on their opinion (usually influenced by their self-proclaimed favorite color).

The good news is that this lesson is easier than the last and that creating color in InDesign is simple. However, I would like you to take the time to not only learn to create color, but try to understand the basic color principles so you can improve your communications and help me make this a more pleasant-looking world.

Color matters

This is how the problem started

Color is one of the most powerful tools a communicator has at their disposal, yet it is often used by many so poorly that it often dilutes or destroys the intended message. One easy design solution is to keep it simple. However, keeping it simple does not mean just using basic red, green, or blue (basic colors). What it means is to not try to use just your favorite color or all the colors at one time and hope it works . . . it won't!

Who influenced our use of color?

The truth is that most people just use the colors they personally like.

Each of us very early in life was encouraged to use color, and this was usually followed by our parents asking us what our favorite color was. What followed was you were now forever associated with that color, which meant:

- You had clothes that color
- Toys that color
- Birthday gifts that color
- Your first bicycle had to be that color
- Your room painted that color
- Do I really need to go on?

Oh yes, I must go on!

Your grandmother asked, your friends asked, your baby sitter asked, your doctor asked, and even the server at the restaurant asked what your favorite color was and thus proceed to give tribute to you and this newfound fact. Even your teachers asked your favorite color and then would proceed to hand you a couple of coloring crayons (which included your FAVORITE color) to create some great art masterpiece.

Solving the problem

I ask you to consider the use of more than your favorite color.

I encourage you to go beyond just using the eight colors from your first box of coloring crayons.

Let's take a big leap of faith and use the colors from the big prized box of 64 colors!

I must insist you go wild and consider even hundreds of colors and maybe mixing them . . . now you have the color tools that will add power to your communications and designs!

The good news is that InDesign allows you to easily make millions of colors, but you will need some basic understanding of the principles and uses of color to create effective communication.

What is color?

Color is part of light. White light is the presence of all color, which Sir Isaac Newton proved with the famous prism that showed light reflecting into the various bands of color (rainbow of colors). Thus, no light (black) is the absence of color. This brings us to the two types of color you will be facing while working on this lesson.

Your notes

Light color: Is that which exists in anything that uses light as the primary source. This would be things such as TVs, projectors, and computer screens. The primary colors for this type of color would be RGB (red, green, blue). Using these three colors in different combinations results in all the colors of the spectrum. Most digital cameras create photographs in RBG color.

Printed color: Color is not an inherent quality of a physical object like an apple. Instead, this fruit's surface has a certain molecular structure that will absorb some light (colors), not letting you see them, and reflect other light (colors) that you do see. We refer to this type of color as reflective color and it is used when creating printed communication in InDesign.

The printed colors have different primary colors used to make all the colors in the spectrum. These are cyan (blue), magenta (red), yellow, and black–CMYK. You will quickly notice that the cyan (blue) and magenta (red) do not look like what you would expect; however, when these primary ink colors are combined together in printing they produce very realistic color.

Combining blue, red, and yellow brings back memories of elementary school when classmates would paint with each of these colors separately and bring their brushes to be cleaned in the shared water can. After a few swishes of each brush color, a very dark brown/black would be created. However, printed colors often include "K," which is black in most cases. Black printing ink is a different color than the combination of all three primary colors. The addition of the separate black ink makes for richer, vibrant full-color printing.

The color white in the printed colors comes from the white of the paper or by adding a separate white ink.

Light color – RGB

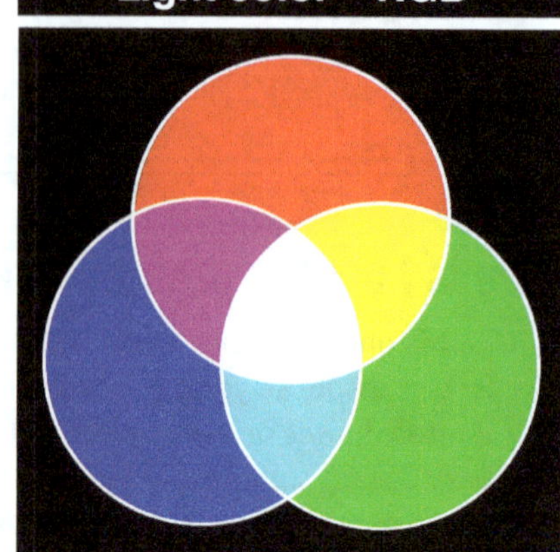

White is created with overlap of colors. **Black** is the result of no light (colors).

Printed color – CMYK

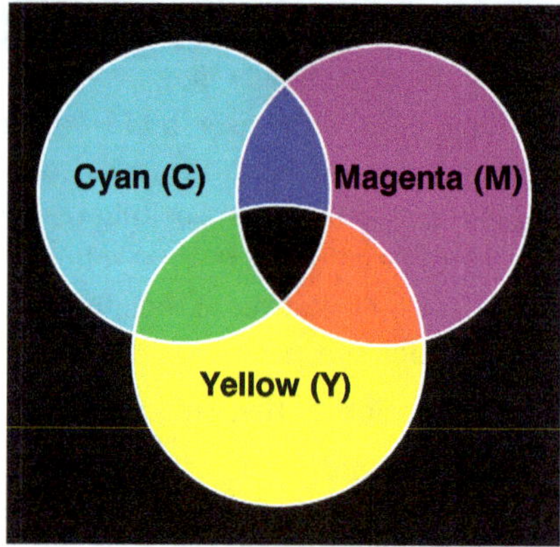

Black is created with overlap of colors. **White** is the result of no color (often paper color).

Why aren't all colors the same?

When you really begin working with color in your designs you very quickly discover how many colors are perceived differently by people. What you need to know is that color does not always conform to physical laws. A person's interpretation of a color often depends on the context. Here are some examples that influence color differences:

Physical: Not all human eyes are created equal. More than seven percent of the population has some form of color blindness. This can be minor with only slight color differences or severe with no color recognition.

Environment: Not all viewing conditions are the same. Viewing a color-printed brochure in the outdoor sun could look different from viewing the same piece inside a building under fluorescent lighting.

Technological: Computer screens are not the same. If you have ever looked at the same color project on two different computers, you would have noticed this fact. Simply the different ages of computer screens could result in different contrast and color balances; thus, the color would look very different.

Physiological: Not everyone's brain processes the stimuli from color the same. Women are more attracted to color, while men do not like color as much and prefer darker colors.

Cultural: Not everyone learns color the same. When you were very young, your mother pointed out an orange (fruit) and told you it was the color orange–when actually the fruit is almost red orange.

Designing with color

Color basics

Let's start with some terminology!

Some of the following terms may be familiar while others might be new to you. One reason is a lot of our use of color has been simplified because of marketing strategies. For example, many retailers, like paint stores, refer to their colors in specific names because they found most of the public had little color knowledge but could remember a distinctive color name. The problem is a "moss green" paint sample at one store might be called "silvery summer green" at another paint company–and that's if you get lucky and the green colors match. The good news is that if you learn the basic color theories and terminology, you will not be at their color-naming mercy and will be empowered to create millions of colors.

■ **Hue** refers to a pure color (example: violet) that has a specific wavelength and does not include tints or shades. In the coming lesson I will often refer to hue and color as the same to make things simpler for you.

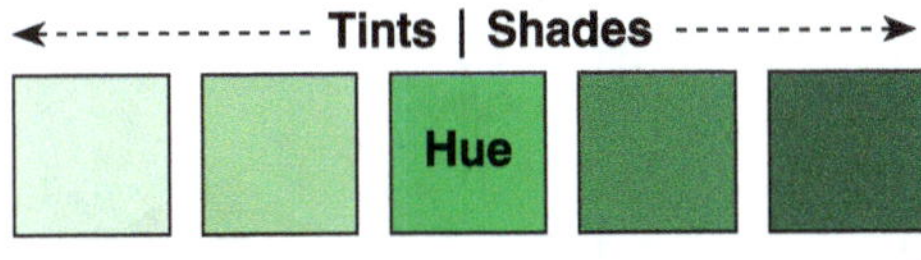

■ **Value** refer to the relative lightness and darkness of a hue (color). We change the value of a color by creating tints (lighter versions of the color) and shades (darker versions of the color). Using printed colors, we can create tints of color in the "Swatches" palette and create the shades of a color by adding black to the original color by using the "Color Picker."

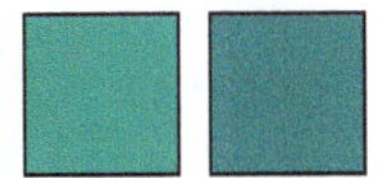

■ **Saturation/value** is the relative purity of the color. Full saturation of the color (example: blue green) would be a bright intense color. To lessen the intensity (saturation) you would add small amounts of an opposite color (complementary color) on the color wheel (example has 20% magenta /red added to one block and 40% to the other).

Too often I see people who do not understand color well not using tints and shades to change the value of the color. Many who use color resort to their early years of using color when they were given praise for bearing down on their crayons and creating bright colors. Good visual communicators will not only consider the color (hue), but also the color's value and saturation to get the most out of the use of the color.

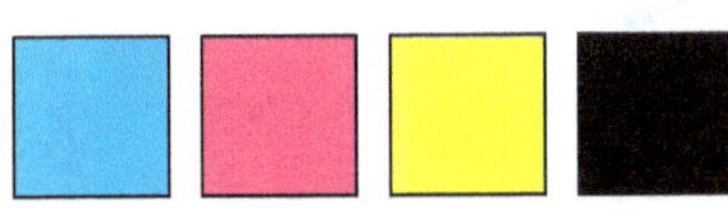

■ **Primary colors** refers to basic colors on the color wheel that cannot be derived by the mixing of colors. In printed color these are cyan (C), magenta (M), yellow (Y), and most often black (K).

NOTE: Cyan (which is blue) and magenta (which is red) will not look like what you have learned. However, both are the pure hues for printed color.

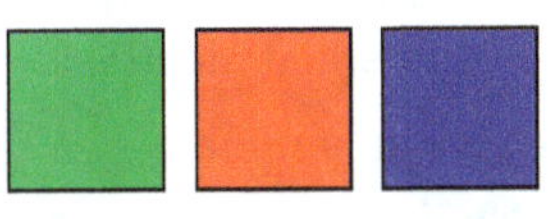

■ **Secondary colors** are colors that are created by mixing equal amounts of two primary colors. When working with printed color, these are green (C+Y), orange (Y+M), and violet (M+C).

■ **Tertiary colors** refer to colors that are created by mixing one primary color with a secondary color. Mixing yellow (primary color) with green (secondary color) will create yellow green. Likewise, mixing cyan (primary color) with green (secondary color) will give you blue green. All other tertiary colors are created the same way.

NOTE: In this example, yellow green is made of 100% yellow plus 50% cyan, while blue green is made by using 100% cyan plus 50% yellow.

■ **Complementary colors** are those that are opposite each other on the color wheel. When these two colors are used together in a design, they have the maximum contrast.

Caution: Be very careful about using equal amounts, because they become very difficult to look at for any extended period. I like to use varied tints and shades of one color and very small amounts of the opposite color to give a bit of a pop of contrast in the design.

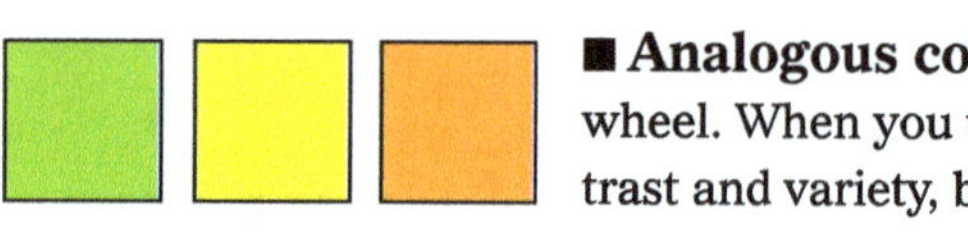

■ **Analogous colors** are those that are adjacent to one another on the color wheel. When you use two, three, of more adjacent colors they give some contrast and variety, but create soothing effect, which is referred to as harmony.

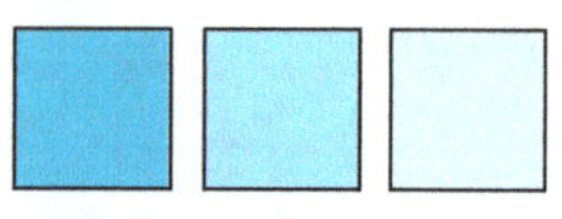

■ **Monochromatic colors** refer to the use of tints and shades of a single hue (color). This use has minimal contrast and is very soothing. Overuse of these colors use can be considered boring at times.

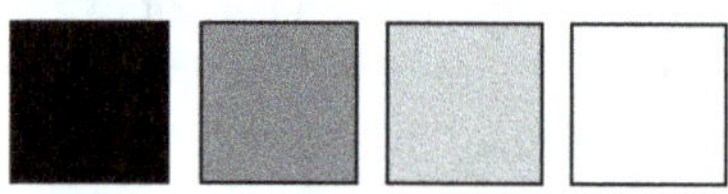

■ **Black and white** are often neglected when color is used, but it can often be the foundation for many good designs. During my years as a graphic artist and designer, I have seen many great designs that only used black and white. Just like using other colors, consider all the variations that can be created with just one color and the bountiful creativity that two colors (black and white) would allow.

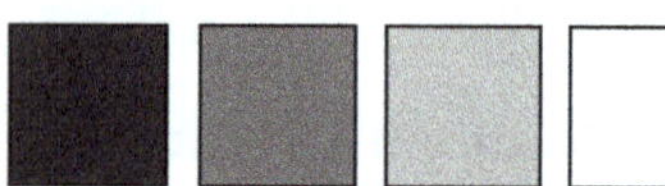

■ **Painters gray** is the creative side of black and white. This color is made from using equal amounts of the primary colors to make a gray that has more depth and is richer than a gray made using only black. I use this type of gray to create much more sophisticated designs. Often, using color is not about being bold but the subtle sophistication you can create.

NOTE: I also will use a light painters gray to determine the quality of the printing. If the painters gray appears a bit red (warm), it means the red (magenta) ink is printing too strong. If the painters gray looks a bit blue (cold), the cyan is printing too much, and likewise with other colors.

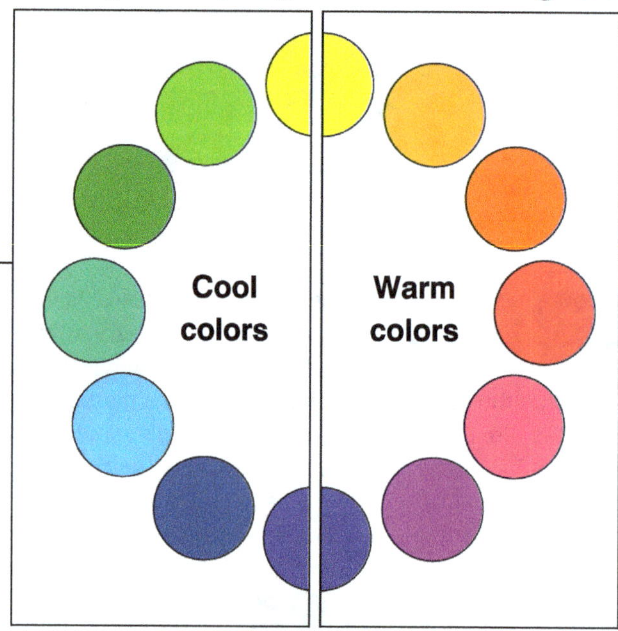

■ **Warm and cool colors** are the colors that denote the sensation of temperature. The warm colors are those that are associated with the sun and fire (include yellow, orange, and magenta). The cool colors are those most associated with water and sky (include green and cyan). These colors are also often referred to as earth colors and are the calming tranquil colors. The warm colors occupy one half of the color wheel while the cool colors occupy the other side.

Color should have a function

Taking your communication to the next level is easier than you think and it often starts with using color more effectively so it matches the information, the media, the client, and the audience. I would challenge you to avoid selecting your favorite color or using color for purely aesthetic purposes. Instead, color should have a function–should do something for the message and/or the design. Here are five potential functions:

Informational: Color can provide more information to the content. Let's say you have an outline drawing that resembles an apple. The shape enables you to see an apple. Take that same shape and apply B&W shading. Now the apple begins to have dimension. Now take that same shape and add red. It denotes a red sweet apple. Color the apple shape green and it tells of a sour apple. Making that same shape yellowish brown and it indicates an apple that is beginning to spoil with a not-so-pleasant taste. Here, color added information and told you much more about the apple.

Symbolic: In this use try to use a color that can denote some symbolism to further the message and use of color. Often when a color becomes part of society's culture it can become symbolic, like a flag or sports team. However, remember that symbolism, while very effective, is not always the same in all communities or cultures.

Affective: Color has the ability to shape a message's tone or mood, thus amplifying the message. Bright tones often will denote activity and fun while a light blue and green can denote tranquility and a peaceful mood. Using the wrong colors could create the opposite effect and make the information less effective.

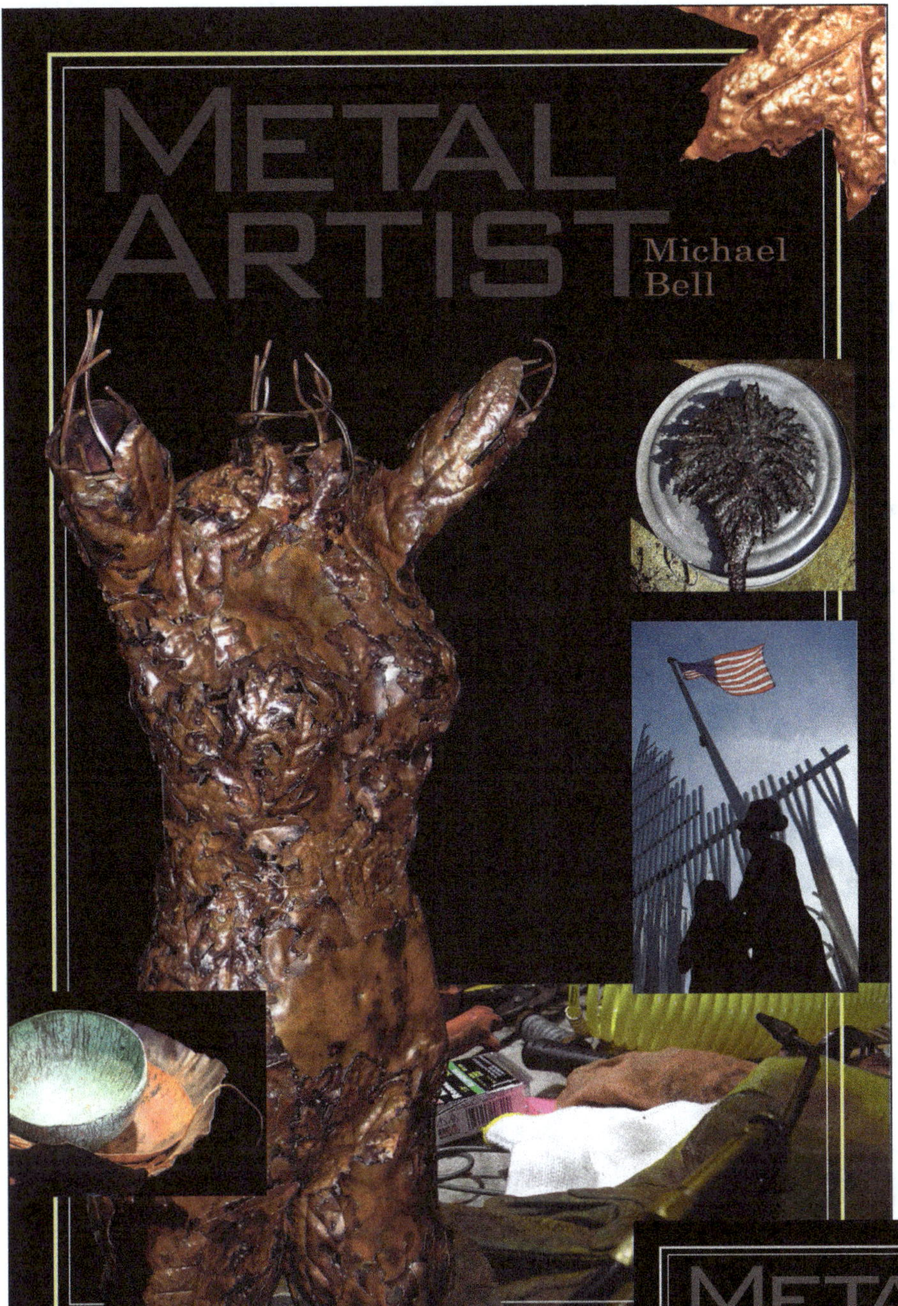

Associational: People tend to associate colors with specific meanings often based on their life experiences. Bright green is often associated with spring, while a vibrant red often denotes something very hot or danger.

Companies often spend a lot of time and money on creating a color association to their company and products and in many cases it works.

Coca Cola = Red

Kodak = Yellow and black

John Deere = Green

Aesthetic: While I encourage not using color for decorative uses only, it can create a visally pleasing effect. If color is used well and you discover a unique approach, this can lift the design from the practical to the artful.

Your notes

Color vs. black and white

These two posters illustrate the power of using color. The black-and-white poster evokes interest with the use of dynamic photographic images, bold type, and contrast.

The color poster goes beyond that and commands attention because of the strong use of color. The use of color in the photographs adds information and helps you understand the materials and techniques used in the artist's metal sculptures. The addition of earth tone colors in the headline and borders helps establish eye movement within the poster, yet providing overall harmony.

Your notes

Color do's and don'ts

DO use color when communicating with women if possible. Females grow up using and being surrounded by color, from notebooks to clothing.

DO use a sophisticated palette of colors. All target audiences have become more visually sophisticated in the last decade.

DO consider using the color white. American Eskimos illustrate how important every color is, especially white. They don't just see white, they have over 17 words to describe different variations of white–think about their white world and the different types of white that must exist.

DO consider using trendy colors when communicating with teens and young adults–they like them.

DO remember that symbolism may be part of a color. However, some color's symbolism is not universal. In America black is the traditional color worn by mourners; however, in China the color is white.

DON'T only use the primary colors. There are millions of colors you can make.

DON'T use just basic colors when designing for kids. Have you seen Saturday morning cartoons and kids' magazines lately? They are accustomed to a sophisticated palette of colors.

DON'T design using all saturated / intense colors. This can be too intense for many viewers.

DON'T place dark or saturated colors behind small typography. It may be hard to read–remember, legibility is everything in communication.

DON'T expect the color on your work to look the same when printed. Your computer monitor is showing you color in RGB while the printed page color is CMYK–often they look significantly different.

Summary

I hope by now you have seen how significant color is to our society. More than 70 percent of all sensory receptors in the human body are in the eyes so they take a commanding role in communication and our perception of the world. While color is one of the most powerful tools you can use to create effective communication, it also can be the most damaging if used poorly. Now that you understand color theory better, it is time to discover how simple it is to create colors using InDesign in the upcoming lesson.

Remember, just experiment and have fun with color while discovering new uses!

DESIGNING with color

LESSON . . .

What InDesign skills will you learn?

- How to create primary, secondary, and tertiary colors
- How to make tints and shades of all colors
- The difference between making gray and painters gray
- How color choices affect a company's logo

Creating color in InDesign

Overview

With the expanded use of desktop publishing has come an explosion of bad use of color. It is essential that all communicators know what good color is and how to create effective color for print and multimedia.

Specifications

■ Use the InDesign "Designing with Color template (A)" to create the color wheel and add color to the illustrations.

■ **Creating circles**
You will need to draw circles for the hues, tints, and shades and place them evenly as seen. Sizes of the circles:

Color/hues = 1.12"

Tints and shades = 0.51"

■ **Creating colors**
You will need to create and assign colors for all the circles based on a color wheel that includes primary, secondary, and tertiary colors. NOTE: These will need to be print color (CMYK).

■ **Label each color** using Arial (bold) 10 pts.

■ **Indicate the mixture** of each color in Arial (plain) 8 pts. type. See the example on the color wheel shown. Place these evenly around the colors.

NOTE: If you are using a computer that does not have the Arial typeface, then use Helvetica or Geneva.

■ **Create a tint** of each color using 25% of each color.

■ **Create a shade** of each color by creating a new color and adding 35% black.

■ **Painters Gray** is a triangle created in the middle of the color wheel. Each point of the triangle should point to one of the primary colors. The color is created by mixing equal amounts (25%) of the primary colors.

Color logos

Each of the illustrations located at the bottom of the template are to be created with a different color scheme (indicated below each logo). The color choices are up to you (be creative).

The final product

■ Print the lesson in color on standard 8.5" X 11" paper.

■ Include your name at the top of the lesson.

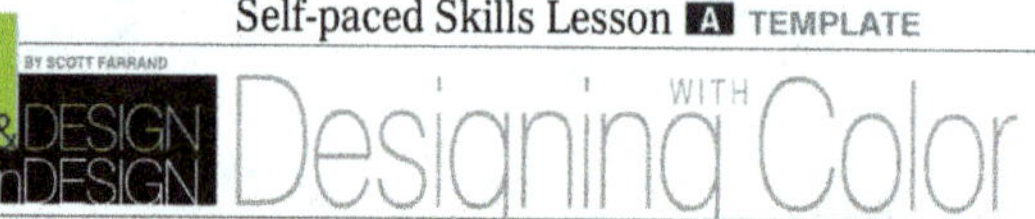

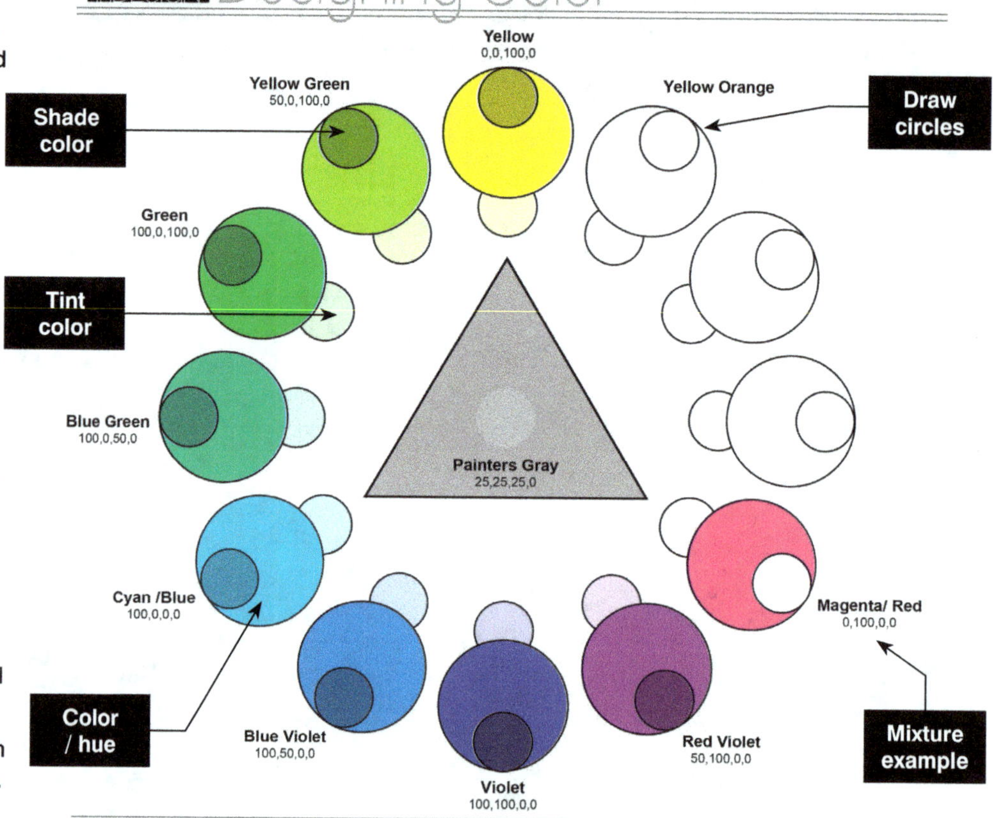

Assessment criteria

■ Are the shapes drawn correctly and evenly spaced?

■ Are the colors on the color wheel mixed correctly?

■ Colors labeled correctly and spaced evenly?

■ Are the Ilustrations created with the correct color schemes?

■ Was the lesson printed in quality color?

Locating lesson template

For this lesson you will be using a precreated InDesign template named "Design Color_A template." This template has guides that indicate the center of the page and will be the starting place to create the color wheel. The template also includes outlines of three illustrations at the bottom of the page, which you will fill with color later.

Getting started

Locate the template and place it on the desktop of your computer.

■ **REMEMBER:** Always drag a copy of the InDesign file to your computer desktop first. Never open and work on a file that is located on a server or your thumb drive. Failure to remember this could result in a file that goes bad and will not open or print later.

Next, highlight the word "template" and replace it with your last name. This will ensure you are always working on your copy and can find the file later if needed.

Open file

If you are using an Apple computer, there is an easier way to open a file! Simply drag the icon of your file on top of the "InDesign" icon located in your dock and the program will be launched and the file opened with one step.

Creating the color wheel design

1. Create a guide to help: Often the ruler guides are not enough help, so do not hesitate to create your own guides and shapes. Give it a stroke of blue (or any other color that is easy for you to see) and delete the guides later.

– **The overall size** of the color wheel is 6 inches wide. Creating a guide to help align the circles and keep the design the correct shape is crucial.

– **Select the "Ellipse Tool"** hidden within the "Rectangle Tool" and create a 6 inch circle in the middle of the page. Remember, once you create the shape you can go to the "Control Strip" and enter 6 inches to get the exact size quickly.

– **Align the center of the circle** (indicated with an "■" in the middle) with the intersection of the two guides. Click on the guide outline (not the handles) with the "Selection Tool" and move to the correct position.

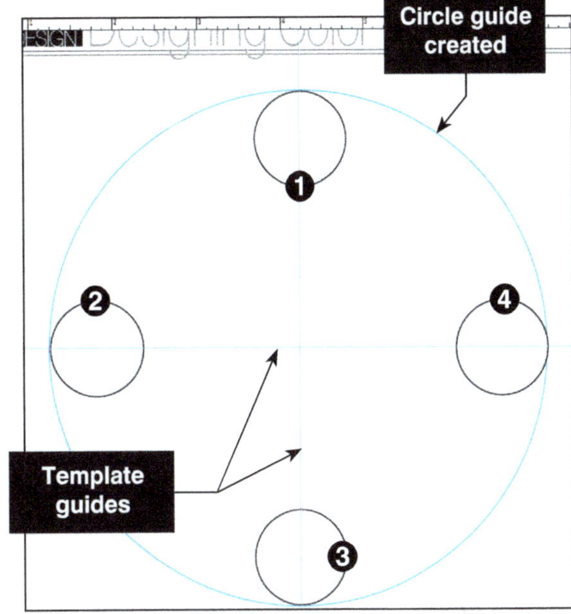

2. Create color (hue) circles: Select the "Ellipse Tool," and create a 1.12 inch circle. Using the "Selection Tool" click and hold on the outline of the circle and move the circle so the outline touches the outline of the large circle guide and the middle handle on the circle intersects with the vertical guide (1).

– With the circle selected, set the circle frame to be .5 pts. Remember, you do this by using the "Stroke" palette or setting the stroke using the "Control Strip."

– **Create a second circle** by duplicating the first circle. Make sure the circle is selected and go to "Control Strip" (at the top) and select "Edit" / "Duplicate." Click on this shape and move it so the outline again touches the outline of the large circle guide and the middle handle intersects with horizontal guide (2).

– **Create circles 3 and 4** by duplicating the first circle and repeat the processes above for circle (3) and (4).

3. Create remaining color (hue) circles: Looking at the color wheel design (on previous page), you will notice that there are two circles between each of the circles centered on the horizontal and vertical guides.

– **Create two new circles** by duplicating one of the existing circles.

– **Visually place them between existing circles** (1) and (2). Make sure the outer edge of your new circles touch the existing large circle guide. Visually space both circles so they are evenly placed between the existing circles.

– **To make spacing perfect**, create a small measure-

Your notes

SAVE

*– **Reminder:** You may want to save your work. **Save often!***

ment circle that fits precisely between the circles (at the closest points). Now move that circle between two other circles and check the spacing. If it is not the same, you will either need to move the color circles or change the size on your newly created measurement circle.

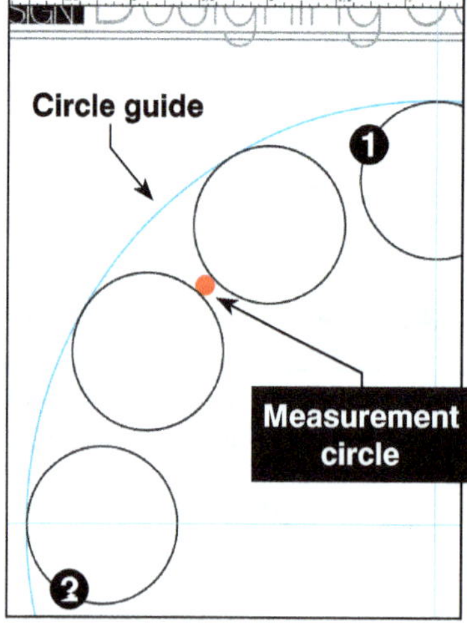

4. Correct stroke: With all the color (hue) circles created now, make sure each has a .5 pt. frame on all.

TIP moving elements »

You may have already discovered that moving small elements can be difficult. Here are some methods that may help:

*– **Method 1 / click & drag:** Using the "Selection Tool," click outside the element you want to move or change. Click on the element and drag in one movement (the secret is to make sure you do not click on a handle and you do this in one quick movement).*

*– **Method 2 / use arrows:** Using the "Selection Tool," click on the element you want to move (again make sure you click on edges but not handles). Now use your arrow keys on your keyboard. While this can be slow, it works!*

*– **Note:** Both of these methods are easier if you use the magnifying glass and zoom in on the object.*

Creating the shades

1. Creating shades: Using the "Ellipse Tool," create a circle that is 0.51 inches in diameter. Remember to use the control strip to get the exact size. Now set the frame to .5 pt.

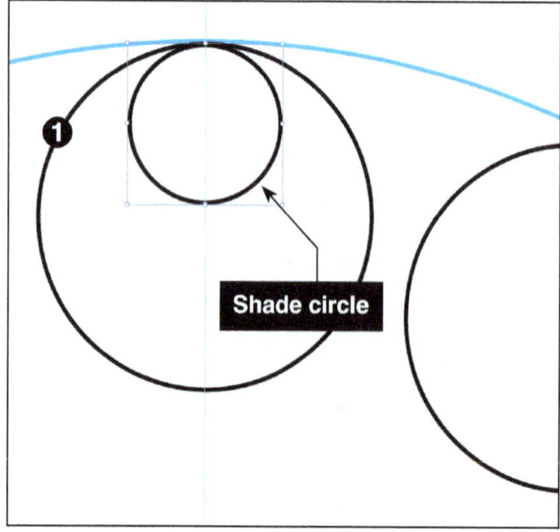

– **Move the shade circle:** Using the "Selection Tool," select the circle and drag the shape so it touches the outside of the large measurement circle and is on top of circle (1) at the top of the design

– **Align the shade circle** so the middle handles intersect with the vertical guide. This will ensure that the circle is centered with the color circle.

NOTE: Zoom in to make this easier.

2. Repeat these steps for shades that are associated with circles aligned with vertical or horizontal guides (circles 2, 3, and 4).

3. Creating remaining shades: Duplicate one of the previously created shade circles. Select and move this shade on top of one of the other large color circles. Make sure that you place the shade circle's outer edge up against the large guide circle's outer edge.

TIP move & see hint »

When moving some elements it would be good to see the element . . . this is possible!

*– **Using the "Selection Tool,"** Click and hold until you see the element and the bonding box. Still holding down on the mouse, now drag your mouse and you will be able to accurately move the element.*

4. Aligning remaining shades: Once all the shades are created and visually placed, you will need to check the alignment to all those that do not have horizontal or vertical guides. Despite how good your eyesight is the alignment is most likely off on a few.

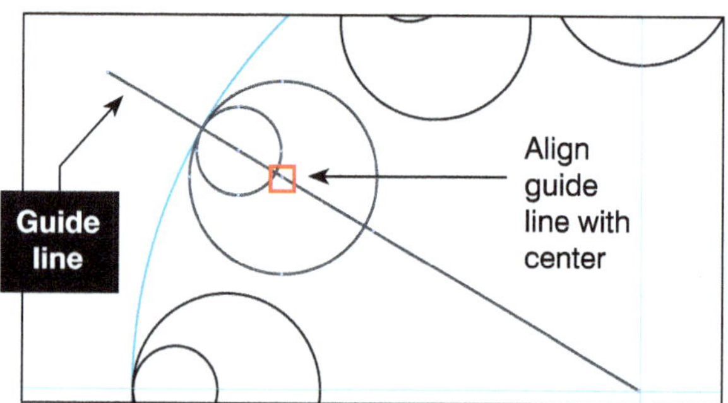

– **Creating a new guide:** Select the "Line Tool" and move your mouse to the center of the design, at the intersection of the horizontal and vertical guides. Now click / hold down / and drag the line tool over the middle of one of the shade and hue circles.

– **Align shades:** Select the "Direct Selection Tool" and click on the hue (color) circle. Does the line you created run through the "X" found in the middle of the circle? If not, using the "Direct Selection Tool," click on the line and you will see white boxes at the end of the line. Click / drag on this white box to move the end of the line to align with center of hue (color) circle.

– Now get the "Selection Tool" and click on the outside of the shade circle to align its center with the line. Remember to make sure the outer edge of the shade circle is still aligned with the outer edge of the large circle guide.

4. Move guide line: Now it is time to adjust the alignment of the remaining shade circles. Using the "Direct Selection Tool," click on the "Guide Line"

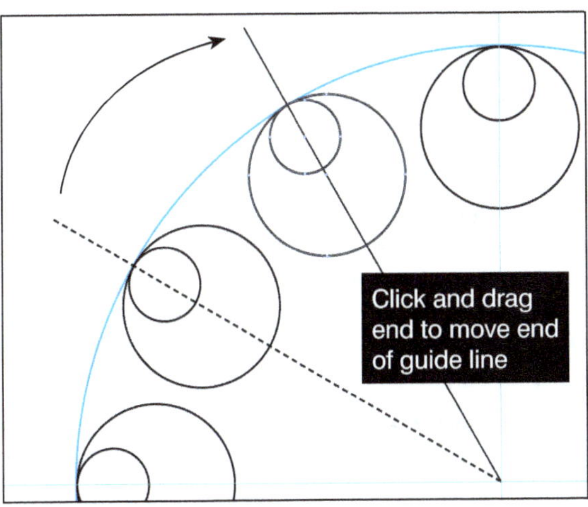

created.

– Now click / hold /drag on the end of the line nearest the circles (the object is to click precisely on the white box at the end of the line). Move the end of the line to the middle of the next hue (color) circle and repeat the alignment steps used earlier.

– When all the shade circles are aligned properly, you can delete the "Line Guide."

Creating the tints

1. Creating tint shapes: The good news is that this is much like creating the shades. Using the "Ellipse Tool," create a circle that is 0.51 inch in diameter. Remember to use the control strip to get the exact size. Now set the frame to .5 pt.

NOTE: An easier way is to duplicate one of the shade circles (these are the same size).

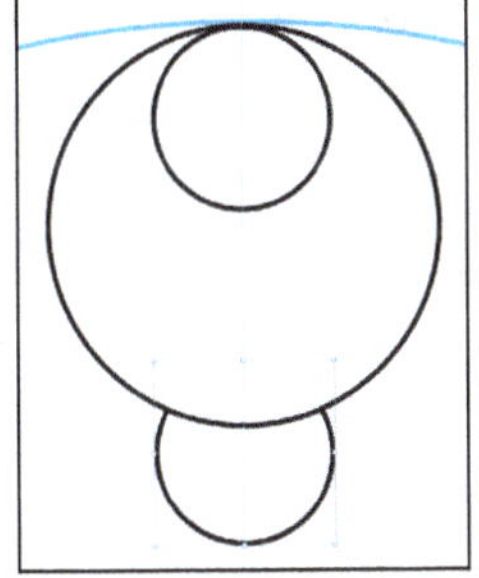

– **Move the tint circle:** Using the "Selection Tool" select the circle and drag the shape so it touches the bottom of the hue (color) circle. Also make sure the middle handle in the shade circle's bounding box aligns with the guide.

– **Move toward color:** Now using your arrow keys on your computer keyboard, move the shade toward the color circle 12 spaces.

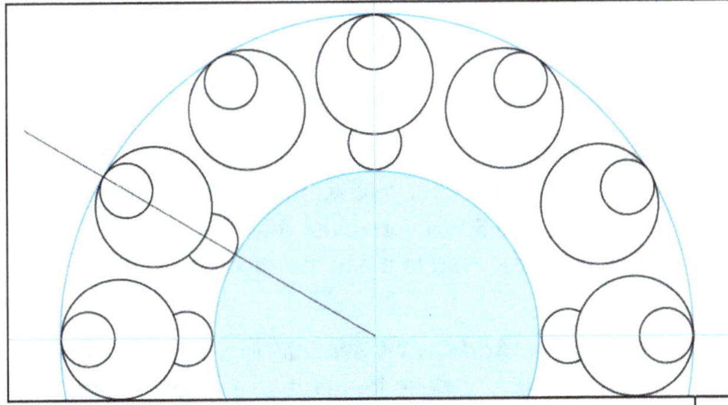

– **Repeat** this process to create the three other tint circles that align with vertical or horizontal guides.

2. Creating more tints: Making them will not be any trouble just duplicate tints already made. However, aligning them accurately is a challenge.

– The easiest way is to **create another circle guide** that extends to the outer edge of the tints already placed.

NOTE: I have added a light blue tone in my example to make it easier to see.

– **Next, create a line guide** (like was created for shades) that starts at the center of the design and extends thrrough the center of one of the color circles.

– **Now move** (using the "Selection Tool") your tint circle so that it just touches the outer edge of the circle guide and the center lines up with the line guide.

3. Creating remaining tints:

– Move line guide to next color circles.

– Duplicate existing tint circles.

– Move to position.

– Repeat process.

4. Finishing: When all the tint circles have been created and placed, you can delete your line guide and tint circle guide you created.

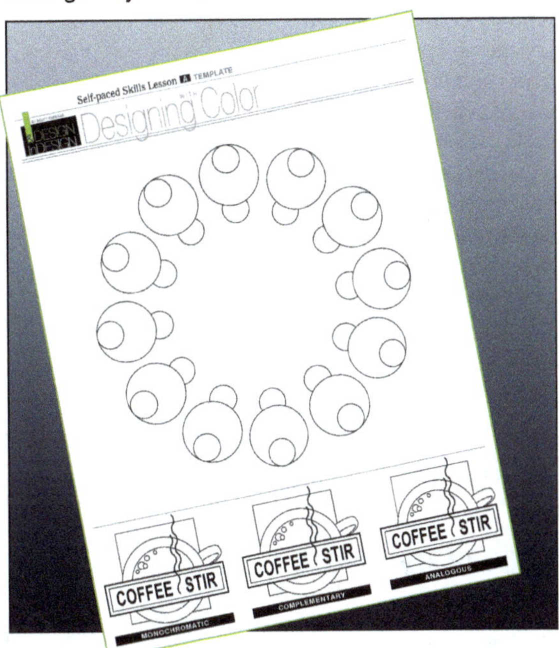

Creating color

The good news is that the hard part of this lesson is done. Creating and placing color in the circles is easy.

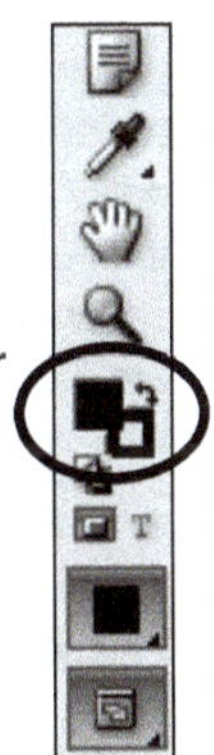

1. Using the "Selection Tool," (black arrow tool) click on the outline of one of the primary color circles (try yellow first).

2. Next, double click the "Fill" box in the "Tool Palette." This brings up the "Color Picker," which allows you to create the color needed. Type in the color mixture needed (100% yellow, 0% of other colors).

3. Create swatch color: With color mixture created, click on **"Add CMYK Swatch"** to add this color to the "Swatches Palette." Next, click on "OK" to finish.

NOTE: Knowing how to add a color to the "Swatches Palette" allows you to use that color repeatedly if needed in the future.

Your notes

Your notes

NOTE: Do not worry if you accidentally created an "RGB" color in the "Swatches Palette" in the last step. Just open the "Swatches Palette" and find the RGB color and double click on the four-color box to the right of the color. This brings up the "Swatch Options" window box, which allows you to change the mode to CMYK.

4. Other primary colors: Locate the cyan (blue) and the magenta (red) circle, which are equal distances from each other on the color wheel. Create these colors as you did when creating the yellow.

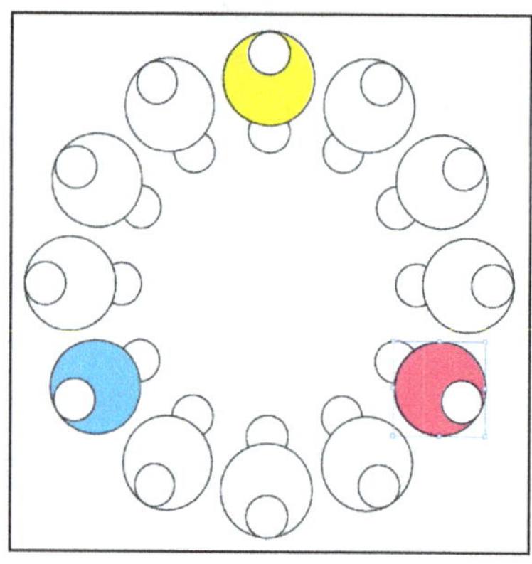

Cyan (Blue): C = 100, M = 0, Y = 0, B = 0

Magenta (Red): C = 0, M = 100, Y = 0, B = 0

Secondary colors

1. These colors are made with equal amounts of two primary colors. Example: 100 percent cyan plus 100 percent yellow equals the secondary color green. On the color wheel secondary colors are found halfway between two primary colors.

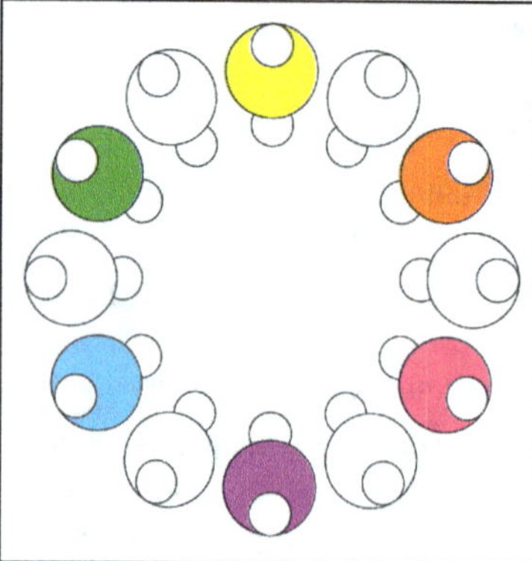

2. Locate and select the green circle on the color wheel design and double-click the "Fill" tool in the "Tool Palette."

– **Color Picker:** When widow appears, create green.
C = 100% (one primary color)
M = 0%
Y = 100% (second primary color)
K = 0%
Now, click on the "Add to CMYK Swatch."

3. Locate and select the violet circle on the color wheel design and double-click the "Fill" tool in the "Tool Palette."

– **Color Picker:** When window appears, create violet.
C = 100% (one primary color)
M = 100% (second primary color)
Y = 0%
K = 0%
Next, click on the "Add to CMYK Swatch."

4. Locate and select the orange circle on the color wheel design and double-click the "Fill" tool in the "Tool Palette."

– **Color Picker:** When widow appears, create orange.
C = 0%
M = 100% (one primary color)
Y = 100% (second primary color)
K = 0%

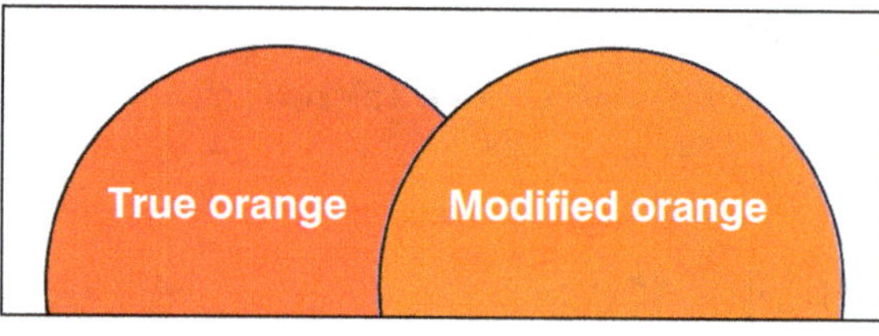

– **PROBLEM:** When the secondary color orange is created, it may appear wrong to you even though it was made correctly. This color has been influenced by our culture. Most of us recognize the color orange as the fruit. Yet the true secondary color orange is much more red. As you gain more experience in visual communication, you will realize that there are a good number of colors that have been influenced by different cultures.

5. Modify orange: We are going to modify this one color on our color wheel to be more visually acceptable to our American culture. Change the orange color to:
C = 0%
M = 70% (modified color)
Y = 100% (second primary color)
K = 0%

Tertiary colors

These are made with primary and secondary colors.

1. Yellow green is between yellow (primary color) and green (secondary color).

– Click on the circle next to the yellow.

– Next, double-click on the "Fill" tool.

– **Using the "Color Picker"** palette, create the yellow green, which is 100% yellow (primary color closest to the color) and 50% cyan (blue) (half the other primary color that was used to make the secondary color green).

– **Click the "Add CMYK Swatch"** to add this new color to the "Swatch" palette for future use. Now click on the "Ok" button.

2. Create the tertiary color blue green, which is the circle closest to the primary color blue and next to the green.

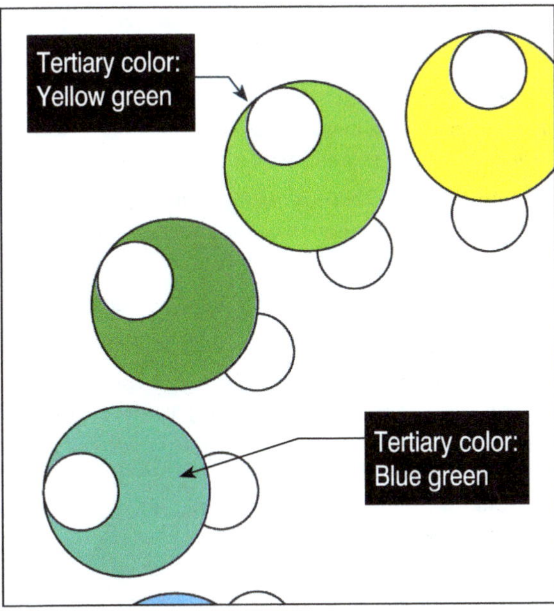

– Click on the circle next to the cyan / blue.

– Next double-click on the "Fill" tool.

– **Create color:** Using the color picker palette, create the blue green, which is 100% cyan (blue), (primary color closest to the color) and 50% yellow (half the other primary color used to make the secondary color green).

– **Click the "Add CMYK Swatch"** to add this new color to the "Swatch" palette for future use. Click "OK" button.

3. Create the other tertiary colors: These colors are created the same as the previous ones and include:

– Blue violet

– Red violet

– Red orange

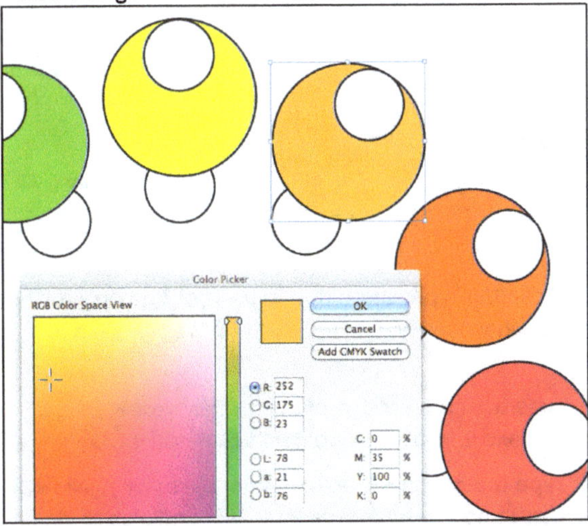

4. Yellow Orange: While this is a tertiary color, remember we adjusted the color orange to make it more socially accepted. Thus, we will need to adjust the color for yellow orange, which is halfway between yellow (primary color) and orange (secondary color).

– **Create color:** We will use all the yellow since it is the primary color closest to the circle. We typically would use 50% magenta (red) (the furthest primary color); however, we need to use half of the red used in the modified orange color created (35%).

Creating tints

These circles are only lighter versions of the color or hue circle on the color wheel. All tints should be 25% of the original color.

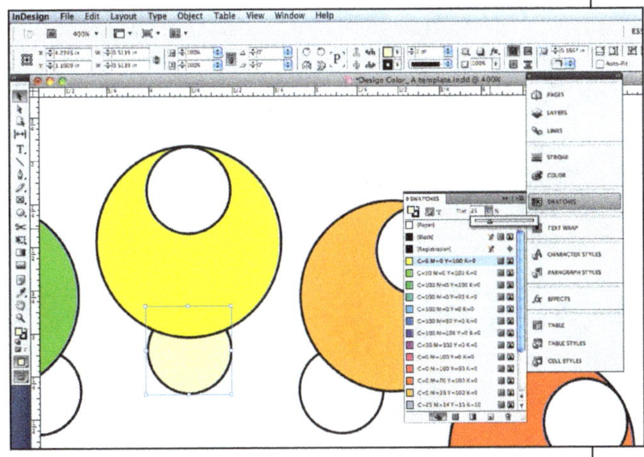

1. Yellow tint is located just below the yellow circle.

– **Select the small circle** using the "Selection Tool."

– **Open the Swatches Palette:** If this is not to the right in the InDesign Palettes, you will need to go to the top and select the "Window" / "Swatches."

– Click on the color (hue) yellow (this will make the tint circle the same color temporarily).

– **Now locate the "Tint"** window in the "Swatches Palette" and enter 25% (or slide the slider to 25%). Was this not easier than you might have thought?

2. All other tints are created the same way by clicking on the tint circle.

– **Locate and select the color** (hue) in the "Swatches Palette."

– **Change tint** window to 25%.

Creating shade colors

The bad news is while shades are not difficult, they are not as easy as the tint colors, because you cannot make each color darker than it was originally without adding black. Thus, you will be creating an additional color for all shades.

– **The shades** are the remaining circles unfilled that are within the color (hue) circles.

1. Yellow shade: Click on the shade circle and double-click on the "Fill" within the "Tool Palette" to create a new fill color.

2. Create shade color: With the "Color Picker" open (from step 1), create the same color as the hue circle (in this case C=0, M=0, Y=100, K=0). Now change the color to a shade by changing the "K" (black) to 35%, which adds black to color. Next, click on the "Add to Swatch" button. Last, click on the "OK" button and you will have created the shade color in the color wheel.

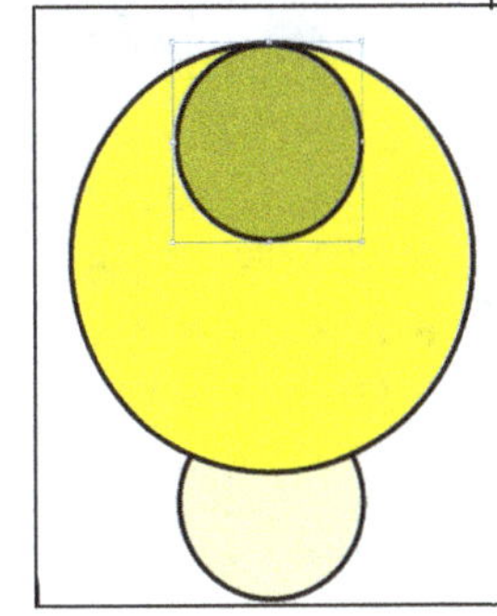

Your notes

*– **Reminder:** You may want to save your work.* ***Save often!***

Your notes

3. All other shades are created the same way by repeating the steps above for each new color on the color wheel.

Triangle

In the middle of the color wheel design is a triangle whose three points are equal distance from the three primary colors. This shape is filled with a color called "painters gray." which is made up of equal amounts of all three primary colors.

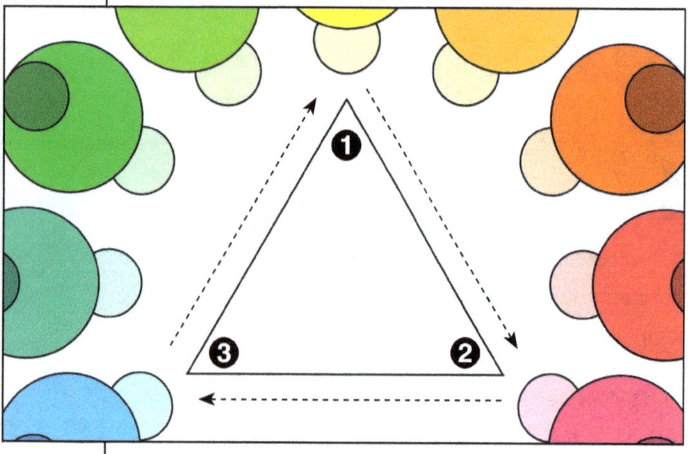

Create the triangle: The triangle will be created using the "Pen Tool."

1. Select the tool and then click and release at the top of the triangle (near the yellow).

2. Move your mouse (pen pointer) to the next point (near the magenta), click, and release again.

3. Move your mouse (pen pointer) to the next point (near the cyan), click, and release again. Now move back to the first point and click and release. The result should be a triangle that can be filled with color.

4. Adjusting the shape: If the triangle is not perfect and needs adjusting, use the "Direct Selection Tool."

– To do this, click on the frame to make the points turn white Now click on any of the points and click and drag to adjust the shape.

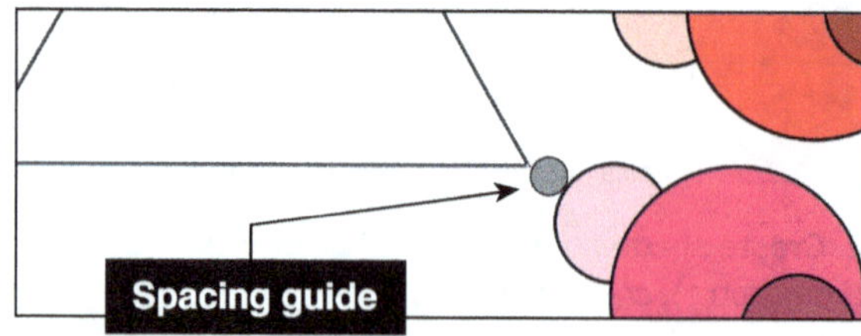

NOTE: If the points do not turn white, click off outside the design and try clicking on a different point on one of the triangle's lines).

5. Aligning the triangle: Create a small circle the width of the distance from one of the triangle points and one of the primary tint circles. Then move that shape to the other side of the triangle so it just touches the point. Is the distance the same? If not, adjust the triangle shape.

NOTE: This is easier and more accurate if you use the "Zoom Tool" and magnify that area.

6. Filling with color: Using the "Selection Tool," click on the triangle and then double-click on the "Fill" tool (using the "Color Picker") to fill the shape with the color

– **Painters Gray:** This color is made of 25 percent of each primary color. Remember to add this color to the swatches.

NOTE: The color "Painters Gray" uses no black.

7. Creating gray circle: Using the "Ellipse Tool," create a 1/2 inch circle and place it in the center of the design, which is at the intersection of the horizontal and vertical guides on the lesson template.

– **Fill:** Click on the circle and double-click the "Fill" tool. Using the "Color Picker," create "Gray" using 25% black ("K").

TIP Swatch palette »

Essential tool to learn for working with color.

– ***Location:*** *In the InDesign Palettes or within "Window" / "Swatches," pull-down tab is at the top.*

– ***Content:*** *Can store all types of colors created to include CMYK, RGB, and gradients for later or multiple uses.*

– ***Attributes:*** *Can easily apply color and color tints to fill, lines, and text using this tool.*

– ***Uses:*** *Can click and move colors for better groupings. Like all palettes, can click on top (gray area) and drag to preferred location on screen.*

Creating names and mixtures

You are nearing the end of creating the color wheel! All you have to do is to give each hue (color) a name and indicate the mixture used to create it.

1. Creating type: Using the "Type Tool," go outside the color wheel design and click and drag to create a text box.

– **Type the name** of one of the colors, "yellow green," and make it 10 pt. Arial bold and centered.

– **Type the mixture** used to create that color ("yellow green") and make the type 8 pt. Arial and also centered.

2. Placing names and mixtures: Click on the handles of the text box and reduce the size so only the type appears (this makes it easier to place and align).

– Using the "Selection Tool," click and drag the type into position so it is close to the correct color circle.

3. Creating other names and mixtures: Is easiest by duplicating the first color.

– **Highlighting the name** and typing the new color.

– **Next, highlight the color mixture** and type in the new

mixture.

– **Move**: Last drag to correct position.

– **Repeat** these steps for all colors.

Aligning names and mixtures

You can try to visually place the names and mixtures and most likely will do a great job. However, I have learned that often it is easier and more precise to use a guide.

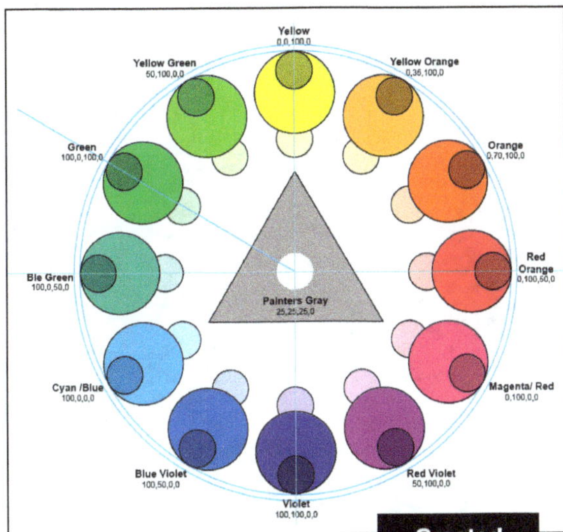

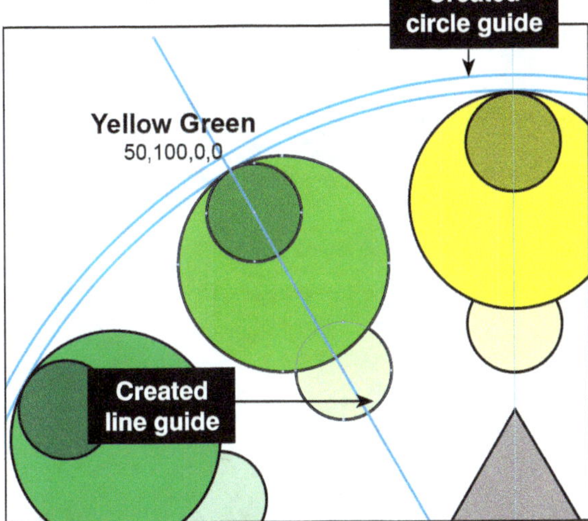

1. Creating a circle guide: Using the "Ellipse Tool," create a circle that extends beyond all the circles a small amount. Make sure you center the circle (align the center with the intersection of the horizontal and vertical guides).

2. Creating a second guide: While the circle guide you created will help assure the text is the same distance from each of the color circles, I would suggest creating another guide to help align the text with the center of each of the color (hue) circles.

– **Select the "Line Tool"** and create a guide line that starts at the center of the design and extends well beyond the color (hue) circles. (I made mine blue, seen in the illustration above). For the line to be in the correct location, it must run through the middle of all circles (hue, tint, and shade).

3. Align the text: Now move the text so it touches the outer circle guide and aligns with the line guide seen above.

4. Align other text: Using the "Direct Selection Tool," click on the end of the line guide and move one end of the line to the middle of the next color (hue) circle.

Remember that you will need to click on the white box (handle) at the end of the line for this to work.

– Select, move, and align the color name and mixture as you did in the previous color.

5. Delete guides: When all the names and mixtures are placed correctly, you will need to delete the guides.

Color logos

At the bottom of the lesson are three logos that you need to apply color according to the specified color scheme indicated with each.

– **You will need to change the color** on all elements that are currently white or black. This will include all fills, lines, and text used in the logo.

1. Monochromatic: Using only one color (hue) and its tints. Black is considered one color so you will not be able to include any black.

2. Complementary: Using only two colors that are opposite each other on the color wheel. There are many variations to consider when you also use tints of these colors.

– **Remember**, these have the greatest amount of contrast so it is wise not to use equal amounts of each color.

3. Analogous: Here, you will need to use two colors adjacent to each other on the color wheel. Again, consider tints. You cannot use the color black.

You are almost finished

Go back and edit your work to perfection!

– Edit content (is it all there?).

– Edit type placement and size.

– Edit colors.

– Save your file and print out in color.

Your notes

– ***Reminder:***
You may want to save your work.
Save often!

DESIGNING with color

LESSON . . .

What InDesign skills will you learn?

- How to create primary, secondary, and tertiary colors
- How to make tints and shades of all colors
- The difference between making gray and "Painters Gray"
- How color choices affect an informational graphic

SCOTT FARRAND

DESIGN & in DESIGN

Designing WITH Color

Creating color in InDesign

Overview

With the expanded use of desktop publishing has come an explosion of bad color usege. It is essential that all communicators know what good color is and how to create effective color for print and multimedia.

Specifications

■ Use the InDesign "Designing with Color template (B)" to create the color wheel and add color to the illustrations.

■ **Creating rectangles**
You will need to draw squares for the colors (hues).
Size = .5768"
Draw rectangles for shades and tints.
Size = Width .14" and height = .5768"

■ **Creating colors**
You will need to create and assign colors for all the colors (hues) based on a color wheel that includes primary, secondary, and tertiary colors. NOTE: These will need to be print colors (CMYK).

■ **Label each color** using 10 pts. Arial (bold) type.

■ **Indicate the mixture** of each color in Arial (plain) 8 pts. type. See the example on the color wheel shown. Place these mixtures evenly around the colors.

NOTE: If you are using a computer that does not have the Arial typeface then use Helvetica or Geneva.

■ **Create a tint** of each color using 25% of each color.

■ **Create a shade** of each color by creating a new color and adding 35% black.

■ **Painters Gray** is a triangle created in the middle. Each point of the triangle should point to one of the primary colors (evenly spaced). The gray color is created by mixing equal amounts (25%) of all of the primary colors.

■ **Informational graphics**
Each of the infographics located at the bottom of the template is to be created with a different color scheme (indicated below each). The color choices are up to you (be creative, but effective and appropriate).

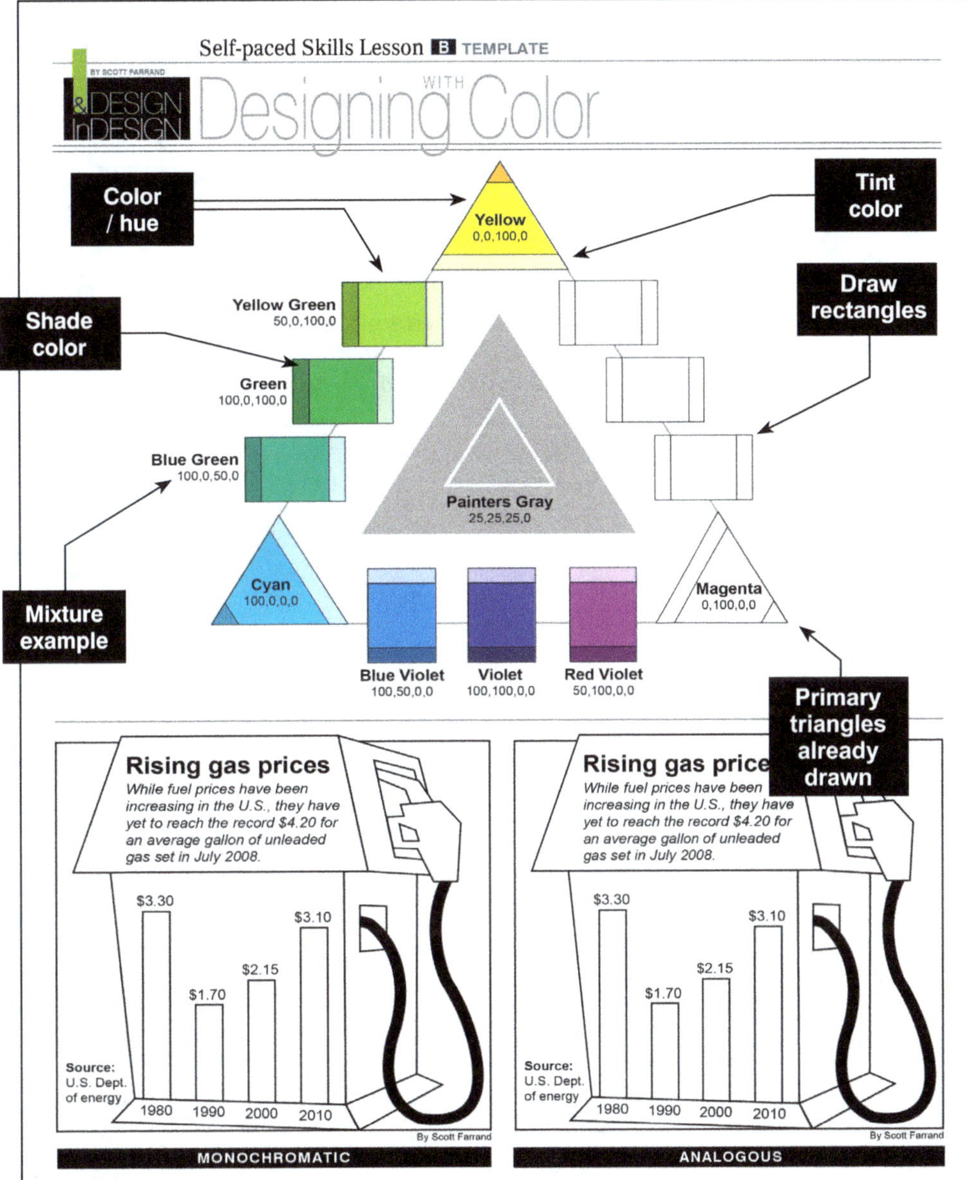

The final product

■ Print the lesson in color on standard 8.5" X 11" paper.

■ Include your name at the top of the lesson.

Assessment criteria

■ Are all the shapes drawn correctly and evenly spaced?

■ Are the colors on the color wheel mixed correctly?

■ Are the colors labeled correctly and spaced evenly?

■ Infographics created with the correct color schemes?

■ Was the lesson printed in quality color?

Instructions Designing with Color

Locating lesson template

For this lesson you will be using a precreated InDesign template named "Design Color_B template." This template has the three primary color (hue) shapes already drawn. The template also includes the outlines of two informational graphics at the bottom of the page, which you will fill with color later.

Getting started

Locate the template and place it on the desktop of your computer.

■ **REMEMBER:** Always drag a copy of the InDesign file to your computer desktop first. Never open and work on a file that is located on a server or your thumb drive. Failure to remember this could result in a file that goes bad and will not open or print later.

Next, highlight the word "template" and replace it with your last name. This will ensure you are always working on your copy and can find the file later if needed.

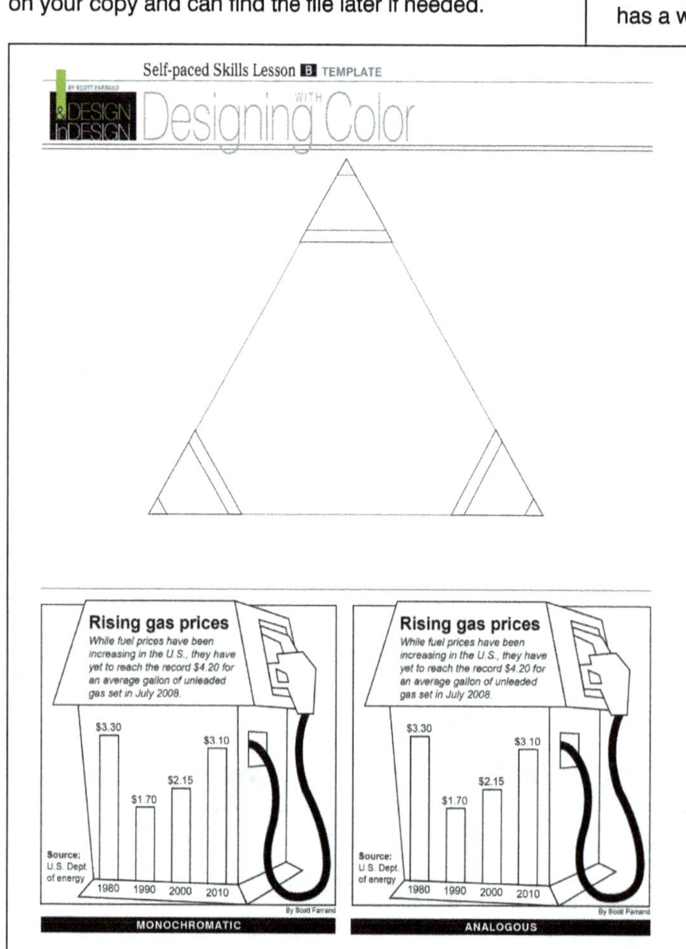

Open file

Double-click the icon to launch the program and open your color lesson.

Creating the color blocks

1. Create color (hue) square: Select the "Ellipse Tool" and create a 0.5768 inch square. After selecting the tool, hold down the "Shift" key while clicking and dragging (this will give you a perfect square). Remember that you type in the exact size in the "Control Strip" to save time.

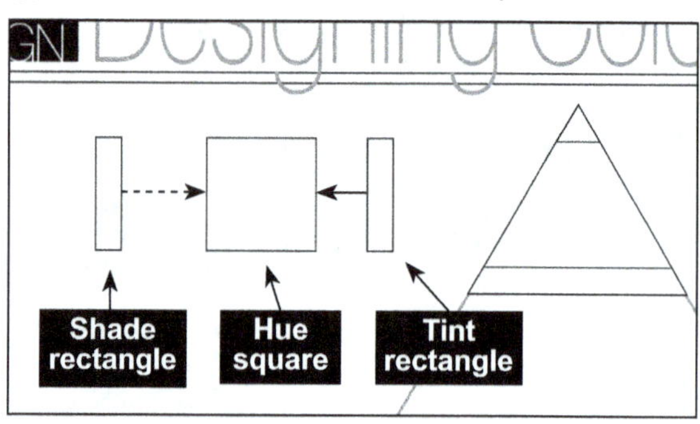

– **Make the frame black** with a stroke of 0.5 pt.

2. Create the color tint rectangle: Using the "Ellipse Tool" again, click and drag to create a rectangle that has a width of 0.1402 inch and a depth 0.5768 inch.

– **Make the frame black** with a stroke of 0.5 pt.

3. Create the color shade rectangle: This step is exactly like creating the tint. Using the "Ellipse Tool" again, click and drag to create a rectangle that has a width of 0.1402 inch and a depth 0.5768 inch.

– **Make the frame black** with a stroke of 0.5 pt.

IMPORTANT: The shade rectangle always goes to the outside of the color (hue) square in the color wheel design.

4. Align elements: Now it is time to combine all three elements into one.

– **Align the tint rectangle** with the inside end of the color (hue) square. Using the "Selection Tool," click on the rectangle and drag into place.

– **Align the shade rectangle** with the other end of the color / hue square (always the outside end of color (hue) square).

IMPORTANT: To make this easier and more accurate, use the "Zoom Tool" to magnify the view when aligning elements. The more you magnify the view the easier this step is (I would suggest about 800% or 1200%).

– **Make sure to overlap** the inside lines of both elements so only one line appears.

– **Use align tool** to align all three elements more accurately. Hold down the "Shift" key and select all three elements. Next, go to the "Control Strip" and

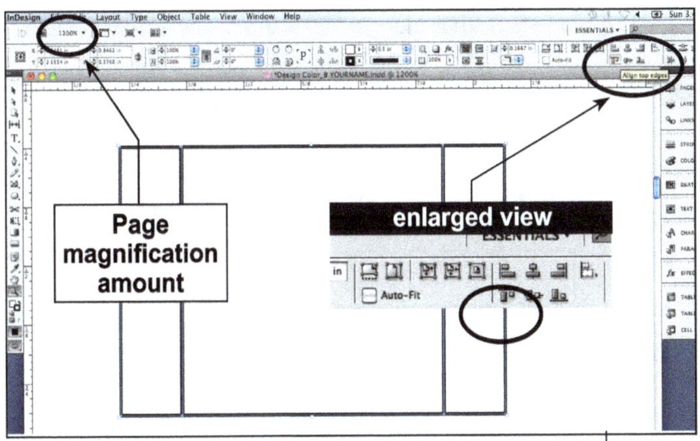

locate the align tools and click on the "Align top edges" tool.
(remember to place you mouse cursor over tool to be sure you selected the correct alignment tool).

6. Group elements: Holding down the "shift" key, select all three elements: color, (hue) square, tint rectangle, and the shade rectangle. With all elements selected, go to the "Control Strip" at the top and group by selecting "Object / Group."

TIP grouping elements »

Grouping is a way to combine several elements into one object to allow easier handling.

– ***What can be grouped?:*** *Anything you can imagine: Lines, shapes, text, photographs, and more.*

– ***Grouping method 1:*** *This way works best with small amounts of elements to group. Using the "Selection Tool," click on one element and that hold down the "Shift" key while clicking (selecting) additional elements.*

– ***Grouping method 2:*** *This technique works best when grouping very small items or a large number of elements. Using the "Selection Tool," move to the upper left-hand corner of the elements (an area with no content). Now click and drag to the right-hand corner of all the elements (any items in or touching the area created will be selected.*

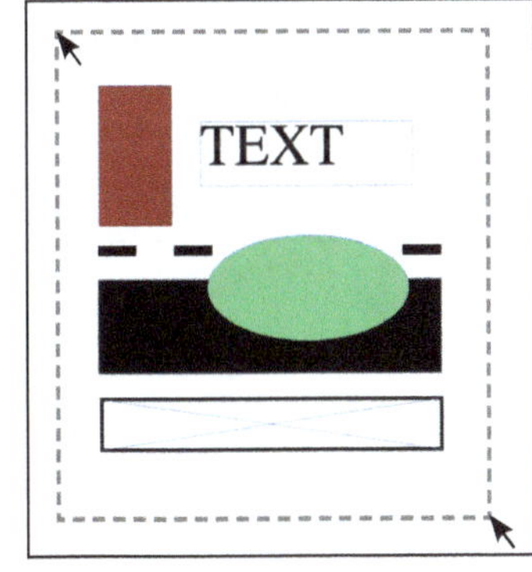

■ **With the elements selected** *(using either method 1 or 2) go to the "Control Strip" and select "Object / Group." Now they are one element and can be moved, sized, or apply another function easier.*

– ***Ungrouping:*** *Using the "Selection Tool," select the grouped elements and go to the "Control Strip" and select "Object / Ungroup." Now move your mouse to an area outside the elements to unselect all elements. Now they are separate items again.*

Creating the secondary color blocks

1. Duplicate the grouped block (shade, hue, and tint grouping) completed in the previous steps. You do this by selecting the element and go to the "Control Strip" and select "Edit / Duplicate."

2. Center the duplicated block between two primary triangle colors. Align this so that the intersection of the tint and hue aligns with the outline of the triangle color wheel design (see illustration).

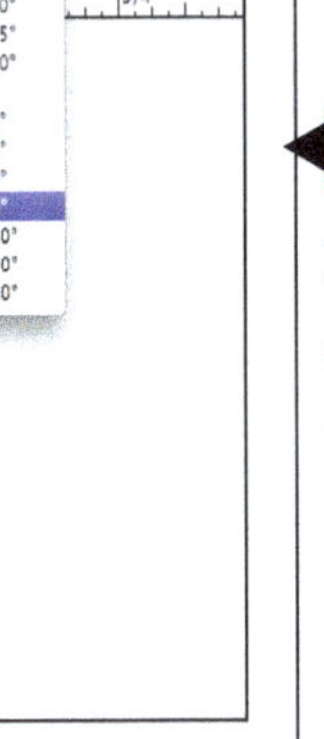

3. Repeat this for the other secondary color blocks on the opposite side of the of the triangle.

4. The final secondary color is located at the bottom of the triangle. However, this one is different. First, duplicate one of the earlier created (shade, hue, and tint) elements. Next, you will need to rotate the element. Select the element and locate the "Rotation" tool in the "Control Strip" at the top and select 90 degrees.

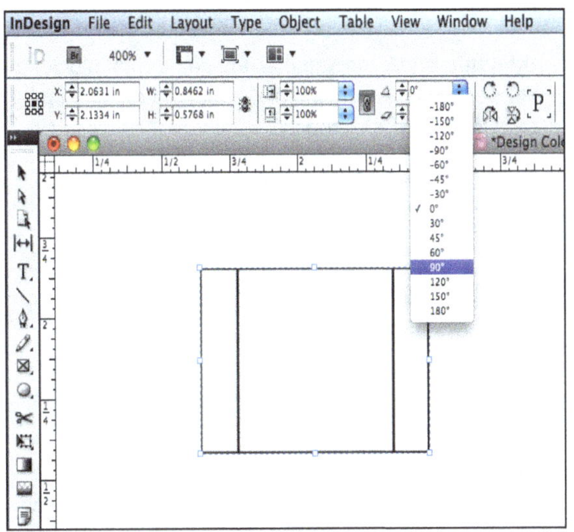

– **Next move the seconday color** to the bottom of the triangle and center between the two primary color triangles on each side.

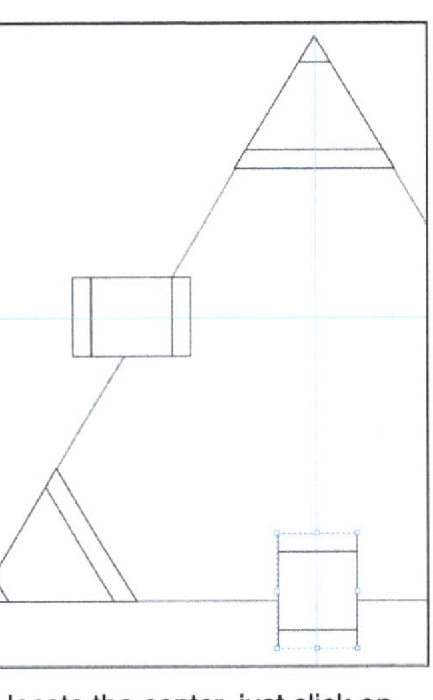

NOTE: The easy way to align this and the other secondary colors is to create guides that align with the vertical and horizontal centers of the triangle color wheel. To locate the center, just click on the large triangle and locate the middle handles.

– **The last step** is to align the secondary color element vertically. Click on the element and using the arrow keys on the keyboard, move the item five spaces up.

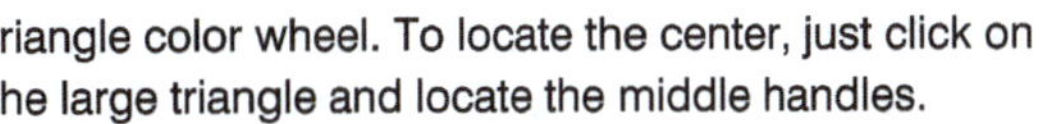

Creating the tertiary color blocks

1. Duplicate one of the secondary grouped blocks

Your notes

SAVE

– ***Reminder:***
You may want to save your work.
Save soon!

Your notes

SAVE – *Reminder: You may want to save your work. **Save often!***

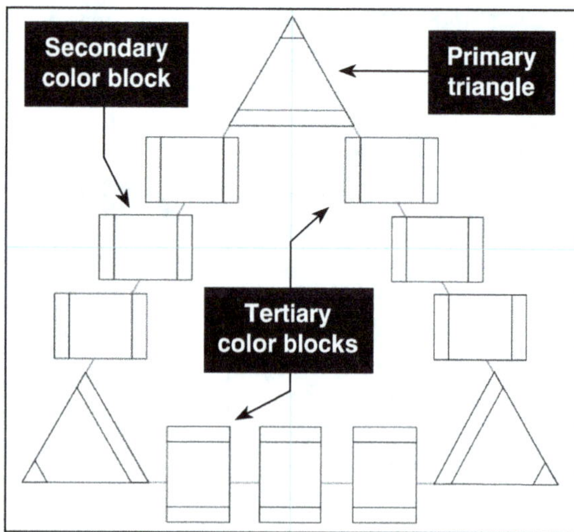

(shade, hue, and tint grouping) completed in the previous steps.

– **Move this new block** so it is centered between one of the primary color triangles and a secondary color block.

– **Align this block** the same as the secondary block so it intersects with the outline of the triangle color wheel design (see previous step 2).

2. **Repeat** these steps to create the remaining tertiary color blocks as seen in the illustration.

Creating the gray triangle

You will be creating a triangle just like in the first lesson. You will be creating a triangle with each of its angles pointing to a primary color, because it is these colors that make this unique gray color.

1. Select the "Pen Tool" and then click and release at the top of the triangle. This is about .30 inch from the edge of the top primary triangle).

2. Move your mouse (pen tool pointer) to the next point (near the second primary triangle), click, and release again.

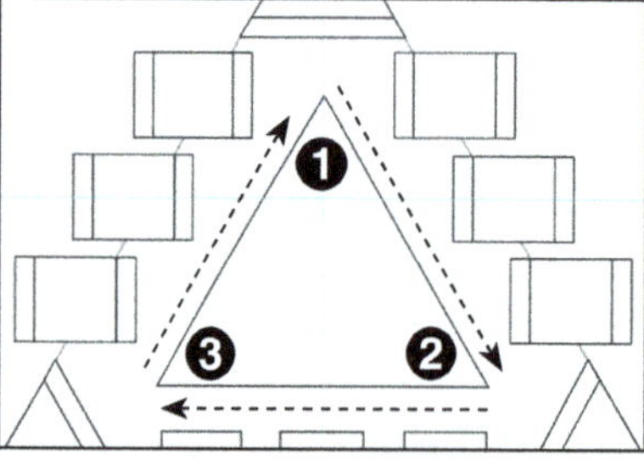

3. Move your mouse (pen pointer) to the next point (near the third primary triangle), click and release again. Move back to the first point and click, and release. The result should be a triangle that can be filled with color.

4. Adjusting the shape: If the triangle is not perfect and needs adjusting, use the "Direct Selection Tool."

– **Edit triangle:** Click on the frame to make the points turn white. Now click on any of the points and click and drag to adjust the shape. The object is to create a uniform painters gray triangle that points to the three primary colors and each of its points are equal distance from the edge of the primary color triangle edges.

Creating the small gray triangle

Using the "Pen Tool" just like in the previous steps, create a small triangle inside the painters gray triangle. This will be filled with gray (made from black) later.

Congratulations!

You have completed all the drawing steps and now it is time to move on to the fun process of making colors.

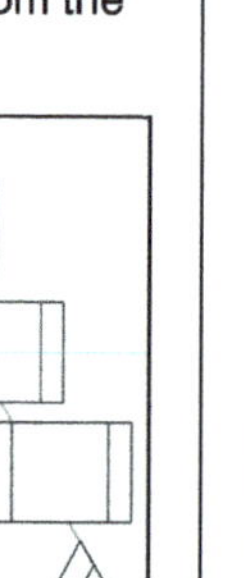

Creating the primary colors

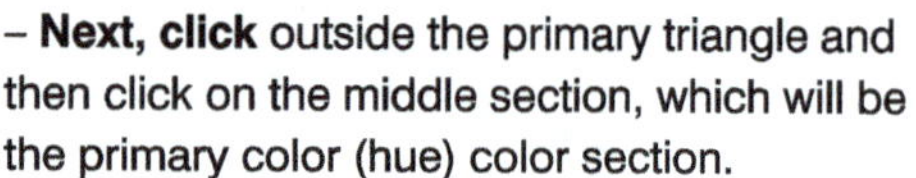

1. Using the "Selection Tool" (black arrow tool), click on the outline of one of the primary color triangles (let's start with the top triangle, which will be yellow). Now go to the "Control Strip" at the top and select "Object / Ungroup."

– **Next, click** outside the primary triangle and then click on the middle section, which will be the primary color (hue) color section.

2. Now, double-click the "Fill" box in the "Tool Palette." This brings up the **"Color Picker,"** which allows you to create the color needed. Type in the color mixture needed (100% yellow, 0% of other colors).

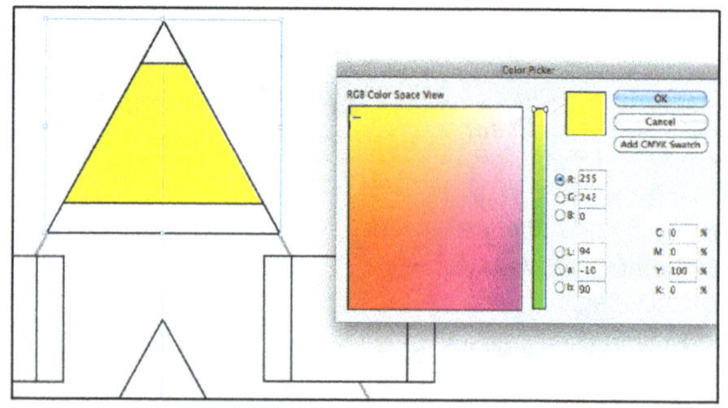

3. With color mixture created, click on **"Add CMYK Swatch"** to add this color to the "Swatches Palette." Now click on "OK" to finish.

NOTE: Knowing how to add a color to the "Swatches Palette" allows you to use that color repeatedly if needed in the future.

NOTE: Do not worry if you accidentally created an "RGB" color in the "Swatches Palette" in the last step. Just open the "Swatches Palette" and find the RGB color and double-click on the four-color box to the right of the color. This brings up the "Swatch Options" window box that allows you to change the mode to CMYK.

4. Create the other two primary colors: Locate the

cyan (blue) and the magenta (red) primary triangles, which are equal distances from each other on the color wheel. Create these colors as you did when creating the yellow.

Cyan (Blue): C = 100, M = 0, Y = 0, B = 0

Magenta (Red): C = 0, M = 100, Y = 0, B = 0

Creating secondary colors

1. These colors are made with equal amounts of two primary colors. Example: 100% cyan plus 100% yellow equals the secondary color green. On the color wheel, secondary colors are found halfway between two primary colors.

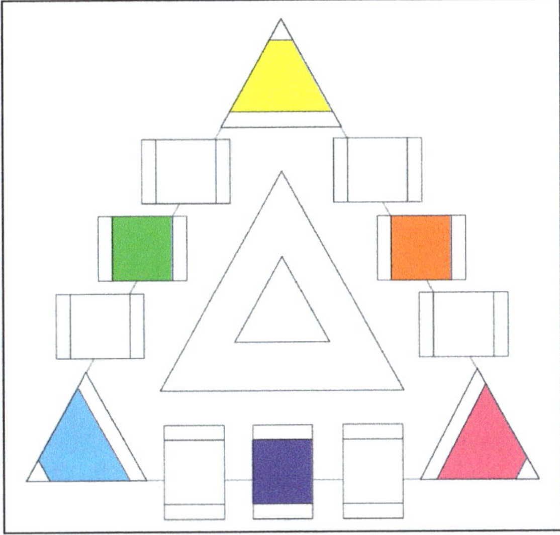

2. Locate and select the green color block on the color wheel design (halfway between the yellow and cyan primary colors). Make sure you only select the larger middle portion, which is the hue. Next, double click the "Fill" tool in the "Tool Palette."

– **When the "Color Picker"** widow appears, create green
C = 100% (one primary color)
M = 0%
Y = 100% (second primary color)
K = 0%
Now, click on the "Add to CMYK Swatch."

3. Locate and select the violet color block on the color wheel design (again selecting only the middle portion) and double-click the "Fill" tool in the "Tool Palette."

– **When the "Color Picker"** widow appears, create violet
C = 100% (one primary color)
M = 100% (second primary color)
Y = 0%
K = 0%
Now click on the "Add to CMYK Swatch."

4. Locate and select the orange color block on the color wheel design and double click the "Fill" tool in the "Tool Palette."

– **When the "Color Picker"** widow appears, create orange.
C = 0%
M = 100% (one primary color)
Y = 100% (second primary color)
K = 0%

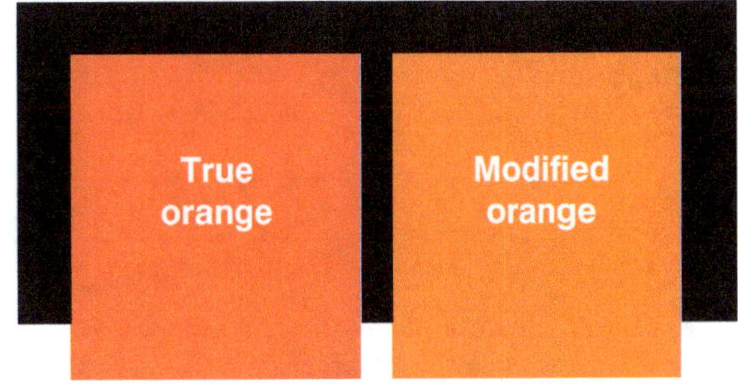

– **PROBLEM:** When you create the secondary color orange, it may appear wrong to you even though it was made correctly. Orange is a color that has been influenced by our culture. Most of us recognize the color orange as the fruit. Yet the true secondary color orange is much more red. As you gain more experience in visual communication ,you will realize that there are a good number of colors that have been influenced by your culture or other cultures.

5. Modify orange: We are going to modify this one color on our color wheel to be more visually acceptable to our American culture. Change the orange color to:
C = 0%
M = 70% (modified color)
Y = 100% (second primary color)
K = 0%

Tertiary colors

These colors are made by combining primary and secondary colors.

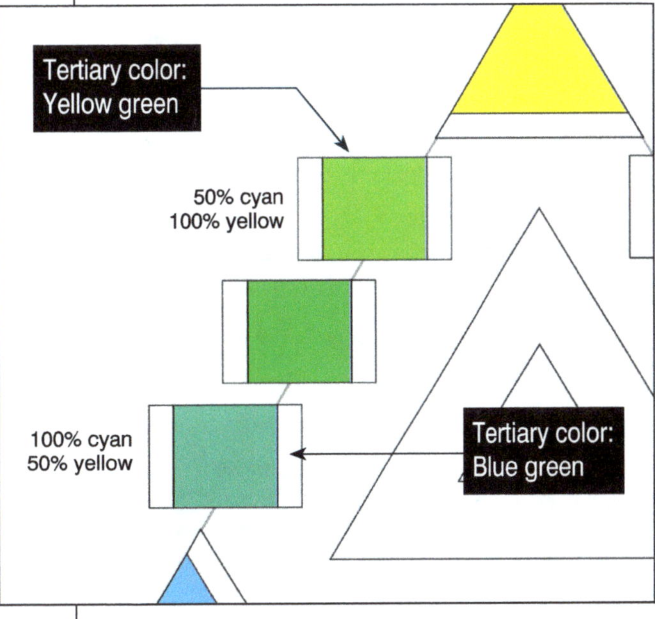

1. Yellow green is between yellow (primary color) and green (secondary color).

– Click on the color block next to the yellow.

– **Fill:** Double click on the "Fill" tool.

– **Using the "Color Picker"** palette to create the yellow

Your notes

Your notes

green which is 100% yellow (the primary color closest to the color) and 50% cyan (blue). This is half the other primary color that was used to make the secondary color green.

– **Click the "Add CMYK Swatch"** to add this new color to the "Swatch" palette for future use. Now click on the "OK" button.

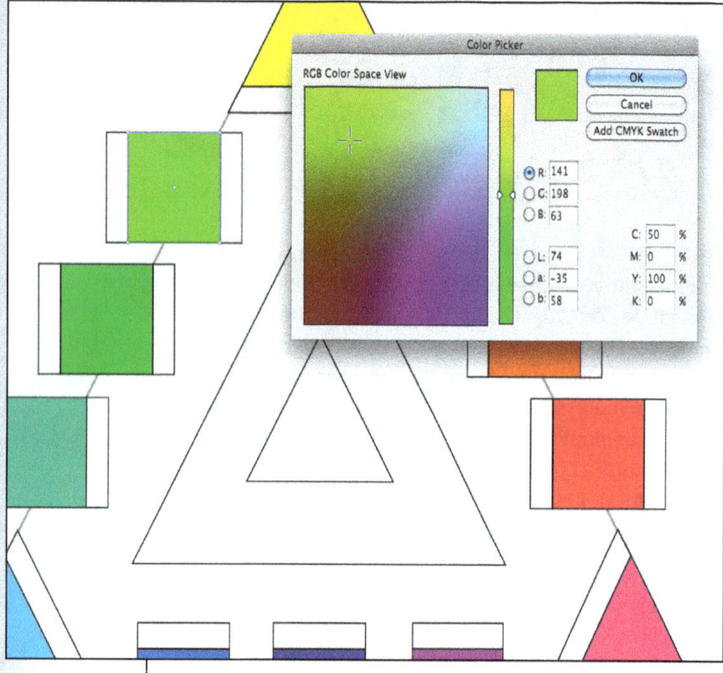

2. Create the tertiary color blue green, which is the color block closest to the primary color blue and next to the green.

– **Click on the color block** next to the cyan (blue).

– Next, double-click on the "Fill" tool.

– **Using the "Color Picker"** palette, create the blue green, which is 100% cyan (blue) (the primary color closest to the color) and 100% yellow (half the other primary color that was used to make the secondary color green).

– **Click the "Add CMYK Swatch"** to add this new color to the "Swatch" palette for future use. Click on the "OK" button.

3. Create the other tertiary colors: These colors are created the same as the previous ones and include:

– Blue violet

– Red violet

– Red orange

4. Creating yellow orange: While this is also a tertiary color, remember we adjusted the color orange to make it more socially acceptable. Thus, we will need to adjust the color for yellow orange, which is halfway between yellow (primary color) and orange (secondary color).

– **Mix the color:** We will use all the yellow (100%) since it is the primary color closest to this color block. However, we typically would use 50% magenta (red) (the furthest primary color). In this case we need to use half (35%) of the red used to create our modified orange.

Creating shades of the colors

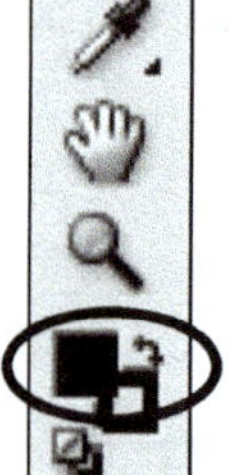

The bad news is while shades are not difficult to make, they are not as easy as creating the tint colors. You cannot make each hue (color) darker than it was originally without adding black. Thus, you will be creating an additional color for all shades.

1. The primary shades are the small triangles at the ends of the primary color triangle blocks.

– **Cyan shade:** Locate the cyan triangle, and using the "Direct Selection Tool" (white arrow), click on the small triangle. Now double-click on the "Fill" within the "Tool Palette" to create the new shade color.

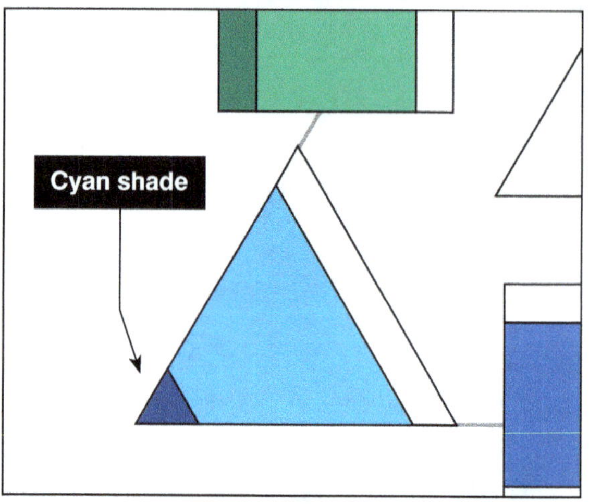

2. Create shade color: With the "Color Picker" open, from step 1, begin by creating the same color as the hue (cyan). In this case the color is C=100, M=0, Y=0, K=0). Now change the color to a shade by changing the "K" (black) to 35%, which adds black to color.

– **Swatch:** Next, click on the "Add to Swatch" button. Last, click on the "OK" button and you will have created the cyan shade color in the triangle.

3. Create secondary and tertiary shade colors: Locate the blue green color block just above the the primary cyan triangle. Using the "Direct Selection Tool" again, select the outside rectangle (the shade segment).

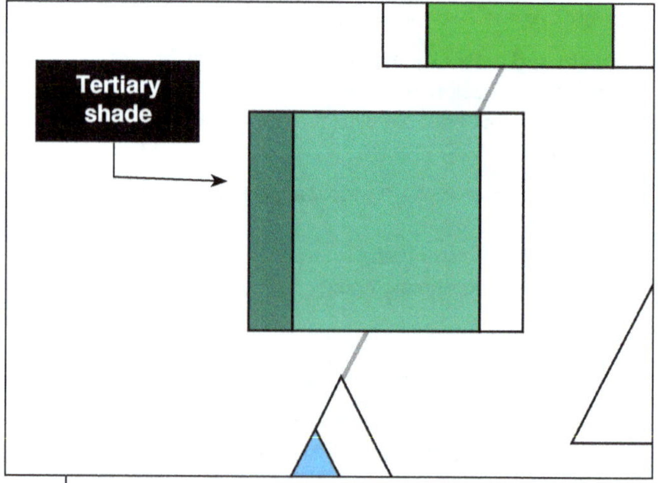

– **Now double-click the "Fill"** tool to get the color picker and create the blue green tertiary color (100%

cyan and 50% yellow). Next, add 35% black to that color to make the blue green shade color.

Creating tints

These are only lighter versions of the colors (hue) on the color wheel. All tints should be 25% of the original color.

TIP using palettes »

These are tools used to create, edit, and manipulate content. Some are visible on the right side of the screen but others are hidden.

*– **Hidden palettes:** To locate the palettes not seen, go to the "Windows" tab in the "Control Strip," at the top of your screen and move down to select the desired palette.*

Note: *Remember when looking in the "Windows" tab that those selections with a small black arrow to the right indicate even more tools and palettes. Simply click and hold down to discover more selections.*

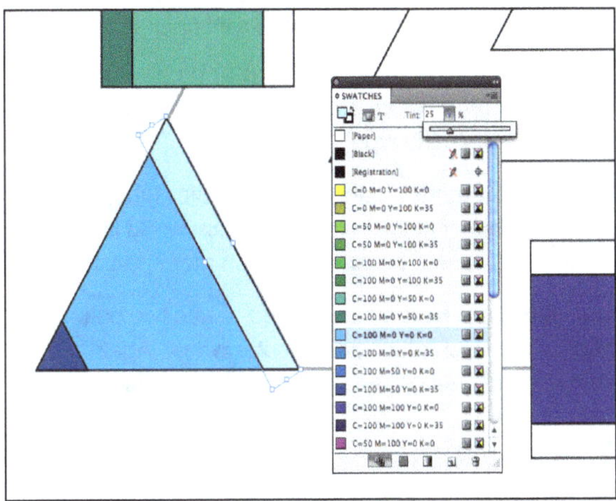

1. The primary tints are the remaining segments of the primary color triangles located at the opposite end of the shade colors.

– **Cyan tint:** Locate the cyan triangle and using the "Direct Selection Tool" (white arrow), click on the unfilled segment of the triangle.

– **Next, open the "Swatches Palette"** by going to the "Control Strip" and selecting "Window" / "Color" / "Swatches." This opens the swatches palette where you have been storing all the colors you have created so far on the color wheel design.

More info »

To learn more about the "**Swatches Palette**" */ Pg. 80*

Click on the color cyan (blue). This will temporarily make the tint shape the same color as the hue.

– **Now locate the "Tint"** window in the "Swatches Palette" and enter 25% (or move the slider to 25%). I told you this would be easier!

– **Continue creating** the other primary tint colors.

2. The secondary and tertiary tints: Create these tints the same way by using the "Direct Selection Tool" to

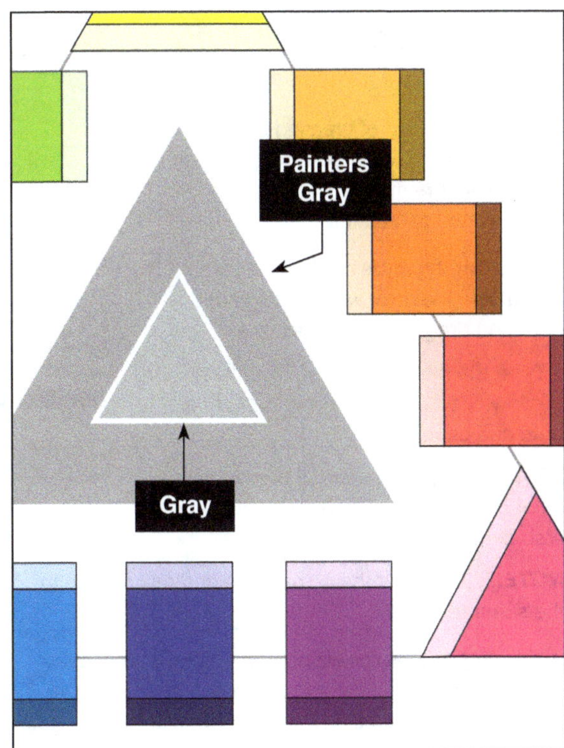

click on the remaining unfilled rectangle that is part of each color's grouped block.

NOTE: All tints face to the inside of the color triangle design.

– **Locate and select the hue (color)** in the "Swatches Palette."

– **Change tint** window to 25%.

Painters Gray

It is now time to color the inside triangles you created earlier with color.

1. Painters Gray: Using the "Selection Tool," click on the large triangle and then double-click on the "Fill" tool. Using the "Color Picker," create the color "Painters Gray" by making a color that has 25 percent of each of the three primary colors. Notice how the triangle points to each of these colors that make this unique gray color. Remember to add this color to the "Swatches Palette."

– **Make sure there is no stroke** on this triangle. Use the "Swatches Palette" to select the stoke and give it no stroke (white color box with a red line).

NOTE: The color "Painters Gray" uses no black.

2. Creating the B&W gray:
Follow the same steps for filling the "Painters Gray" triangle, except fill this shape with 25 percent of black. You will use the color swatches palette and select black and create a tint of 25 percent.

– **Create a stroke of 2 pt. white** on this triangle only. Again, you can do this by selecting the stroke while in the "Swatches Palette" and clicking on the white color. You can set the stroke at the top in the "Control Strip" or by opening this "Stroke" palette.

■ **Can you see the difference** between the two types of gray colors?

Your notes

Your notes

SAVE

*– **Reminder:** You may want to save your work. **Save often!***

Creating names and mixtures

You are at the end of creating the color wheel! All you have to do is to give each hue (color) a name and indicate the mixture used to create it.

1. Creating type: Using the "Type Tool," go outside the color wheel design and click and drag to create a text box.

– **Type the name** of one of the colors, "Yellow Green," and make it 10 pt. Arial bold and centered.

– **Type the mixture** used to create that color (Yellow Green) and make that type 8 pt. Arial. Also center the type.

NOTE: It is easier if the color name and mixture are in the same text block.

2. Placing primary color names and mixtures: Click on the handles of the text box and reduce the size so only the type appears. This makes it easier to place and align.

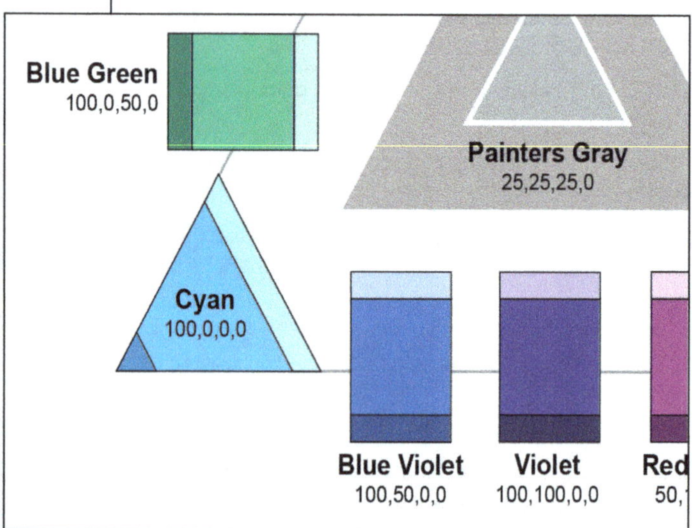

– **Center the type within the text box** (using the body composition tools at the top in the "Control Strip."

– **Move:** Using the "Selection Tool," click and drag the type into position so it is centered within the primary color (hue) triangle.

3. Placing secondary and tertiary color names and mixtures: Duplicate one of the primary text blocks and enter in the new name and mixture. Change the text body composition to match those on the design.

NOTE: To do this, highlight the text using the "Type Tool" and go up to the "Control Strip" and click on the appropriate text composition.

- Color blocks on the left side: Align right
- Color blocks on the right side: Align left
- Color blocks on the bottom: Align enter
- Painters Gray triangle: Align center

4. Aligning names and mixtures: The goal will be to place the mixtures consistently beside each color. You can do this visually or you can create a specific size shape that you can use as a temporary spacer to be more accurate.

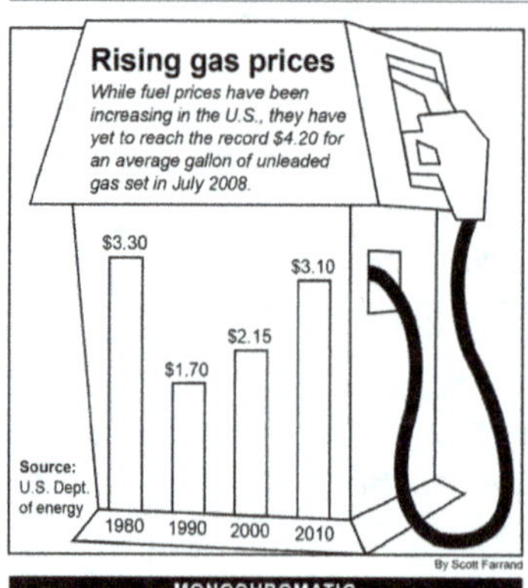

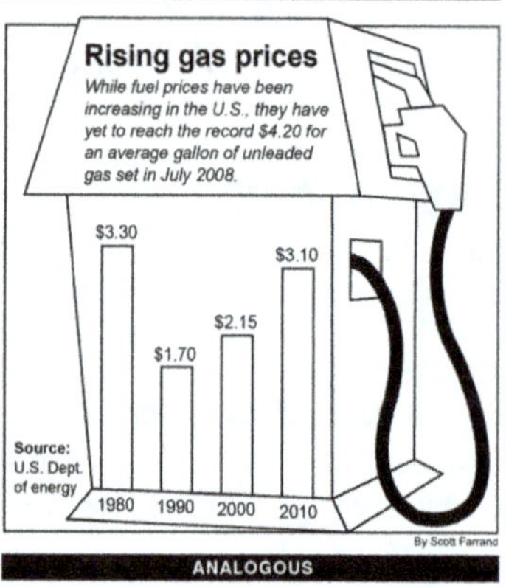

Color informational graphics

At the bottom of the lesson are two informational graphics that you need to apply color according to the specified color scheme indicated with each.

– **You will need to change the color** on all elements that are currently white or black. This will include all fills and lines (leave the type all black).

1. Monochromatic: Using only one color (hue) and its tints. The use of black in the journalism world is often a staple, so also use black to give you more possibilities.

3. Analogous: Here you will need to use two colors adjacent to each other on the color wheel. Again, consider tints and you can also again use black.

You are almost finished

Go back and edit your work to perfection!

– Edit content (is it all there?).

– Edit type placement and size.

– Edit colors.

– Now save your file and print out the completed lesson in color.

Congratulations, you have learned the basics of color. You now know how to make any of the millions of colors that you might need for future projects.

DESIGNING with photos

"**Good design** uses photographs to communicate, not decorate."

Are you packing a camera? In 2005 I asked my class of 75 students this question and was surprised to find that all but three students were carrying some device on them that could create a photograph. In 2006 Facebook began allowing users to upload photos, and this was an instant success. This year Facebook may reach 100 billion photos on the site and nearly 6 billion images are being uploaded monthly. We have become a very visual society and the photographic image has been a very big reason for this change.

During the last several years newspapers have been declining and laying off staff, including photographers–wrong move! I have been encouraging media companies to increase their number of photographers, videographers, and use of images in their communications to match society's hunger to communicate more in this form. The problem I see is more photos being used poorly rather than correctly.

The challenge for designers is not to decorate with photographs, but to learn to use them well.

Photos & photos

Your notes

The photo evolution

It is amazing to see how that small pin hole camera used by Joseph Niepce in the early 1800s has progressed.

– Americans discovered their love of creating photos with the introduction of Kodak's Brownie camera.

– 1963 color Polaroid images illustrated the public's desire for photographic instant gratification and their poor ability to follow directions, resulting in thousands of poorly developed images.

– Yeah, I got a copy of Photoshop for my Apple computer in 1989. Many photographers thought I was wasting my money creating digital images, since nothing could compare with their quality darkroom prints.

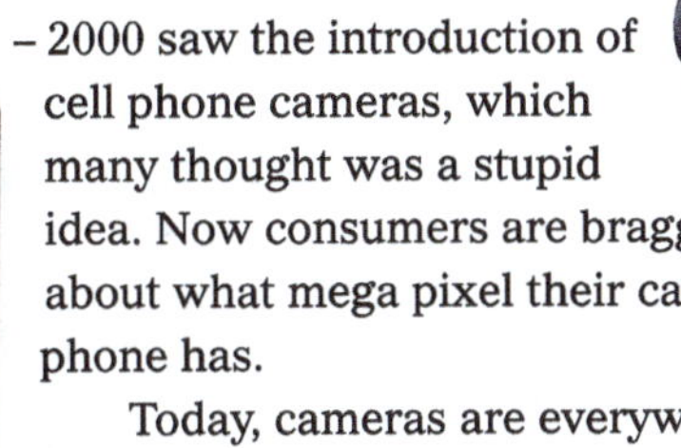

– 2000 saw the introduction of cell phone cameras, which many thought was a stupid idea. Now consumers are bragging about what mega pixel their camera phone has.

Today, cameras are everywhere! You will find them on your laptop computer, on the rear of your SUV, and even your kid's Nintendo 3DS, which can snap a photo of your face and turn you instantly into a game figure. Have we seen the end of the evolution? No! Photographic and video images have become a significant part of our life and how we communicate so there will be more new ways to create and use them.

All photographs are not created equal

Yes, even I can get lucky and snap a great photo at times; however, after years of working with professional studio and news photographers I have learned that there is much more behind those images than luck. Photographers manipulate light to create images that appear simple, but are complex in the information or story they tell.

To be a successful professional photographer will have to be part scientist, a creative genius, great composer, and a multifaceted story teller all in one. They will spend hours shooting hundred of images to get that one perfect image that can reach out and grab the viewer. It is said that a photograph represents a thousand words–true. A brilliant photograph can say just a few words at first glance, but if examined closer it will convey thousands of words. That is why photographers hate those who are quick to tilt, crop, or downsize a photograph, because they often destroy the message that was intended.

Advertising

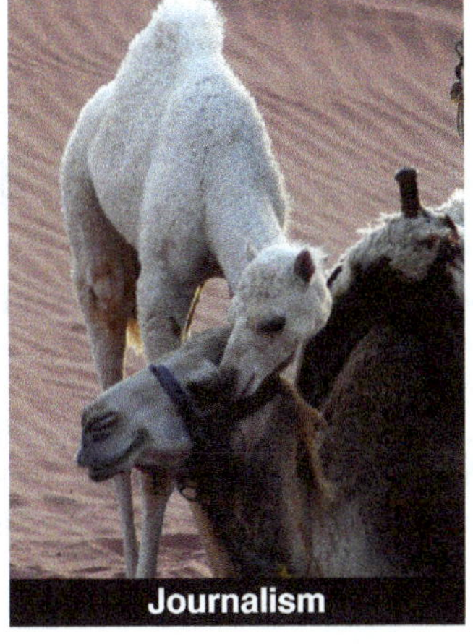

Journalism

Journalism vs. advertising

Designers use photographs more often than any other type of visual. Why? Because this medium is great at conveying reality, has strong emotions, is very credible, is not language specific, and can effectively communicate to all ages. To understand the basics of photographs, you first need to understand the two very different perspectives that are approached when they are created.

Advertising and public relations

These are photographs that have a persua-

Your notes

sive thrust and strive to show the subject in the best context.

– Images are often preconceived.

– Targets a specific audience.

– Often use models and props in image.

– Retouching done to make the photograph perfect.

Journalism

These photographs strive for realism. The photojournalist often strives to become a fly on the wall and capture images that transport the viewer to the location.

– Deals in reality

– Tells a story

– Models and props rarely used (in feature illustrations)

– No editing of content (cropped carefully)

– Retouching done only to correct technical problems (red eye, scratches)

How to determine the good vs. the bad photograph

Imagine that you are at the end of the day where you helped host this great public relations event for your charity organization. The local newspaper texts you that they are interested in publishing a story about the event tomorrow and wanted to know if you had any photographs to share since they were unable to send a photographer. The good news is that you hired a photographer to capture all those great moments and they provided you with a collection of 35 photos. How do you pick three good ones?

Art directors, photo editors, and many others in the communication industry face this problem almost daily. They know that many of the same qualities that make a good design also make excellent photographs. Designers know that without good content they cannot achieve good design. You will need to learn to weigh a variety of factors to select the best photographs to use.
Here are three simple things to consider:

Technical quality

I most often start with this factor because I rarely use images that have technical problems. Keep in mind that quality standards are often significantly different depending on the media that is being used. Take, for instance, the difference from a photograph used in a PowerPoint presentation to an image needed for a high-quality printed magazine.

– **Poor lighting:** Is content too dark?

– **Sharp:** Is the photo image out of focus? This problem can damage the message significantly.

– **Correct color:** Is the color realistic or badly unbalanced? A common problem is the photo is too blue.

– **Good contrast:** Does the photo have a range of tone from white to black?

Your notes

Content

After technical quality, I look for photographs with great content. To me this is the most important factor, because images that have little or no information leave you with nothing to say to your audience.

- **Relevant:** Does it advance the message to be communicated?
- **Too simple or too complex**?
- **Redundant:** Does image and other content add to each or does it just duplicate what is seen visually?
- **Unique** or too common?
- **Human interest appeal:** People like to see people or cute animals.
- **Newsworthiness:** What new information does the image convey to the audience?

Composition

After a photo appears to have good technical quality and content, you look for the images that have the best composition. This quality can make the image easier to comprehend, provide greater interest and eye movement–all helpful in creating an effective design.

- **Everything centered is boring.** Try using the "Rule of Thirds" by dividing the photo into three equal portions horizontally and vertically. Now position the photo (by cropping) so the focal point of the image falls not in the center, but at the intersection of one of the other third portions. This will create more eye movement (interest in the photo).
- **Body parts cut off** in photos is not good. This looks unnatural and creates tension.
- **A lot of small detail** will get lost. This also reduces contrast and proportion, which are elements of a good image.
- **Wasted space** (little image with a lot of background that adds no information) results in a photo with poor composition.

Original photograph

Improved photograph using "Rule of Thirds" composition

Criteria of good photographs

These are just some of the aspects that you should look for when trying to determine a good persuasive or journalism image.

- Eye-stopping appeal.
- Tells a story (worth a thousand words).
- Unique.
- Strong emotional impact.
- Human interest appeal.
- Free of ethical concerns: Photograph is appropriate for the target audience and client.
- Free of legal concerns: Image capture/created appropriately and has clear ownership and copyright.

Your notes

Designing with photos

Often you have been taught incorrectly

Your biggest problem will be to undo what you have been taught for many years by your schoolteachers and parents–to use photos as decoration. This goes back to when you were assigned a research project in elementary school and told to include photographs. Using lots of them often meant a higher grade. This endeavor often included a trip to the local store to purchase a large, brightly colored poster board (often your favorite color) to display your research findings. You then would proceed to paste your words, mixed with images, on the poster board and the goal was to make sure every corner of the board was decorated because that meant praise and a good grade. This is so wrong!

A good photograph is one of the most powerful tools a designer has at their disposal. However, using too many, the wrong size or used just to decorate can lead to confusion and destruction of the message. I will encourage you to fight that urge to use photographs as decorations.

Sizing them correctly

A photograph's dimensions should not be determined by the shape that is needed for design. Rather the photograph's size, should be set by what size is required for the image's content to be conveyed appropriately to the audience. Size often helps or hurts the content of the image.

- Larger tells the audience it is more important
- Larger is more emotional
- Larger increases impact
- Size can determine sequence
- Smaller means less, quieter
- Size differences can create more contrast

How big can you make them?

The size that is best for the content is up to you as the designer, but there are some physical constraints that you must be aware of.

Original size: When an image is captured in a digital camera, it is created at a specific size and quality determined by the camera's ability and settings. The image is next worked in a digital photo software program (most commonly Photoshop) to a proper size, resolution, and format for a specific media use (this book's lessons use .tif files). This photograph, when saved and placed in InDesign, is referred to as the "Original" and comes in at 100% (the size created).

Original (4 inches wide X 3 inches deep)

Resizing / scaling terminology: InDesign makes it easy to enlarge or reduce the size of an image, but you need to understand the terminology associated with this action.
- When the image changes dimensions, it is represented in a percentage of the original size.
Examples:
- A size of 100% is the actual size of the photo brought into InDesign (assume a 4" X 3" image).
- A size of 50% is that same photo reduced to half the size of the origi-

Reduced (2 inches X 1.5 inches)

nal dimension (now 2" X 1.5"). A size of 150% is a photo that is enlarged to one half the size than the original size (now 6" X 4.5").

Resizing / scaling quality: When an image is resized from the original, often there will be a significant change in quality. Here are some general rules to follow when scaling photographs:

■ **Enlarging photo size**

– I suggest using the photo the original size when possible.

– You can enlarge an image up to 115% with minimal quality loss (in most cases it is hardly noticeable).

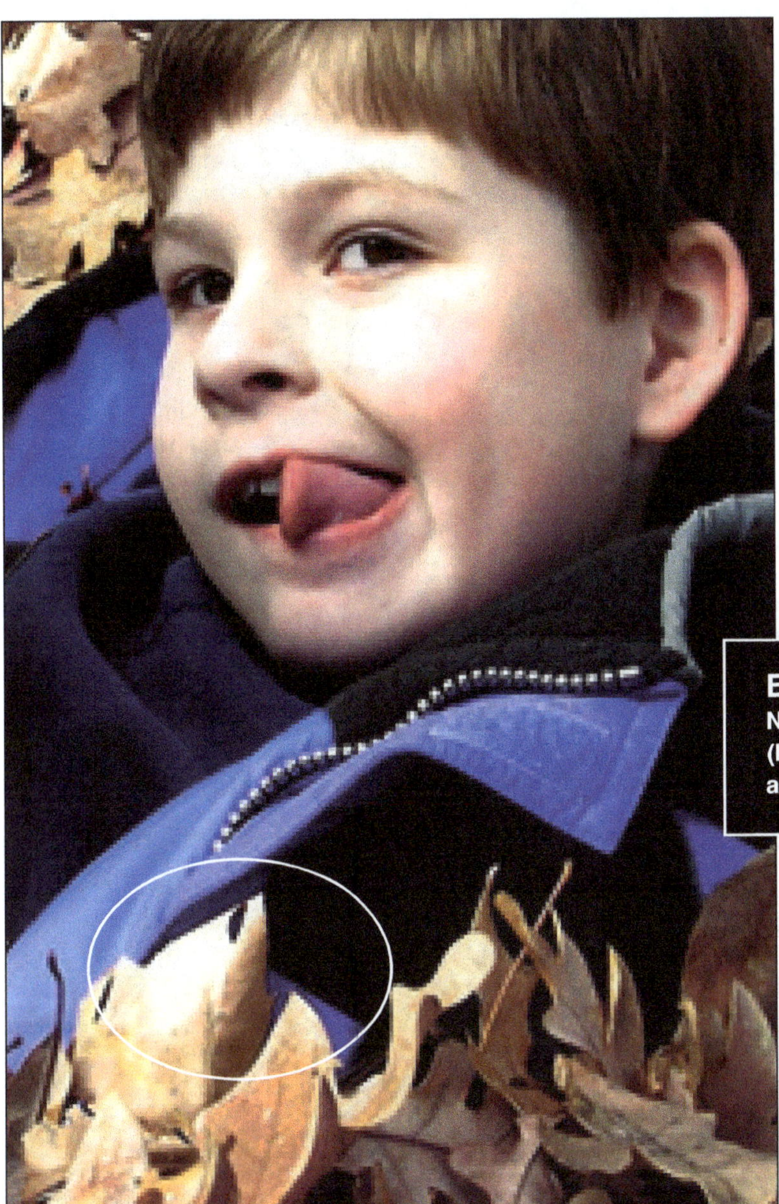

Enlarged too much
Notice how the image begins to pixilate (looks fuzzy), destroying image quality and impact of photograph.

– Enlargements greater than 120%, you will observe significant quality losses that will hurt your communication. When needing to enlarge a photograph significantly, go back to the original image that came from the camera and attempt to rework it in Photoshop to a higher resolution and size and then placed in InDesign.

■ **Reducing photo size**

– Often, reducing an image a small amount (100%-80%) will visually strengthen a technically weak photograph. Images that are slightly fuzzy or have minimal color and contrast problems are helped the most. However, it will not help photographs that have significant technical problems–these will hurt your message and should not be used.

– Reductions smaller than 80% may significantly reduce the visual effect of the photograph. In these cases I suggest cropping the image and reducing the size when possible.

Photograph scaled incorrectly

Scale them proportionally

There is nothing worse than to not realize that you distorted someone's face because you did not scale a photograph correctly. Do this to a celebrity or politician and they will never talk to you again! To avoid this problem, make sure that you enlarge or reduce an image proportionally.

– The horizontal and vertical scale amounts need to be the same percentage.

– To manually scale a photo proportionally with InDesign, hold down the "Shift" key when dragging the corner handle of a photograph.

NOTE: This will be explained further in the upcoming lesson.

Your notes

Your notes

Why cropping images is important

This is the act of changing the shape and content of the photograph to improve its composition. Editing the image can improve the photograph's focal elements, thus improving the message.

The benefits are:

– Improve composition (do not center everything, use the "Rule of Thirds").

– Magnify emotion (crop tighter on a face to see the expression).

– Simplify information (too often photos include too many details, information).

– Improve shape (creates a stronger vertical or horizontal image).

– Eliminate distractions (taking unnecessary elements out).

– Greater impact (cropping to leave negative space adds drama and can be effective).

Not all cropping is good:

– Be careful cropping body parts. Avoid clipping off the tips of fingers, heads, feet, etc.

– Do not just crop to fit a preconceived shape in a design.

– Avoid crops that change the meaning of the image.

Left:
Original photo has many distracting elements in background that are competing with the focal point (girl).

Bottom:
Cropped photo simplifies content and gives greater impact to the subject.

Photo captions

While a photograph often tells a story, there are many times that the image can benefit from the assistance of words to help clarify or add information. These words that often accompany photographs are commonly referred to as captions or cutlines.

Do all photographs need captions?

No, but this answer needs explaining.

Advertising: Images that are used in persuasive forms rarely do use captions because the photograph is usually accompanied by a display headline and ad copy that work together to relay the message.

Public relations: In this use, photographs sometimes do and do not have captions. The use, message, audiences, and media vary so much that there can be made cases for and against the use of captions.

Journalism: Is all about efficiently telling a story or conveying information so captions/cutlines play a significant role. Magazines and newspapers as a general rule always use them. Readership surveys indicate that photographs are often viewed before other content, so captions play an important part of conveying information.

How long are captions?

Again, it depends on the photograph and if it is used in a persuasive or journalistic aspect. In journalism the caption should use as few words as possible but be brilliantly written to add to the photograph's story. When using small photos of a single person, the cutline may be just the name of the person. However, in other photographs the caption may be one or two sentences. Any caption that is longer than two sentences begins to lose the effect of delivering quick information.

What should captions say?

Remember, the caption works in unison with the photograph. Together, the image and caption should answer the five "Ws"–who, what, where, when, why, and lets add "what is the news."

– **Avoid poor captions** that are vague and only state what is seen in the photograph.

Where to place captions?
The best position is below each photograph, which is the natural place most viewers will glance first.

– **I will on occasion group images together and create one caption** that refers to both photographs. However, I rarely combine more than two captions, because it causes the viewer to refer back to the photo or memorize the caption, thus significantly slowing down communication.

Captions to left: I would suggest using this location sparingly, as it is the least comfortable for the viewer because of how the type is read. The text here is best designed so it is flush right and ragged left.

Captions to right: This is the second best location and the words are usally aligned flush left and ragged to the right. Do not make side captions too wide or too narrow or they become more difficult to read.

Captions below: This is the best location and they usually align with the left side of the image and do not extend past the image. Just remember to add to the photograph and keep the captions short.

Using multiple photographs

Using more than one photograph requires the designer to consider the relationship, the content, and the design of the project, which is harder than it may seem at first. The problem is that our old habits of decorating rather than designing (for function) take over. The result is often many small photographs randomly dispersed throughout the project, which dilutes the message. Here are some options for using multiple photographs that will give your message greater impact:

– **Go big:** Make one image the dominant photo that commands attention and gives the project the "wow" factor. Make sure to pick the best photograph that is unique and has good content.

– **Less is more:** Often using one or two good-sized images is a better option than using many photos. Using too many can make the design busy and lack visual impact.

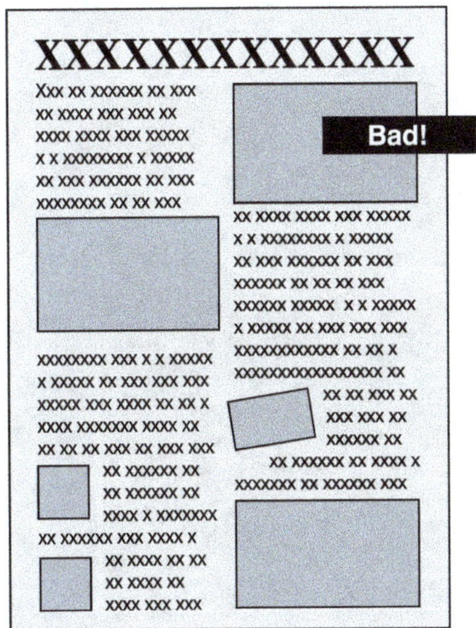

■ Too many photos competing for attention (decorating, not design).

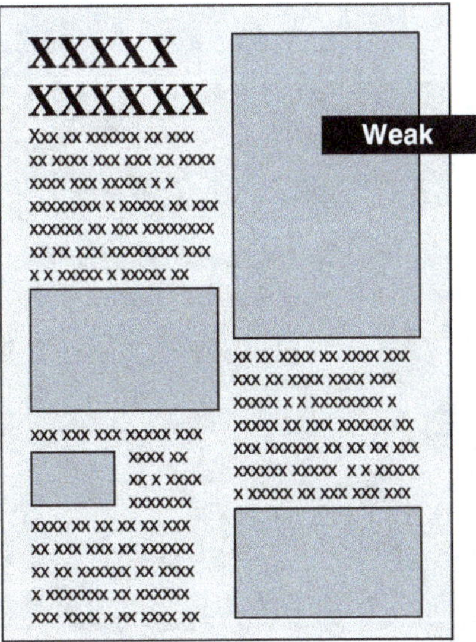

■ More impact, but photos spread out too much (still decorating).

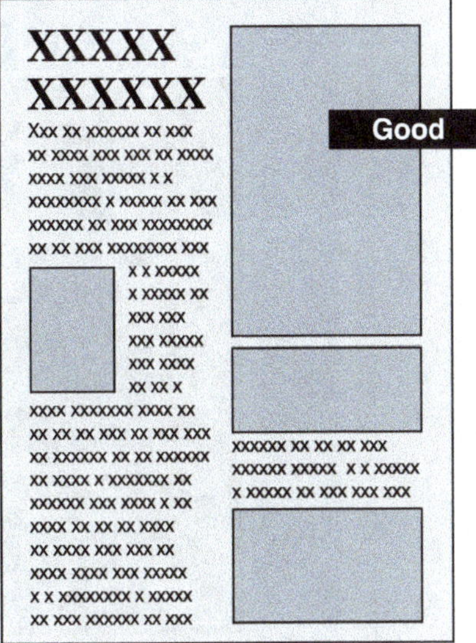

■ Varied shapes and grouping can give more impact.

Your notes

Best

■ Has impact! Larger photos, varied shapes, grouped elements, and captions with photos. This is designing.

Caption xxx xx xx xxxxxxxx xxx xx xxxx xxx xxx xx xxxx xxxx xxx xxxxx x x xxxxxxxx x x x.

Headline goes here xxxxx xxx xxxxxxx

Story xxx xx xx xxxxxxxx xxx xx xxxx xxx xxx xx xxxx xxxx xxx xxxxx x x xxxxxxxx x xxxxx xx xxx xxxxxx xx xxx xxxxxxxx xx xx xxx xxxxxxxxxxx x x xxxxx x xxxxx xx xxx xxx xxx xxxxxxxxxxxx xx xx x xxxxxxxxxxxxxxxxx xx xx xx xxx xx xxx xxx xx xxxxxx xx xx xxxxxx xx xxxx x xxxxxxx xx xxxxxx xxx xxxx x xx xxxx xx xx xx xxxx xx xxxx xxx xxx xx xxxx xxxx xxx xxxxx x x xxxxxxxx x xxxxx xx xxx xxxxxx xx xxx xxxxxxxx xx xx xxx xxxxxxxxxxx x x xxxxx x xxxxx xx xxx xxx xxx xxxxxxxxxxxx xx xx x xxxxxxxxxxxxxxxxx xx xx xx xxx xx xxx xxx xx xxxxxx xx xx xxxxxx xx xxxx x xxxxxxx xx xxxxxx xxx xxxx x xx xxxx xx xx xx xxxx xxx xxxx xxx xxx xx xxxx xxxx xxx xxxxx x x

Caption xxx xx xx xxxxxxxx xxx xx xxxx xxx xxx xx xxxx x xx.

Caption xxx xx xx xxxxxxxx xxx xx xxxx xxx xxx xx xxxx xxxx xxx xxxxx x x xxxxxxxx x xxxx xxxx xx xxxxxxxxx.

– **Vary the shapes:** Using all vertical or all horizontal photographs can reduce the viewer eye movement, thus diminishing the impact of the message. However, using too many shapes can create even bigger problems by distracting from the content of the photos.

– **Avoid these shapes:** Have you noticed that professional photographers rarely compose their images in the shape of squares? The reason is that this shape is so strong that the viewer will often notice the shape more than the content of the photograph. Also, be very careful shaping photographs in circles or triangles.

– **Group images:** Often combining images together in a designed grouping will have greater impact than placing them separately throughout the design. Make sure you do not place them randomly together, but consider the sequences, sizes, and common visual lines.

Summary

Recently, a student of mine got his first freelance job. After completing the design to the client's satisfaction, he dropped it off at the printers to be produced. Hours later, he got a scathing email from the printer, charging him hundreds of dollars to correct all the errors in the project–most of them with photographs. Today, it is essential to design communication that is functional. It is equally important to learn the theories and skills needed to publish. Pay attention, because the next lesson will test your design skills along with teaching you how to correctly use photographs.

DESIGNING with photos

LESSON . . .

What InDesign skills will you learn?

How to place, crop, and size photographs

Importing text methods

Using text wrap to flow copy around boxed content

Checking links to make sure your work prints properly

Use clipping paths and text wrap to flow text around photographs

Designing WITH Photographs

Photos are powerful elements

Overview

Images can add information, attract viewers, and give more impact to the message. They are often used incorrectly and obstruct the communication they were intended to help. To do this lesson well, research effective and creative uses of photographs.

Specifications

The assignment: The publisher's research shows that young adults, ages 17-32, are not reading the ads. Your job is to use your design skills and create an advertisement that lists upcoming entertainment offerings in the area. Your ad should grab the audience's attention!

■ **Size:** The ad should be 7.5" wide by 9.75" deep. There is no InDesign template for this lesson. You can change the orientation of this project if you like.

■ **Content:** Entertainment photographs and text for this lesson can be found in the "Design Photo_A Lesson" folder. Place this folder on your computer.

■ **Number of photos:** A minimum of three photographs must be used; however, there is no maximum number. You can crop and manipulate the images any way that is deemed appropriate for the content.

■ **Text wrap:** The lesson must use at least one text wrap around a photograph. Remember to control the amount of text wrap and be aware of leading and text column gutters. In most cases 1 pt. text wrap is wrong.

■ **Text:** Set the body copy of the entertainment events in "Times" 9 pts. with 12.8 pts. leading (regular text and 0 tracking).

– The body composition is your choice.

– Must have all six events, but you can edit, cut, add, or arrange the copy any way that is appropriate.

■ **Event titles:** Include headlines on each entertainment listing. The lesson includes headlines, but they need to be edited to reflect content and your design.

– Be careful of the font, size, leading, and color you use.

■ **Ad headline:** You must include a display headline for the ad. The wording, font, and size are your choice, but must be appropriate for your design.

HINT: Give it some size!

■ **Be creative:** Include any rules, borders, screens, boxes, icons, special typography, or other design elements you would like. Remember, we are designing effective advertisement, not decorating.

The final project

■ **Print the design** in color centered on a 8.5" X 11" paper and include your name on the lower left corner of the page.

Assessment criteria

■ Is the project the correct size and centered on the page?

■ Are the photographs sized and cropped effectively?

■ Is the typography legible, and does it have impact?

■ Was color used effectively?

■ Is the assignment complete (six events, correct fonts, and text wrap used)?

■ Does the ad communicate to the target audience?

■ Is the design creative and uses white space effectively?

Locating lesson template

This lesson does not include an InDesign template. Instead, you will be starting from the beginning and creating your own InDesign document. The good news is that there is a lot of text and photographs for you to work with to create your stunning design.

Use your design skills!
This lesson will differ from previous lessons, because you will not be trying to duplicate an example, but asked to come up with an original design using the theories and skills you have learned. In this lesson I will explain many new InDesign techniques and skills for you to consider when creating your design (several are not in specific order).

To be successful, stay organized!
When working with documents that have more than text, keeping everything organized is crucial. Once an image is placed on your document, InDesign creates a path to the image. If the location, name, or the image content has been changed, InDesign will not have the correct information needed when printing . . . BIG PROBLEM! This lesson will show you how to work with images and larger amounts of text in the correct manner. Keeping organized so you can print successfully is not hard, but it is essential.

Getting started

1. Locate the "Design Photo_A Lesson" folder containing the working text and images, and place the entire folder (with its contents) on the desktop of your computer.

■ **REMEMBER:** Always drag a copy of the lesson folder to your computer desktop first. Never open and work on content that is located on a server or your thumb drive. Failure to remember this could result in a file that goes bad and will not open or print later.

2. Highlight part of the folder's name "A Lesson" and replace it with your last name. This will ensure you are always working on your copy of the lesson and can find the folder later.

Creating a new document

1. Launch the InDesign program: Remember, this can take a while. Often an InDesign pop-up window will appear with "Open a Recent Item," "Create New," and other options. This feature was created to get to files and create new content quicker. We could actually create our new document here, but I will show you a second method.

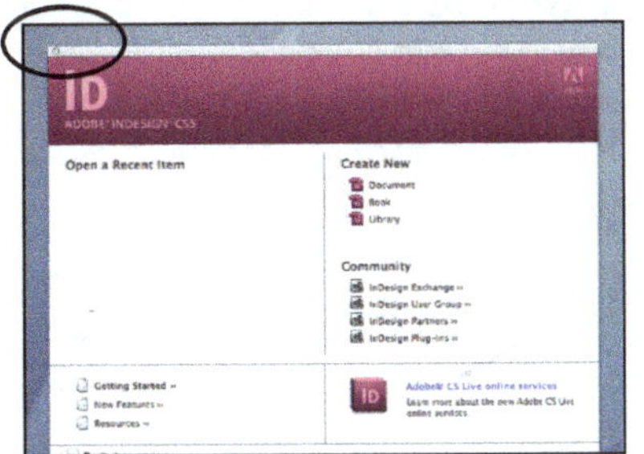

– **Close the InDesign pop-up window** by clicking on the small button in the upper left-hand corner.

2. New document: With InDesign running, go to the top controls and select "File" / "New" / "Document" to begin creating a new document. A pop-up window appears, allowing you to set up the size, type, and specific setting for your document.

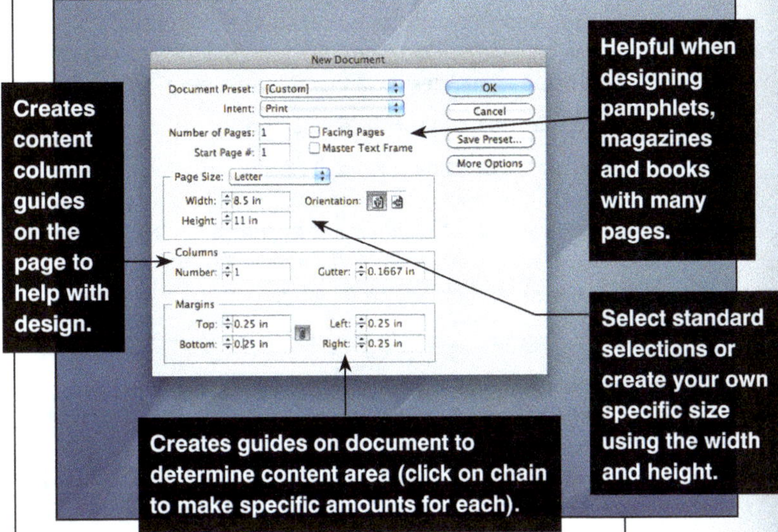

Here are the settings you need to use:

– Document Preset: (no change)
– Intent: Print
– Number of pages: 1
– Start page#: (no change)
– Facing pages: unselect box (no check mark)
– Master text frame (no change)
– Page size: Letter
– Width: (no change)
– Height: (no change)
– Orientation: You select!
– Columns: (no change)
– Gutter: (no change)
– Margins: Change to 0.25 inch for all
– Now select "OK" to go get our new document

NOTE: If you make a mistake at this stage, just close the document and repeat the steps to create a new document.

Ad size

The first thing I do on all projects is create the shape of the element and then create guides on all sides. Why, you ask? There is nothing worse than finishing a project to find out that you created it in the wrong size. I put

Your notes

guides on all edges and lock the guides because it is so easy to accidentally click on the project edges and change the size or move it to the wrong location.

So you think this will never happen to you? Ask printers, Web publishers, and professors what percentage of work comes to them the wrong size . . . a lot!

1. Turn page rulers on by going to the top and selecting "View" / "Show Rulers."

2. Create ad shape: Referring to the lesson requirements, use the "Rectangle Tool" to create a shape the required size of the project. This can be done several ways:

– **Using page rulers:** Click and drag "Rectangle Tool" to desired size, watching the page rulers as you progress.

– **Control Strip:** Using the "Rectangle Tool," click and drag to create any size box. Next, type in the exact dimensions needed in the "W" (width) and "H" (height) located in the left side of the "Control Strip."

NOTE: This is my preferred method.

– **Rectangle pop-up window:** Select the "Rectangle Tool" and holding down on the "option" or "alt" key on the keyboard, click anywhere on the document. Now type in the exact width and height in the "Rectangle" pop-up window that appeared.

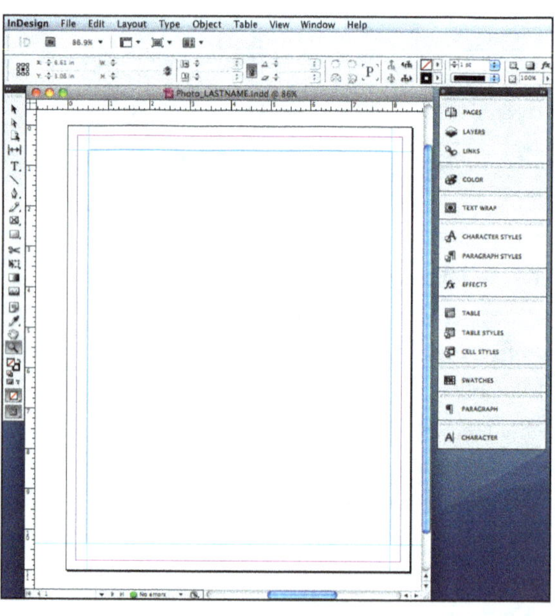

3. Center document: With the rectangle selected, use your keyboard's arrow keys or your mouse to move rectangle so it is centered within the InDesign document.

4. Create guides: Get the "Selection Tool" (black arrow) in the "Tool Palette." Next, click and hold down within the middle of the document rulers and drag the guide to one of the rectangle's edges

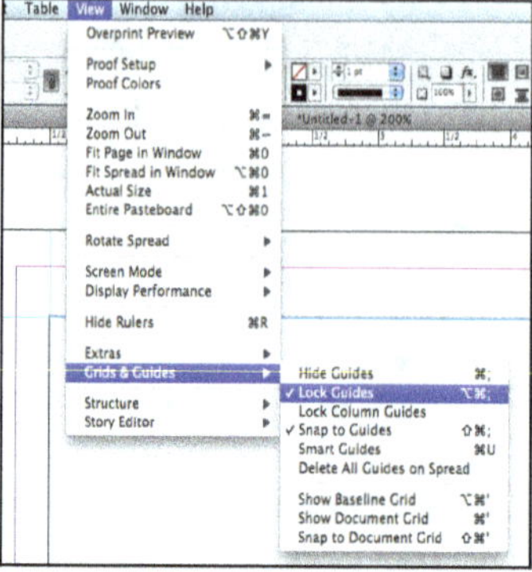

and release. Repeat this process until you have created guides on each side of the rectangle.

5. Lock guides: Go to the top and select "View" / "Grids & Guides" / "Lock Guides."

ore info »

To learn more about the **Guides** */ Pg. 25*

6. Save document: We do not want to lose any work, and we want to make sure the document is saved in the correct location before we create any more content.

– Go to top and select "File" / "Save." Name your file "Photo_YOURLASTNAME" and save the file to your lesson folder or save the document to your desktop and move it to your lesson folder.

IMPORTANT: Double check to make sure that your InDesign document is located inside the lesson folder! Failure to do this will cause problems in the future.

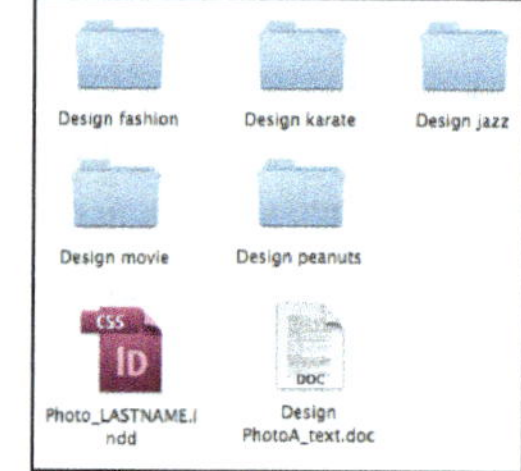

– You should now see seven things in your lesson folder.

Placing text

Text can be imported into InDesign from many other programs. When working within an advertising or other communication company, this is the best way. However, if you get content from a wide variety of sources, it may be more reliable to first copy and then place that copy in InDesign. The good news is that there are many ways to get text and the goal will be to discover the most efficient for you.

■ For this lesson I have created the text in a Microsoft Word document. There is a duplicate file created in InDesign for those who do not have that program.

1. Select text: Open the "Design PhotoA_text.doc" file by double-clicking on the file in your lesson folder. Highlight the text by dragging the mouse over all the text.

– A better way I have found is to click at the beginning of the text; now hold down the "command/apple" key and the "A" key to select all the copy. This ensures all the copy is selected, even overfill text on additional pages that you cannot easily see.

2. Copy the text: With all the text highlighted, go to the top and select "Edit" / "Copy." All computers have internal temporary memory (often referred to as the clipboard) that makes it possible to remember the text content while going to another software program.

3. Close the text file and open your InDesign document that you already created.

4. Text box: Using the "Type Tool," create a large text box in the middle of your ad (do not worry about the exact size and location now) and select "Edit" / "Paste." The copy now exists in your InDesign document and is ready for you to manipulate.

Working with the word content

Very shortly when you move the text onto your design you will discover you have a problem–too much text!

You will discover later that you have too many photographs. If you use all the text you are guaranteed to have a poor design that no one would look at. Choose your content wisely!

– **Solution:** You are required to use all six events, but you will need to edit, condense, and change the order to produce a successful design.

Another problem: The typography for all the events has many problems, which include:

– Wrong typeface

– Wrong type size

– Wrong leading

– Maybe even some poor grammar and spelling

Solution: Read the instructions and make all the events' body text meet the lesson requirements. Remember, the headlines for the events are another element and can be whatever typeface and size that is deemed appropriate for a good design.

Fixing body text inconsistencies

There are many ways to manipulate text in InDesign. We will explore some of the more common ways so you can choose the ones that work for your design.

1. Place text: First, let's get the text onto our document. Select the "Type Tool" from the "Tool Palette," and click and drag to create a large text box that fills our ad design area. Go to the top and select "Edit" / "Paste."

– **Adjust text box size:** If you did not make the text box the desired size or shape, go to the "Tool Palette" and get the "Selection Tool" to allow you to click on the text box handles to adjust the shape.

– **Text overset:** If you look closely at the bottom right corner of your text box, you most likely will see a small red box with a red plus in the middle. This indicates that all of your text is not visible and there is an overflow.

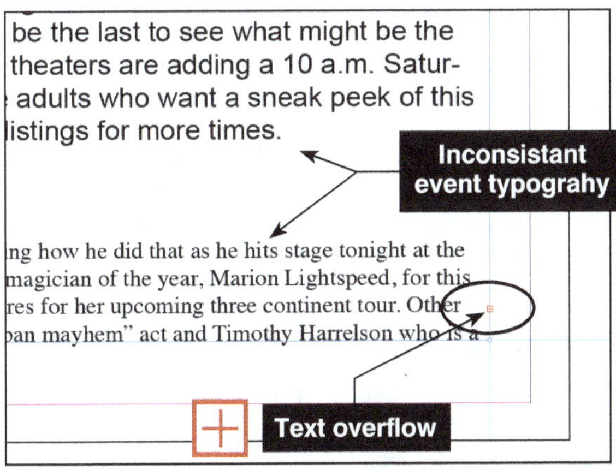

2. Fix text problems: Using the "Type Tool," click within your text box and press the "Apple" / "A" key to select all the text (including the overflow content). If you look at the "Control Strip," you will notice several controls are blank, which indicates conflicting attributes.

– **Using the "Control Strip," change the typeface** to Times, size to 9 pts., leading to 12.8 pts., and make sure the other font attributes are set to regular text with 0 tracking.

Designing with text columns

InDesign makes it easy to work with large amounts of words by enabling large type boxes to be evenly divided into columns easily. The advantage of using large text boxes with columns over smaller individual text boxes is the ease of changing the design and the flow of copy from one column to another.

1. Creating text columns: Select the text box. Next, go to the "Control Strip" and select "Object" / "Text Frame Options" to get the "Text Frame Options" palette.

– **Number of columns:** Change the text columns "Number" from one to any number. I would suggest trying two, three, or four for this lesson. Also, if you were to change the size of the text box, the column widths would adjust automatically.

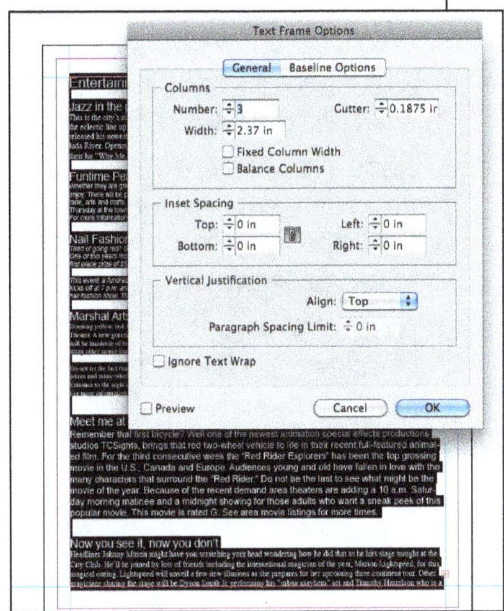

■ Using text columns can make designing and editing easier. When photos or new text are added within any column, the content will automatically readjust to the other columns.

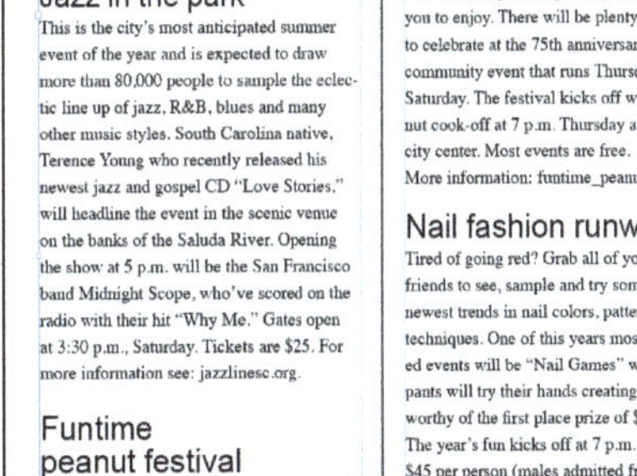

Jazz in the park

This is the city's most anticipated summer event of the year and is expected to draw more than 80,000 people to sample the eclectic line up of jazz, R&B, blues and many other music styles. South Carolina native, Terence Young who recently released his newest jazz and gospel CD "Love Stories," will headline the event in the scenic venue on the banks of the Saluda River. Opening the show at 5 p.m. will be the San Francisco band Midnight Scope, who've scored on the radio with their hit "Why Me." Gates open at 3:30 p.m., Saturday. Tickets are $25. For more information see: jazzlinesc.org.

Funtime peanut festival

Whether they are green, roasted, toasted, ter, there is a peanut specialty waiting for you to enjoy. There will be plenty for you to celebrate at the 75th anniversary of this community event that runs Thursday thru Saturday. The festival kicks off with the peanut cook-off at 7 p.m. Thursday at the town's city center. Most events are free. More information: funtime_peanutparty.org

Nail fashion runway

Tired of going red? Grab all of your girl friends to see, sample and try some of the newest trends in nail colors, patterns and techniques. One of this years most anticipated events will be "Nail Games" were participants will try their hands creating a new look worthy of the first place prize of $5,000. The year's fun kicks off at 7 p.m. and costs $45 per person (males admitted free) and includes light snack, pedicure, nail polish samples and the great nail fashion show. Information: www.fashionDEleague.org

Marshal arts celebration

Donning yellow, red, blue, brown and black belts the kids learning marshal arts show off their new skills Friday evening at the city township Theater. A new generation of youth is dreaming of being the next "Bruce Lee" or "Karate Kid" and will be celebrating their success. There will be hundreds of boys and girls giving demonstrations of various disciplines of marshal arts that include karate, Judo, Tae Kwon Do and many other newer forms. Do not let the fact that you might not be sporting a marshal arts belt stop you from coming out and enjoying the games, food,

2. Type gutters: When changing the number of columns of text, the gutters (space between the columns of type) remain at the default width setting. This is usually good for some newsletters and newspapers designs. However, for many magazine, advertising, and other creative uses, different gutter widths are more desirable.

– **Change gutters:** Go to the "Control Strip" and select "Object" / "Text Frame Options." Here, you can change the gutter width.

– **Preview changes:** If you check the "Preview" button at the lower left corner of the "Text Frame Options" palette, you can see your changes as you make them before having to hit the "OK" button.

NOTE: If you want to make your design more vertical, consider adding significantly more gutter width. Then add vertical lines in the gutters.

Your notes

Your notes

Designing with separate text boxes

Using separate text boxes allows you to create multiple varied text box shapes, something that the traditional column method does not. A good technique is to use both methods together.

1. Identify content: Using the "Type Tool," click and drag over (highlighting the text) the content of one of the entertainment events within the large text box created earlier.

2. Copy: Go to the top pulldown tabs and select "Edit" / "Cut" (you also could select "Copy").

3. New text box: Create another text box outside your design using the "Type Tool." Next, go to the top pull-down tabs and select "Edit" / "Paste."

NOTE: I often will make elements outside my design or document area to make it easier to work with the content. I then will move the element to the desired location.

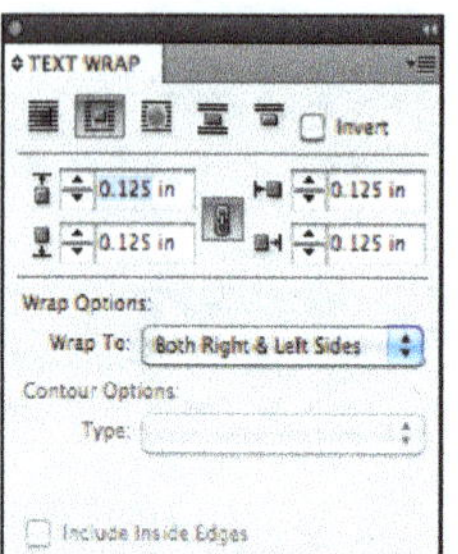

4. Text wrap: With the new text box still selected, go to the top and select "Window" / "Text Wrap," which will bring up a new palette.

– **Next, select** "Wrap around bounding," and set the mount you want the text to flow from the edge of the text box.

TIP text wrap amount »

When applying a text wrap, you must also indicate the amount. The default is none . . . which most often is the wrong amount!

*– **"Text Wrap Offset:"** Click on the arrows or type in the exact amount. A good starting point to determine the amount is to match the amount of leading or gutter space used in the design.*

More info »

To learn more about the types of ***Text Wraps*** */ Pg. 110*

Creating text boxes with frames

One method to draw even more attention to content is to add a frame to the text box. You see this often when ads are competing with other ads for attention.

NOTE: The first three steps are the same as the "Separate text box" instructions (above).

1. Identify content: Using the "Type Tool," click and drag over (highlighting the text) the content of one of the entertainment events within the large text box created earlier.

2. Copy: Go to the top pull-down tabs and select "Edit" / "Cut" (you also could select "Copy").

3. New text box: Create another text box outside your design using the "Type Tool." Next, go to the top pull-down tabs and select "Edit" / "Paste."

4. Create frame: With the text box still selected, go to the "Control Strip" and select the stroke thickness.

5. Inset text: You will notice that when you added the frame, it is butted up against the text, which is uncomfortable and creates tension. The solution is to inset the text.

– **Get palette:** Go to the top and select "Object" / "Text Frame Options."

Text needs to be inset

Now you see it, now you don't

Headliner Johnny Muson might have you scratching your head wondering how he did that as he hits stage tonight at the City Club. He'll be joined by lots of friends including the international magician of the year, Marion Lightspeed, for this magical outing. Lightspeed will unveil a few new illusions as she prepares for her upcoming three continent tour. Other magicians sharing the stage will be Dyson Smith Jr. performing his "urban mayhem" act and Timothy Harrelson who is a juggler extraordinaire and comedian. The magic begins at 8 p.m., Saturday. Tickets are $35 for adults and $15 for children.

Information: www.cityclubsched.com

– **Inset spacing:** Next, select the amount to inset the text within the text box (and the frame in this case). Click on the arrows or enter the exact amount.

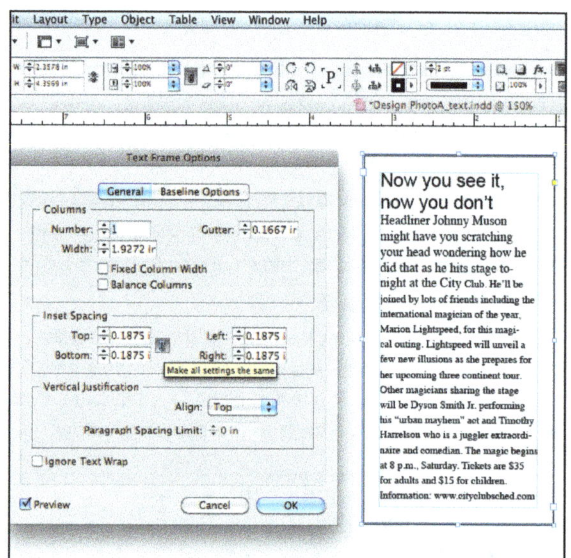

NOTE: Clicking on/off the chain icon allows you to set all the same amounts or different amounts. Also, check the "Preview" box at the bottom to see your selections before hitting "OK."

Uniquely shaped text

At times there is a need to form text into unique shapes to attract attention to the content. InDesign makes this very easy to accomplish.

1. Create standard text box: This text box starts off the same as the other two previous ones.
– Create a text box shape and fill with content.
– Next, chose to inset the text within the frame or not.

2. Edit shape: Select the "Direct Selection Tool" (white arrow) and click on a corner of the frame of the text box. The result is that the corner points turn white and become editable.

3. Reshape: Next, click and drag on any one of the box

corners to change the shape.

4. Add points to shape: With the text box still editable, select the "Add Anchor Point Tool" (hidden under the "Pen Tool").

– Click on the text box frame to add points.

5. Reshape text box: After all points are added, get the "Direct Selection Tool" and click and drag on each new point to create the new shape.

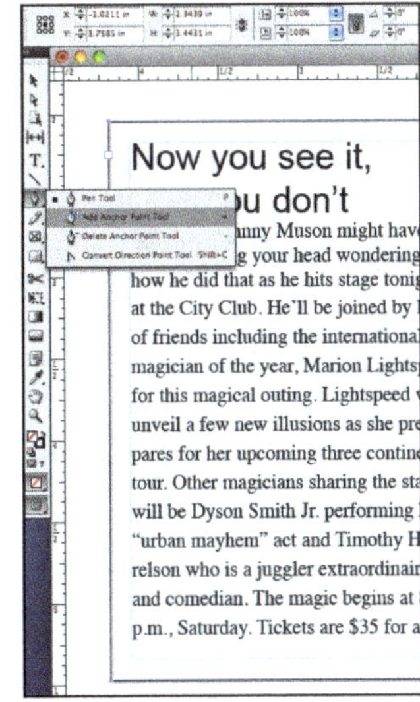

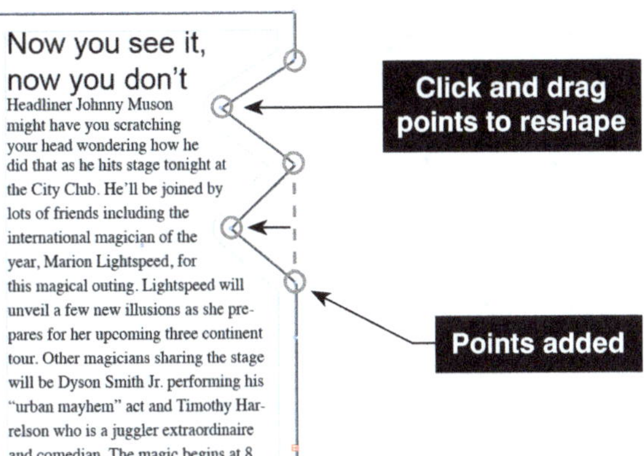

Obisqui quatias porpori beatur, cum, ulliqui adistrum volupta ne ped quaecab il escium nobis nem rectoremquae voluptatet mosa si quiam aut magnihi temquam quae culparc illique simi, accullaciae eum aut omniaes enes eos essunt aut prat magnate mpores sin re nosamentisi amenece pratium imus, offici cor alignimus aut aut et que aut ea voloreius eost et Obisqui quatias porpori beatur, cum, ulliqui adistrum volupta ne ped quaecab il escium nobis nem rectoremquae voluptatet mosa si quiam aut magnihi temquam quae culparc illique simi, accullaciae eum aut omniaes enes eos essunt aut prat magnate mpores sin re nosamentisi amenece pratium imus,

How was this text box shape created?

1. Create a standard text box with the content.

2. Using the "Ellipse Tool," create a circle shape.

3. Highlight and copy the words from the standard text box.

4. Using the "Type Tool," click on the circle shape created and go to "Edit" / "Paste" to put the words into this shape.

5. Highlight all the text and go to the "Control Strip" and select the "Justify with last line aligned center" text composition.

Essential knowledge for using photographs in InDesign

Photographs taken directly from a camera ARE NOT typically ready to be used in InDesign. Those new to desktop publishing often make this mistake, which more often than not results in production and quality problems later.

Images work best when they make the trip from the digital camera to a photo editing software like Photoshop. Here, they are taken from a raw form captured in the camera and transformed into a digital image that has the correct size, mode, quality, color saturation, and format for the media and use. A photograph used for a 1 inch web thumbnail is not the same digital image used in a centerspread of a high-quality printed magazine.

– **The solution:** Never use images directly from the digital camera or the Internet–work them in Photoshop.

Size does matter

While InDesign can resize images easily, any image that is increased will have some quality loss. Those images enlarged more than 120 percent will begin to have significant quality loss that will often be noticed by the audience.

– **The solution:** Make sure that images that are considered for use in InDesign are sized slightly larger than the largest possible size in your design.

What you see is not what you get

InDesign actually uses a lower resolution viewing image in the document to speed up the design process. The result is that some images may not appear to the quality that you anticipate.

– **Solution:** Ignore this fact, and know that if the digital image looks great in Photoshop then it will most likely look great when printed in the InDesign document.

Photoshop, your turn!

One of the hardest concepts to learn is that when you place text on an InDesign document, it becomes part of that file. When you use a photograph, however, it does not work the same. At the time you place a photo on the document, it is actually recording the file name and creating a link to the external image file (often a photo.tif or photo.eps). When this document, with a photograph, is printed it comes to the image container and says,

Your notes

"Hey Photoshop, it's your turn to print this part!"

The problem: If you move the Photoshop file, move the InDesign file, or change the name of either of these files you will get what is referred to as a "busted link." Which means you have a big problem! Now when InDesign prints this document, it will come to the image container and say "Hey, I can't find the file!" InDesign's next action will be to print the photograph from the low-resolution file it used as a visual to design the page. The result is that you have a photograph that looks very bad.

The solution: Before you place a photograph on the InDesign document, make sure you have named all the files and placed the images and InDesign document in locations that will not change.

Placing images in InDesign

Remember, keeping the photo links working is essential. Make sure you have a copy of the "Design Photo_A Lesson" folder on your desktop. Next, make sure you replaced your last name with the "A Lesson" words on this folder. Last, make sure you have saved the InDesign document you created in this folder. Now you are ready to successfully add photographs to your lesson! There are several ways to get photographs and other images (which include vector graphics and others) into InDesign. However, I am going to explain two of the most common techniques.

Method one

1. Select the "Rectangle Frame Tool" from the "Tool Palette." Click and drag on the document (moving the mouse diagonally) to create a container for the photograph. A box with handles (for resizing) and diagonal lines identify the type of container (these lines do not print).

NOTE: There are other picture box styles available by clicking on the small black arrow within the tool box (ellipse and polygon).

2. Place image: With the image box created, go to the top drop-down menu and select "File / Place." Now locate the photograph file to be placed in the box. Click on the file name and select the "Open" button.

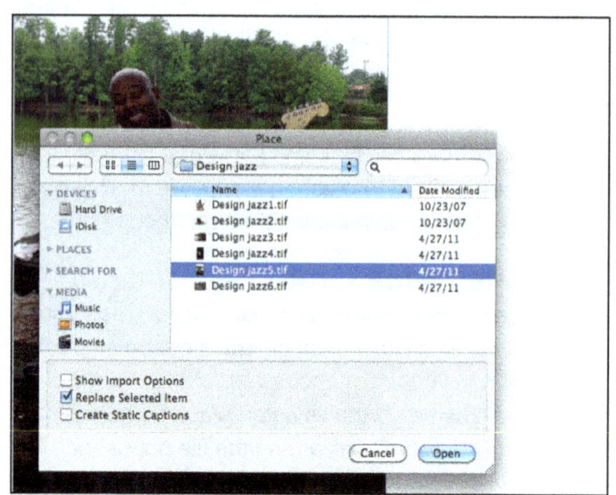

NOTE: It is important that you know where your files are located and what they are called (organization and consistent naming is essential, especially with large projects).

3. Image content: When you place the photograph within the rectangle frame, you will see only what is possible within the size shape you created–often not the entire image. The reason is that the image is brought in the size that it was created, often the size saved in Photoshop. Do not worry we will address sizing and cropping later.

– **I use this method** when I have specific-sized photo images needed for the design, because it is quicker and more accurate.

Method two

1. Place: Use the "Selection Tool" (black arrow) to the top drop-down menus and select "File" / "Place." Here, you will navigate to your lesson folder to locate the desired image, just like the previous method.

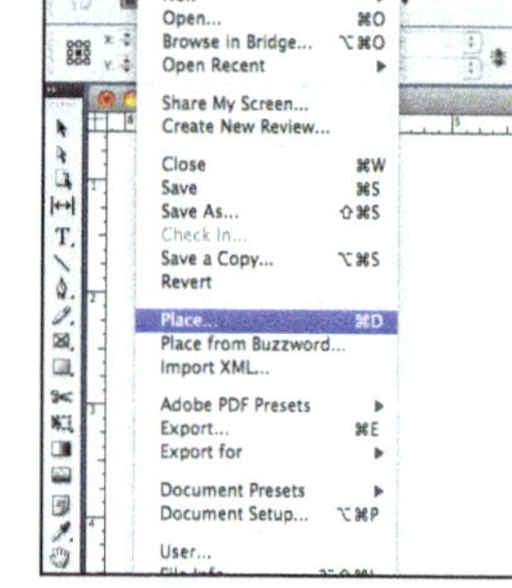

2. Move image: Once you have selected the image, click on the "Open" button. Now you see that your computer mouse's arrow has a very small image attached.

– **Move your mouse** to the desired location and click to release the image to the InDesign document.

3. Image content: This method brings in the image at the exact dimensions it was created.

– **I use this method** the most, because it allows me to see the entire photograph composition quickly.

ore info »

To learn more about the ***photo quality issues*** */ Pg. 96*

Sizing photo frames

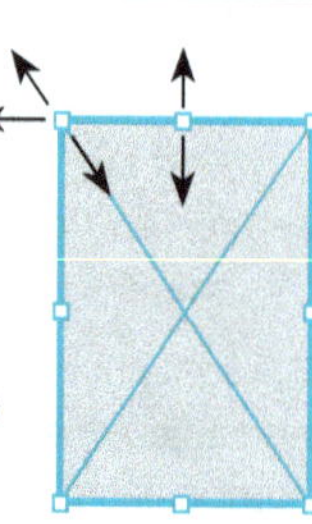

Changing frame dimensions:
Using the "Selection Tool," click on the photo image and then click and drag on the handles to change the size of the container.

– **Change proportionally:** Hold down the "Shift" key while selecting one of the photograph's corner handles. Dragging the mouse will change the frame size while maintaining the same proportions.

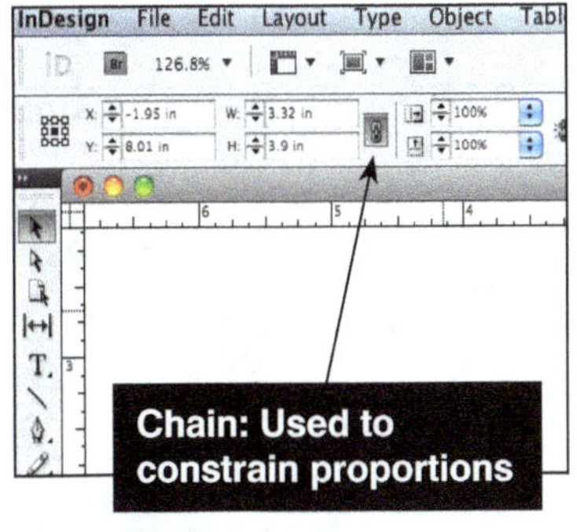

– **Change frame to exact size:**
If you are having trouble getting the photo frame an exact size, try this method: With the image selected, go to the "Control Strip" and type the specific dimensions in the "W" (width) and "H" (height) controls.

NOTE: To constrain proportions, click on the nearby chain (locks or unlocks width and height constraints).

Sizing photos to fit

Often, you have created a specific size photo frame and placed the image. You want to quickly fit the image content to the frame. The good news is that InDesign has several features that help you do this quickly.

1. Create frame: Using the "Rectangle Frame Tool" (or any other image tool), create a shape.

2. Place photo: With the shape still selected, go to "File" / "Place" and select the photo.

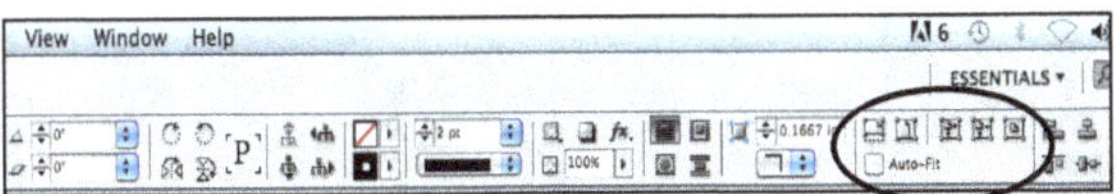

3. Resize image: Fit image content to frame using any one of the five tools located in the "Control Strip."

Example: Here is how four of the most common tools resized the image to the same-sized photo frame.

Fill frame proportionally

Fit content proportionally

Fit content to frame

Center content

■ With the photo still selected, use the scaling tools in the "Control Strip" to change the size of the image within the container. The size can be set by highlighting the amount or entering a specific amount.

– Scale X percentage = width

– Scale Y percentage = height

NOTE: Use the "Constrain Proportion for Scaling" tool to change the size proportionally (clicking on chain turns constrain on or off).

4. Photo frame: Using the "Selection Tool," click on the photo and select the type of frame and the stroke weight found in the "Control Strip."

■ **Second method:** Use the "Stroke Palette" (if it is not in view, go to "Window / Stroke"). Here you will find more line options.

■ **Color:** To create the frame (or lines) in color, select the photo with the "Select Tool." Next, double click on the stroke box in the "Tool Palette." This brings up the "Color Picker" window to select a color. You also can click once on the stroke box and then pick an existing color in the "Swatches Palette."

More info »

To learn more about ***editing photographs*** */ Pg. 122*

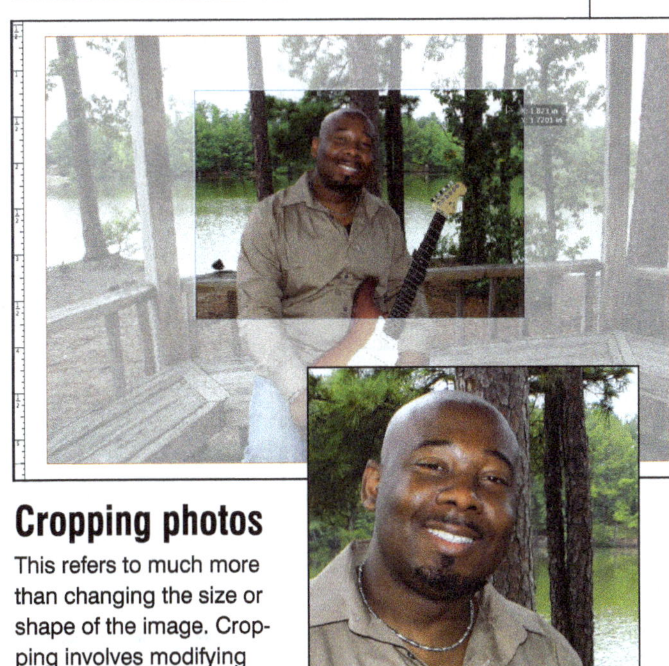

Cropping photos

This refers to much more than changing the size or shape of the image. Cropping involves modifying the size, proportion, and composition to simplify and strengthen an image.

1. Place image: Place photograph on the InDesign document using one of the two methods used earlier.

2. Crop image: Select the "Direct Select Tool" (white arrow) in the "Tool Palette." Move the tool over the photograph, and you will notice the arrow changes to a hand. Click and drag to move the image within the frame. This is cropping of the photograph.

NOTE: When you clicked and dragged (the "Direct Selection Tool") on the photograph, you can see the photo (darker tones) and the cropped portion (screened lighter tones) at the same time.

Your notes

Your notes

Types of text wraps

"No text wrap"

Ⓐ This allows you to put a text box or an image box directly on top of other content. In this case the underlying text would not wrap around the image.

– **Creative use**: Try overlapping several text boxes to create interesting display headlines.

■ The top image has no text wrap and is simply placed above the text box below. I suggest using no text wrap on content unless you need it.

"Wrap around bounding box"

Ⓑ This text wrap allows the type to wrap around the image box created on top. If the image dimensions or location change, the text wrap will automatically readjust.

– **Text wrap amount:** It is important to control how closely the text wraps around the image. The default setting has the image and text touching (most often seen on the left and right sides) and is not correct in most cases.

■ This image was placed on the upper left-hand corner of the text box and has text wrap applied.

"Wrap around object shape"

Ⓒ This method requires a few more steps but is worth the effort. This type of text wrap gives you the ability to flow copy around intricate shapes.

– **Text wrap amount:** Again, you must set an amount to keep the text from touching the image.

■ This photograph was placed on top of the lower right-hand corner of the text box and the "Wrap around object shape applied."

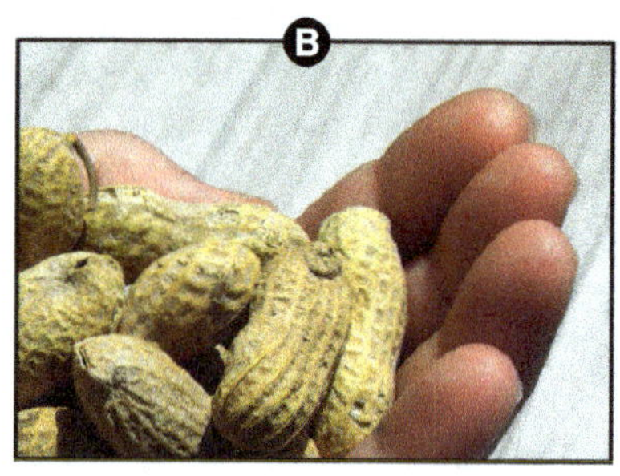

Funtime Peanut Festival

Whether they are green, roasted, toasted, candied, boiled or mashed into peanut butter, there is a peanut specialty waiting for you to enjoy. There will be plenty for you to celebrate at the 75th anniversary of this community event that runs Thursday thru Saturday. A parade, arts and crafts, food and live entertainment are planned for the weekend. The festival kicks off with the peanut cook-off at 7 p.m. Thursday at the town's city center. Most events are free. More information: funtime_peanutparty.org

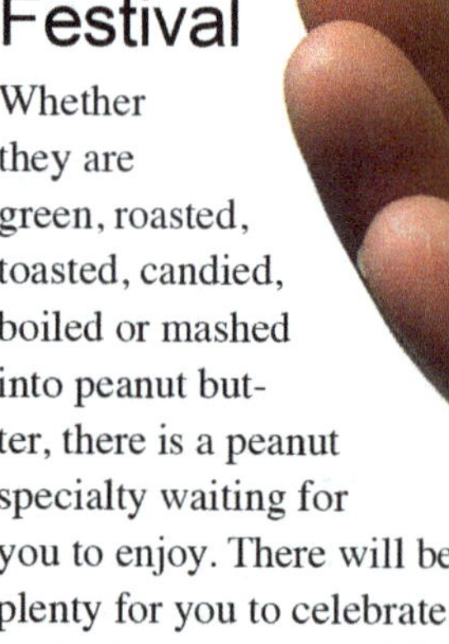

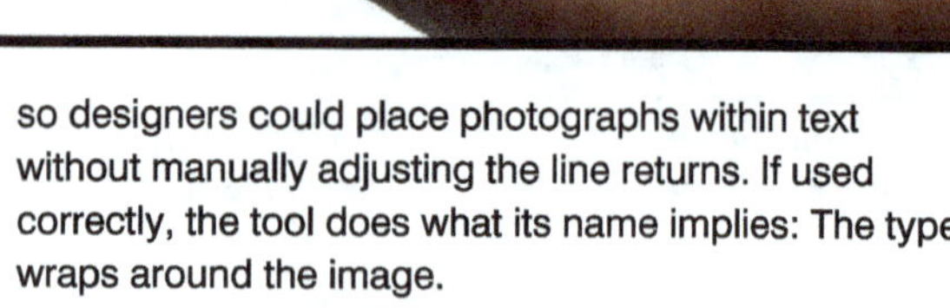

Using text wrap

The "Text Wrap" feature in InDesign is a very powerful and time-saving tool. This feature was created so designers could place photographs within text without manually adjusting the line returns. If used correctly, the tool does what its name implies: The type wraps around the image.

■ This section will introduce you to several different ways to use this tool. This lesson also requires you to use a text wrap, so learn the steps well.

Creating bounding box text wrap

1. Place photo: Using the "Rectangle Frame Tool," create an image shape and go to the top drop-down menus and select "File" / "Place" and locate the image. The location of the image rectangle does not matter at this point. I often place my images outside the document area to allow me to design the page easier later.

2. Move image: Select the photo using the "Selection Tool." Make sure that the photo is the layer in front of the text by going to the top pull-down menus and selecting "Object" / "Arrange" / "Bring to Front." Now, move the image to the desired position.

More info »

To remember how to work with ***layers*** */ Pg. 28*

3. Text wrap palette: Open this palette by looking to the right of your InDesign document and clicking on "Text Wrap," which is within the other palettes.

NOTE: Remember, if the palette is not visible, go to the top and select "Window" / "Text Wrap" to open this palette.

4. Types of text wrap: There are five different types of text wraps and each makes the image and text work together in different ways.

– With the photo still selected and the "Text Wrap" palette open, click **"Wrap around bounding box,"** which is the second text wrap icon.

5. Amount of text wrap: In this step you will indicate how much space you want between the image and text.

– **Set the amount** for the top, bottom, left, and right by clicking on the arrows or typing in specific amounts. The amount to set will depend on the images, text gutters, and your design. I often set this amount to match the text gutter width. A good starting amount is 0.125."

NOTE: Not setting a text wrap amount is often the wrong choice.

– Click on the middle chain link (will appear as whole or broken chain link) to set all amounts the same.

6. Wrap options: This setting gives more control over how the wrap will work. Set this to "Both Right & Left Sides," which is the setting used most often.

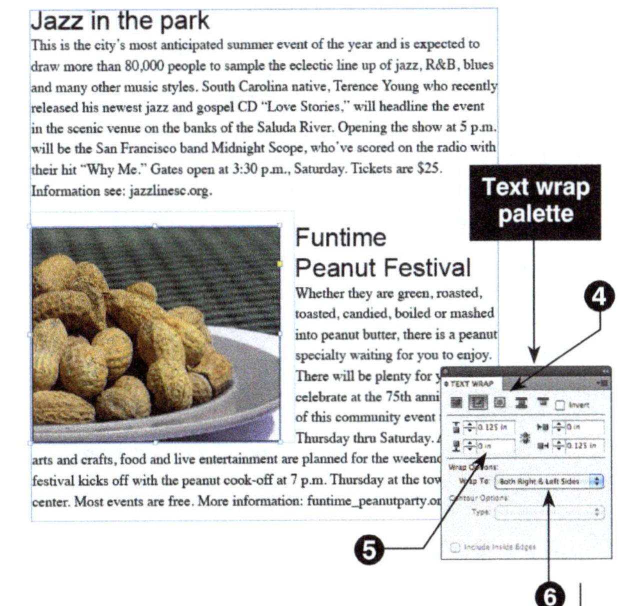

Creating object shape text wrap

This method allows you to flow text around the specific image within the photographic container created; however, this technique will not work on all photographs. Since InDesign must be able to identify the image within the photo box (rectangle frame created) that you made, content with distinctive foregrounds and backgrounds work the best.

NOTE: Often I modify the photograph's background in Photoshop, making it white, black, or some other solid color to make using this type of text wrap easier.

1. Place photo: The first two steps are the same as creating the bounding box text wrap. Using the "Rectangle Frame Tool," create an image shape and go to the top drop-down menus and select "File" / "Place" and locate the image. The location of the image rectangle does not matter at this point. I suggest placing the images outside the document area at first.

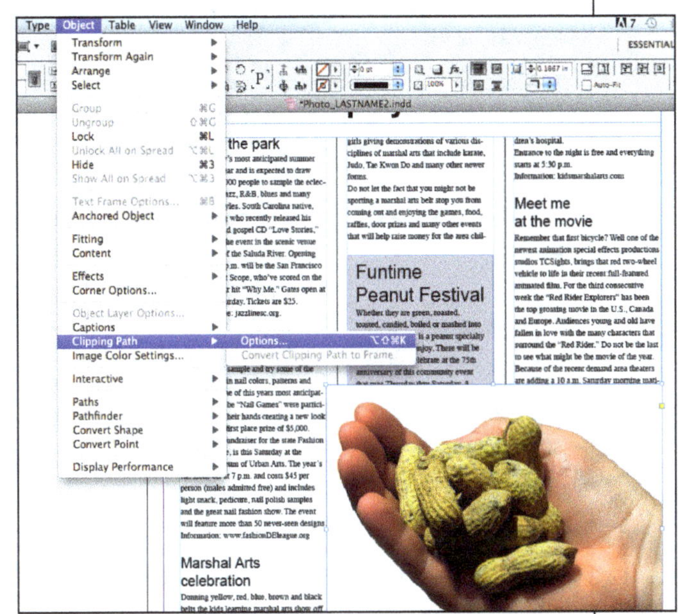

2. Move image: Select the photo using the "Selection Tool." Make sure that the image rectangle you created is in the front layer (select "Object" / "Arrange" / "Bring to Front)."

3. Clipping path: Set the photograph's clipping path, which will be used to determine the text wrap around the image. With the image still selected, go to the top and select "Object" / "Clipping Path" / "Options." This brings up the "Clipping Path" palette.

– **Now change the "Type" selection** from "None" to "Detect Edges." To see if the clipping path is detecting the outside edges, click on the "Preview" box to see.

NOTE: If the edges are not defined well, it may be necessary to adjust the "Threshold" and "Tolerance" levels. In most cases when there is a well-defined background color, you will not need to touch these settings.

4. Text wrap: The final step is to set the type of text wrap and the amount. With the image still selected, open the "Text Wrap" palette.

Your notes

Your notes

– **Select the "Wrap around object shape."**

– **Set the amount of text wrap** (amount of space between the text and the image). This amount will depend on the image, typeface, type size, and column width used in the design. I usually begin with approximately the amount of the leading used or the gutter width.

– **"Wrap Options:"** Most often I use the "Both Right & Left Sides" (often the default setting).

Modified text wrap shape

This method allows you to customize the text flow around an image container created. This is very helpful when neither the basic bounding box wrap or the object shape wrap do not give you the specific look you want.

1. Place photo: Using any of the image "Frame Tools" (such as the rectangle, ellipse, or polygon frame tools), create an image shape and go to the top drop-down menus and select "File" / "Place" and locate the image.

NOTE: This is the same start as other text wrap options.

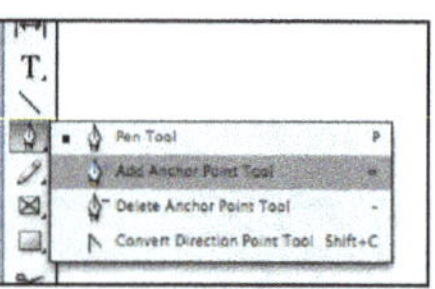

2. Adding image frame points: Go to the InDesign "Tool Palette" and locate the "Pen Tool." Using your mouse, click and hold to locate additional tools and select the "Add Anchor Point Tool." This tool adds additional points to the rectangle frame.

– **Using the "Add Anchor Point Tool,"** click repeatedly anywhere on the image outside the frame and add as many points as you would like. Add just a few points at first, because you can add more at anytime.

3. Moving new points: Next, go to the "Tool Palette" and get the "Direct Selection Tool" (white arrow).

– **Click and drag any of the image frame points** to a new preferred location.

NOTE: You cannot move the points unless they are white boxes. If the box's handles are not white, use the "Direct Selection Tool" and click on any point or outline edge.

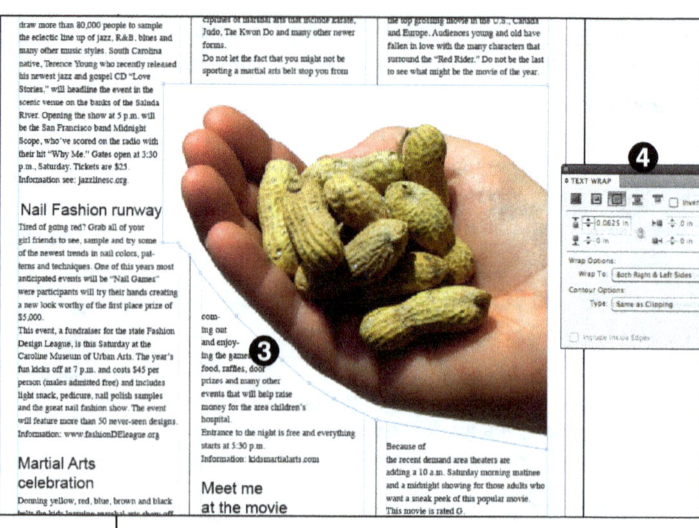

4. Adding text wrap: With the new photo shape defined, you will need to add additional space between the text and the image. Open the "Text Wrap" palette and select "Wrap around object shape" icon.

– **Next, add the text wrap amount** directly below by clicking on the arrows or entering a specific amount.

REMEMBER: Select or unselect the link in the middle to make all text wrap amounts the same or different.

Are your images linked?

InDesign and other desktop publishing programs require you to be very organized. Failing to do so will result in printing problems.

– **REMEMBER:** When you placed a photograph onto an InDesign document, the image was not embedded, but a link to the image was created. If you did any of the following things while creating your project, you may have busted links:

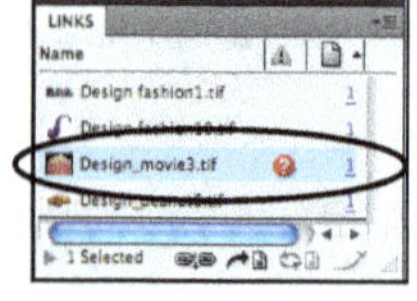

– **Moved elements** outside the lesson folder.

TIP Links palette »

This InDesign tool allows you to check to make sure your images are linked correctly to your document. Bad links can cause significant problems when printing or creating a PDF file.

*– **Bad links:** A yellow or red icon will be found next to a problem image. The palette allows you to be able to identify the bad image link and its location.*

*– **Fixing links:** At the bottom of the palette are tools that will help relink the images. You can just delete and replace the problem image if necessary.*

– **Changed the name of your InDesign** document?

– **Changed the name of any of the images**?

– **Added additional images** to your project that are located in places outside the lesson folder? The good news is that InDesign has a feature that allows you to check your document to see if it will print correctly.

1. Checking links: With your document open, go to the “Palettes” or to the top and select “Window” / “Links.”

2. Identifying bad links: Examine all the images within the “Links” palette. Those with icons to the right indicate potential problems, which if not fixed, will result in printing problems.

3. Fix bad links: The first option is to click on the relink tool located at the bottom of the “Links” palette and relink (locate) the correct image.

– **The second option** is to locate and delete the problem image within the InDesign document and replace it with a new image

– **Last step:** Save the document before printing.

Finishing this lesson

Review the lesson requirements carefully to make sure your design meets all the specifications. The goal is to produce a design that has impact and uses photographs well (sized, cropped and placed effectively).

– **Check spelling:** Go to the top and select “Edit” / “Spelling” / “Check Spelling.”

– **Edit the colors, edit the type and edit the design.**

– Does your design have the **wow factor** needed?

Your notes

SAVE

– ***Reminder:*** *Do not wait until the end to save your work.*

Save often!

Good design or bad design?

To be a successful communicator, you wil need to be able to edit and evaluate your own work. Here are a few of the many problems that should have been avoided on this lesson . . . hopefully you will edit your work.

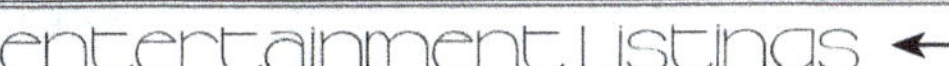

JAZZ IN THE PARK

This is the city’s most anticipated summer event of the year and is expected to draw more than 80,000 people to sample the eclectic line up of jazz, R&B, blues and many other music styles. South Carolina native, Terence Young who recently released his newest jazz and gospel CD “Love Stories,” will headline the event in the scenic venue on the banks of the Saluda River. Opening the show at 5 p.m. will be the San Francisco band Midnight Scope, who’ve scored on the radio with their hit “Why Me.” Gates open at 3:30 p.m., Saturday. Tickets are $25. Information see: jazzlinesc.org.

NAIL FASHION RUNWAY

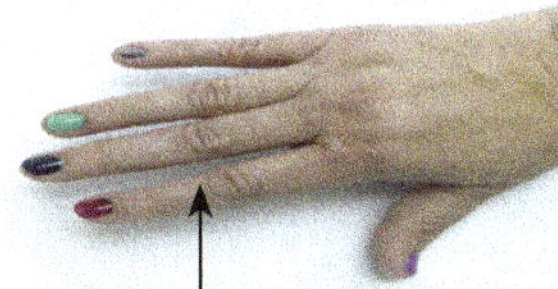

Tired of going red? Grab all of your girl friends to see, sample and try some of the newest trends in nail colors, patterns and techniques. One of this years most anticipated events will be “Nail Games” were participants will try their hands creating a new look worthy of the first place prize of $5,000. This event, a fundraiser for the state Fashion Design League, is this Saturday at the Caroline Museum of Urban Arts. The year’s fun kicks off at 7 p.m. and costs $45 per person (males admitted free) and includes light snack, pedicure, nail polish samples and the great nail fashion show. The event will feature more than 50 never-seen designs. Information: www.fashionDEleague.org

FUNTIME PEANUT FESTIVAL

Whether they are green, roasted, toasted, candied, boiled or mashed into peanut butter, there is a peanut specialty waiting for you to enjoy. There will be plenty for you to celebrate at the 75th anniversary of this community event that runs Thursday thru Saturday. A parade, arts and crafts, food and live entertainment are planned for the weekend. The festival kicks off with the peanut cook-off at 7 p.m. Thursday at the town’s city center. Most events are free. Information: funtime_peanutparty.org

NOW YOU SEE IT, NOW YOU DON’T

Headliner Johnny Muson might have you scratching your head wondering how he did that as he hits stage tonight at the City Club. He’ll be joined by lots of friends including the international magician of the year, Marion Lightspeed, for this magical outing. Lightspeed will unveil a few new illusions as she prepares for her upcoming three continent tour. Other magicians sharing the stage will be Dyson Smith Jr. performing his “urban mayhem” act and Timothy Harrelson who is a juggler extraordinaire and comedian. The magic begins at 8 p.m., Saturday. Tickets are $35 for adults and $15 for children. Information: www. cityclubsched.com

MEET ME AT THE MOVIE

Remember that first bicycle? Well one of the newest animation special effects productions studios TC-Sights, brings that red two-wheel vehicle to life in their recent full-featured animated film. For the third consecutive week the “Red Rider Explorers” has been the top grossing movie in the U.S., Canada and Europe. Audiences young and old have fallen in love with the many characters that surround the “Red Rider.” Do not be the last to see what might be the movie of the year. Because of the recent demand area theaters are adding a 10 a.m. Saturday morning matinee and a midnight showing for those adults who want a sneak peek of this popular movie. This movie is rated G. Seeareamovielistingsformoretimes.

Problem
Poor wording and the type size is too small.

Problem
Background color is too dark–very hard to read.

Problem
Text wrap problems. Needs more space between words and element.

Problem
Poor design lacks dominant image or element. All photos used about the same size.

Problem
Image is scaled wrong – not proportional.

Problem
Poor use of white space.

Problem
Body text is the the wrong size and has the incorrect leading.

DESIGNING with photos

LESSON . . .

B

What InDesign skills will you learn?

- How to place, crop, and size photographs
- Using text wrap to flow copy around boxed content
- Checking links to make sure your work prints properly
- Use clipping paths and text wrap to flow text around photographs

Designing WITH Photographs

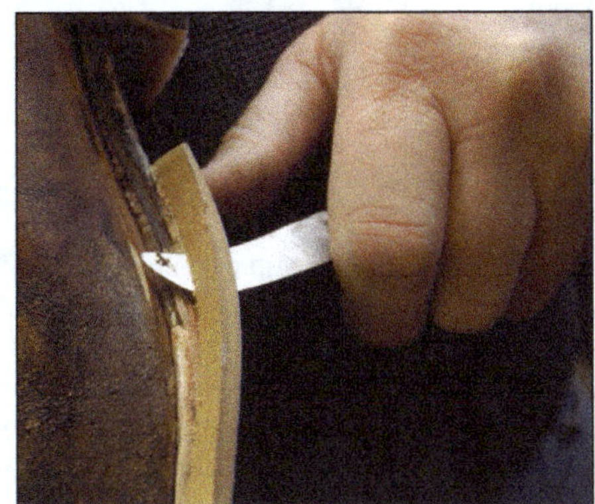

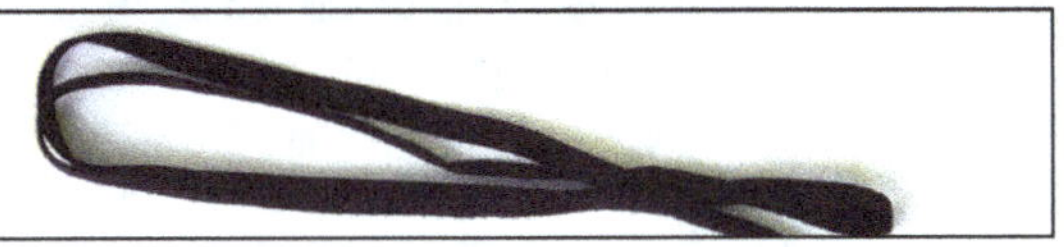

Photos are powerful elements

Overview

Images can add information, attract viewers, and give more impact to the message. They are often used incorrectly and obstruct the communication they were intended to help. To do this lesson well, research effective and creative uses of photographs.

Specifications

The assignment: The publisher's research shows that young adults, ages 17–32, are not reading the magazine. Your job is to use your design skills to create a photo story that grabs the audience's attention!

■ **Size:** The magazine story design should be 7.75" wide by 9.5" deep. There is no InDesign template for this lesson. **NOTE:** You can change the orientation of this project.

■ **Content:** The photographs and text for this lesson can be found in the "Design Photo_B Lesson" folder. Place this folder on your computer.

■ **Number of photos:** A minimum of three photographs must be used; however, there is no maximum number. You can crop and manipulate the images any way that is deemed appropriate for the content.

■ **Photo captions:** Included in the photo story are captions for many of the photographs. You must use at least some of the captions, but you can edit, cut, add, or arrange the captions any way that is appropriate.

– The captions can be any typeface and size that is appropriate (be careful).

■ **Text wrap:** The design must use at least one text wrap around a photograph. Remember to control the amount of text wrap and be aware of leading and text column gutters. In most cases 1 pt. text wrap is wrong.

■ **Text:** Set the body text of the photo story in "Times" 9 pts. with 12.5 pts. leading (regular text and 0 tracking).

– The body composition is your choice.

– Must use some portion of the story, but you can edit, cut, add, or arrange the copy any way that is appropriate. Check grammar and spelling.

■ **Headline:** You must include a display headline for the photo story. The wording, font, and size are your choice, but must be appropriate for your design (Hint: Give it some size).

■ **Be creative:** Include any lines, borders, screens, boxes, icons, special typography, or other design elements you would like. Remember, we are designing a magazine photo story, not decorating.

The final project

■ **Print the design** in color centered on a 8.5" X 11" paper and include your name on the lower left corner of the page.

Assessment criteria

■ Is the project the correct size and centered on the page?

■ Are the photographs sized and cropped effectively?

■ Is the typography legible, and does it have impact?

■ Was color used effectively?

■ Is the assignment complete (six events, correct fonts, and text wrap used)?

■ Does the ad communicate to the target audience?

■ Is the design creative and uses white space effectively?

Instructions Designing with Photographs

Locating lesson template

This lesson does not include an InDesign template. Instead, you will be starting from the beginning and creating your own InDesign document. The good news is that there is a lot of content for you to work with to create your stunning magazine page design.

Use your design skills!
This lesson will differ from previous lessons because you will not be trying to duplicate an example, but you will be asked to come up with an original design using the theories and skills you have learned. In this lesson I will explain several new InDesign techniques and skills for you to consider when creating your design (some instructions are not in any specific order).

To be successful, stay organized!
When working with documents that have more than text, keeping everything organized is crucial. Once an image is placed on your document, InDesign creates a path to the image. If the location, name, or the image content has been changed, InDesign will not have the correct information needed when printing . . . BIG PROBLEM! This lesson will show you how to work with images and larger amounts of text in the correct manner. Keeping all your files in the correct location so you can print successfully is not hard, but it is essential.

Getting started

1. Locate the "Design Photo_B Lesson" folder, which contains the working text and images. Place the entire folder (with its contents) on the desktop of your computer.

■ **REMEMBER:** Always drag a copy of the lesson folder to your computer desktop first. Never open and work on content that is located on a server or your thumb drive. Failure to remember this could result in a file that goes bad and will not open or print later.

2. Highlight part of the folder's name "B Lesson" and replace it with your last name. This will ensure you are always working on your copy of the lesson and can find the folder later.

Creating a new document

1. Launch the InDesign program: Remember, this can take a while. Often an

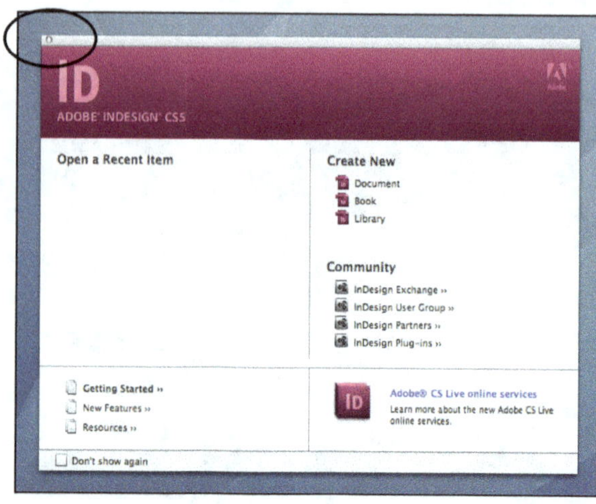

InDesign pop-up window will appear with "Open a Recent Item," "Create New," and other options. This utility was created to allow easy access to InDesign documents and to create new content quicker. We could actually create our new document here, but I will show you another method.

– **Close the InDesign pop-up window** by clicking on the small button in the upper left-hand corner.

2. New document: With InDesign running, go to the top controls and select "File" / "New" / "Document" to begin creating a new document. A pop-up window appears, allowing you to set up the size, type, and specific setting for your document.

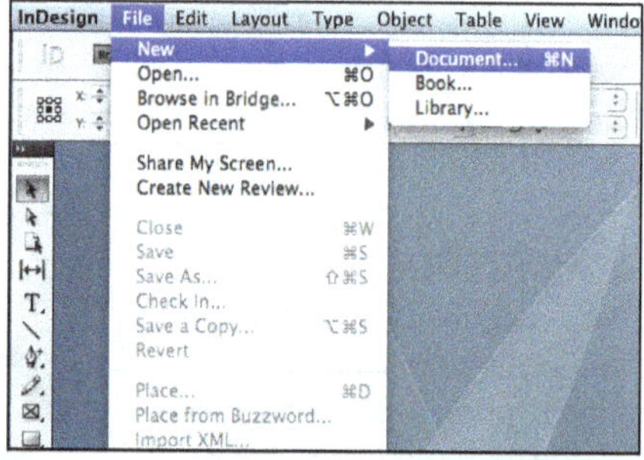

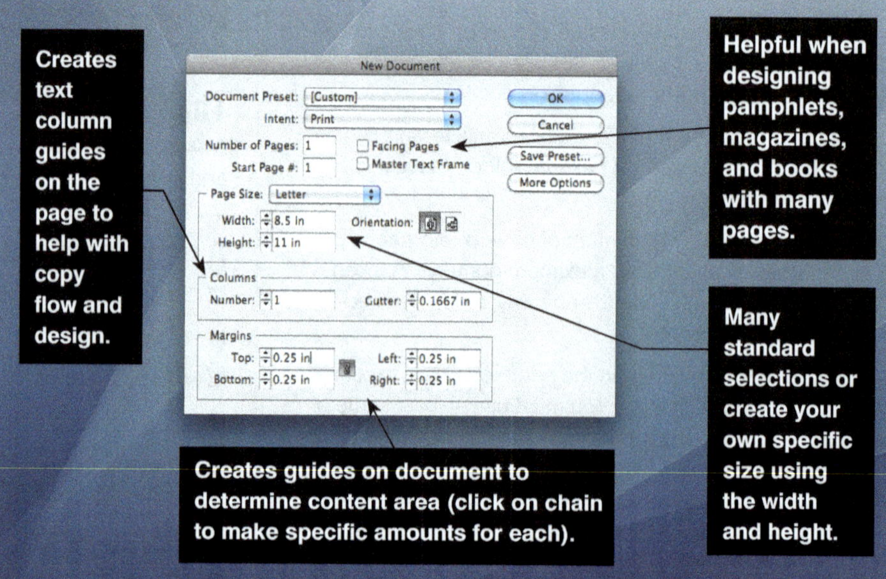

Here are the settings you need to use:

– Document Preset: (no change)

– Intent: Print

– Number of pages: 1

– Start page#: (no change)

– Facing pages: unselect box (no check mark)

– Master text frame (no change)

– Page size: Letter

– Width: (no change)

– Height: (no change)

– Orientation: You select!

– Columns: (no change)

– Gutter: (no change)

– Margins: Change to 0.25 in for all

– Now select "OK" to get our new document.

NOTE: If you make a mistake at this stage, just close the document and repeat the steps.

Magazine story size

The first thing I do on all projects is create the shape of the project and then create guides on all sides. Why, you ask? There is nothing worse than finishing a project to find out that you created it the wrong size. I put guides on all edges and lock the guides, because it is so easy to accidentally click on the project edges and change the size or move it to the wrong location.

You think this will never happen to you? Ask printers and publishers how many projects come to them in the wrong size . . . a lot!

1. Turn page rulers on by going to the top and selecting "View" / "Show Rulers."

2. Create photo story shape: Referring to the lesson requirements, use the "Rectangle Tool" to create a shape the required size of the project. This can be done several ways:

– **Method one: Using page rulers:** Click and drag "Rectangle Tool" to desired size, watching the page rulers as you progress.

– **Method two: Control Strip:** Using the "Rectangle Tool," click and drag to create any size box. Next, type in the exact dimensions needed in the "W" (width) and "H" (height) located in the left side of the "Control Strip."

NOTE: This is my preferred method.

– **Method three: Rectangle pop-up window:** Select the "Rectangle Tool," and holding down on the "option" or "alt" key on the keyboard, click anywhere on the document. Now type in the exact width and height in the "Rectangle" pop-up window that appeared.

3. Center document: With the rectangle selected, use your keyboard's arrow keys or your mouse to move it so it is centered within the InDesign document.

4. Create guides: Get the "Selection Tool" (black arrow) in the "Tool Palette." Next, click and hold down within the middle of the document rulers and drag the

guide to one of the rectangle's edges and release. Repeat this process until you have created guides on each side of the rectangle.

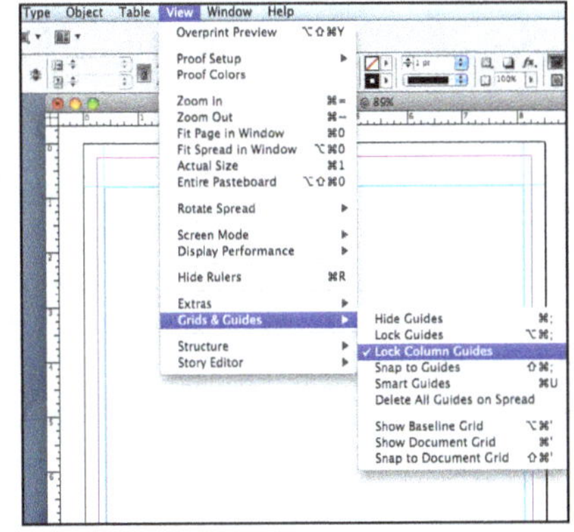

ore info »

To learn more about the ***Guides*** */ Pg. 25*

5. Lock guides: Go to the top and select "View" / "Grids & Guides" / "Lock Guides."

6. Save document: We do not want to lose any work and we want to make sure the document is saved in the correct location before we create any more content.

– **Go to top and select "File" / "Save."** Name your file "Photo_YOURLAST-NAME" and save the file to your lesson folder or save the document to your desktop. Next, move it to your lesson folder.

IMPORTANT: Double check to make sure that your InDesign document is located inside the lesson folder!

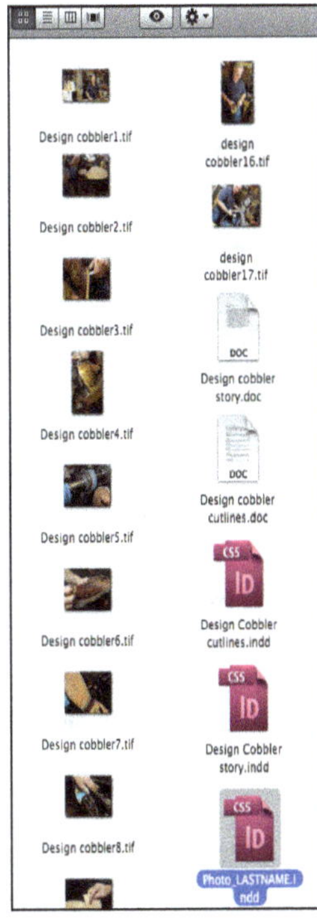

Your notes

Your notes

Failure to do this will cause problems in the future.

– You should see many things in your lesson folder, incuding your new InDesign document.

Placing text

Words can be imported into InDesign from many sources. When working within a newspaper, magazine, or other publishing company, importing the content into the InDesign document might be the best method. However, if you get content from a wide variety of sources, it may be more reliable to open the word document in whatever program it was created and "Copy" / "Paste" the copy within a text box in InDesign. The good news is there are many ways to get text.

■ For this lesson I have created the text in a Microsoft Word document. There is a duplicate file created in InDesign for those who do not have Microsoft Word.

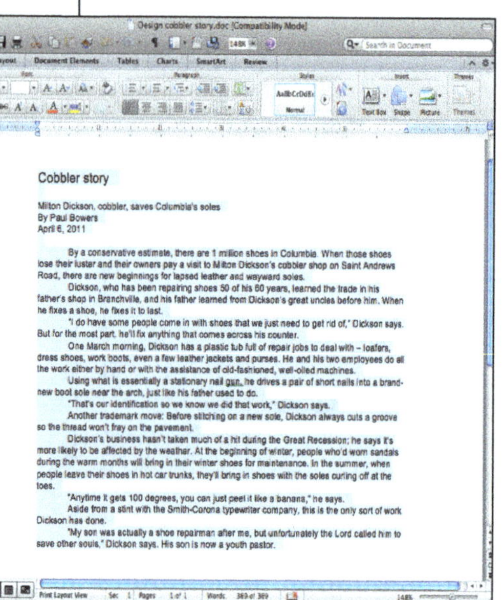

Cobbler story

Milton Dickson, cobbler, saves Columbia's soles
By Paul Bowers
April 6, 2011

By a conservative estimate, there are 1 million shoes in Columbia. When those shoes lose their luster and their owners pay a visit to Milton Dickson's cobbler shop on Saint Andrews Road, there are new beginnings for lapsed leather and wayward soles.

Dickson, who has been repairing shoes 50 of his 60 years, learned the trade in his father's shop in Branchville, and his father learned from Dickson's great uncles before him. When he fixes a shoe, he fixes it to last.

"I do have some people come in with shoes that we just need to get rid of," Dickson says. But for the most part, he'll fix anything that comes across his counter.

One March morning, Dickson has a plastic tub full of repair jobs to deal with – loafers, dress shoes, work boots, even a few leather jackets and purses. He and his two employees do all the work either by hand or with the assistance of old-fashioned, well-oiled machines.

Using what is essentially a stationary nail gun, he drives a pair of short nails into a brand-new boot sole near the arch, just like his father used to do.

"That's our identification so we know we did that work," Dickson says.

Another trademark move: Before stitching on a new sole, Dickson always cuts a groove so the thread won't fray on the pavement.

Dickson's business hasn't taken much of a hit during the Great Recession; he says it's more likely to be affected by the weather. At the beginning of winter, people who'd worn sandals during the warm months will bring in their winter shoes for maintenance. In the summer, when people leave their shoes in hot car trunks, they'll bring in shoes with the soles curling off at the toes.

"Anytime it gets 100 degrees, you can just peel it like a banana," he says.

Aside from a stint with the Smith-Corona typewriter company, this is the only sort of work Dickson has done.

"My son was actually a shoe repairman after me, but unfortunately the Lord called him to save other souls," Dickson says. His son is now a youth pastor.

1. Select text: For this lesson you will be working with two different word files. One file contains a short story and the other document contains some photo cutlines. Both of these files are located in the "Design Photo_B Lesson" folder.

– **Open the "Design cobbler story.doc" file** by double-clicking on the file in your lesson folder. Highlight the text by dragging the mouse over all the text.

– **A better way** I have found is to click at the beginning of the text; now hold down the "command/apple" key and the "A" key to select all the copy. This ensures all the copy is selected, even overflow text on additional pages that you cannot easily see.

2. Copy the text: With all the text highlighted, go to the top and select "Edit" / "Copy." All computers have internal temporary memory (often referred to as the clipboard) that makes it possible to remember the text content while going to another software program.

3. Close the text file and open your InDesign document that you already created.

4. Text box: Using the "Type Tool," create a large text box somewhere on the InDesign page your created (do not worry about the exact size and location now). Next, go to the top and select "Edit" / "Paste." The text now exists in your InDesign document and is ready for you to manipulate.

Working with the story content

Very shortly, when you move the text onto your design you will discover you have a small story–so use it wisely! Later you will discover I have given you too many photographs, which poses a different problem to solve. If you use all the content, you are guaranteed to have a poor design with little impact. Choose your content wisely!

– **Solution:** Become familiar with all the content. Read the story and look at all the images.

Another problem: The typography for the story and the captions has problems that may include:

– Wrong typeface

– Wrong type size

– Wrong leading

– Maybe even some poor grammar

Solution: Read the lesson instructions and make all the text meet the lesson requirements. Remember, the headline is an element that can be whatever typeface and size that is deemed appropriate for a good design.

1. Adjust text box size: If you did not make the text box the desired size or shape, go to the "Tool Palette" and get the "Selection Tool" to allow you to click on the text box handles to adjust the shape.

2. Set typeface, size, and leading: Using the "Type Tool" click and drag to highlight all the text or click within the text box and press the "Apple" / "A" key to select all the text (including the overflow content).

– **Using the "Control Strip,"** change the typeface to Times, size to 9 pts., leading to 12.5 pts. Make sure the other font attributes are set to regular text with 0 tracking.

3. Setting text columns: Select the text box. Next, go to the "Control Strip" and select "Object" / "Text Frame Options" to get the "Text Frame Options" palette.

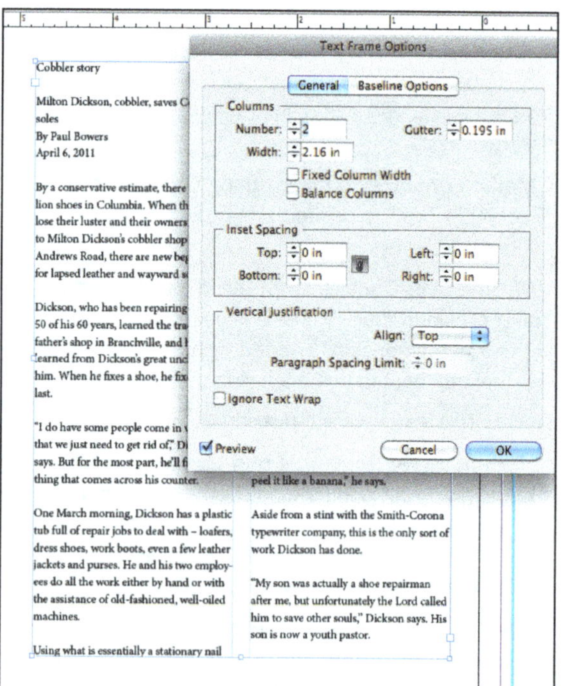

– **Number of columns:** Here, you can change the text columns from one to any number. I would suggest using one, two, or three depending on your design.

NOTE: If you change the size of the text box, the column widths will adjust automatically. When photos or new text are added within any column, the content will automatically readjust to the other columns.

4. Gutter width: When changing the number of columns of text, the gutters (space between the columns of type) remain at the default width setting. This is usually good for some newsletter and newspaper designs. For many magazine, advertising, and other creative uses, different gutter widths are more desirable.

– **To change gutters:** Look for "Gutters" within the "Text Frame Options" window. Here, you can change the gutter widths.

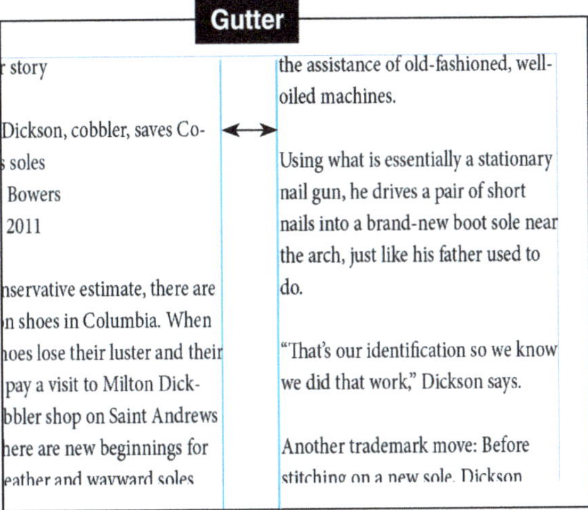

– **Preview changes:** If you check the "Preview" button at the lower left corner of the "Text Frame Options" palette, you can see your changes as you make them before having to hit the "OK" button.

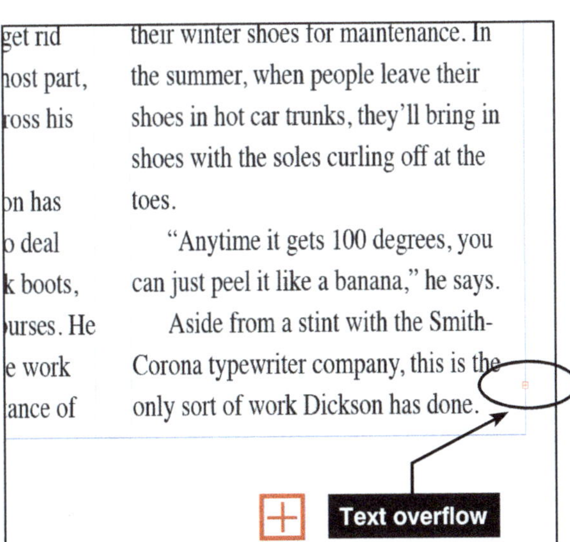

5. Text overset: If you look closely at the bottom right corner of your text box, you might see a small red box with a red plus sign in the middle. This indicates that all of your text is not visible and there is an overflow. You have two solutions:

– **Use more story** by enlarging the text box.

– **Edit and cut** your story to reduce the amount of text.

NOTE: You must use the story, but the amount of text in the design is up to you.

Story composition & paragraphs

1. Text composition: With the story selected, go to the InDesign palettes (to the right) and click on the "Paragraph" palette. If that palette is not there, go to the top "Control Strip" and select "Window" / "Type & Tables" / "Paragraph."

– **Now click on your preferred story composition.** There are two most commonly used choices:

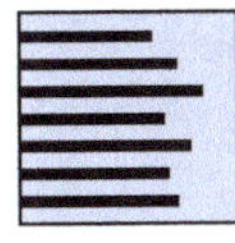

Align left (also commonly called ragged right), aligns the left side but has the right side ragged. This body style is one of the easiest and quickest to read.

Justified with last line aligned left aligns the left and right side except the last line. The body composition is also used often in newspapers. While this works well with a lot of copy, it can be harder to read at times because of letter spacing used to align the right side of the copy.

2. Paragraph indentures: With the text box still selected and the "Paragraph" palette still open, use the "Type Tool" and click at the beginning of the paragraph.

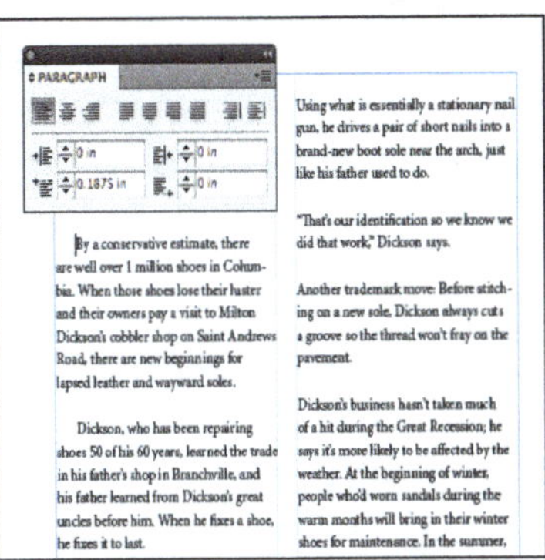

– **Next, go to the "First Line Left Indent" setting** in the "Paragraph" palette and click on the up arrow to apply an indent amount to the first line. I would suggest setting the amount between 0.125 inch to 0.25 inch.

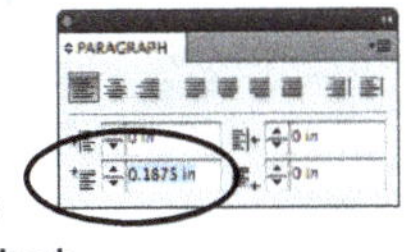

– **Now click at the front of each new paragraph** and repeat, adding the indent amount.

– **The last step** is to delete the additional line spaces between each paragraph.

Story byline

This refers to who authored the story. Often this includes the publication name or the company the writer works for.

By Paul Bowers
Special Editor / BigE Magazine

By a conservative estimate, there are well over 1 million shoes in Columbia. When those shoes lose their luster and their owners pay a visit to Milton Dickson's cobbler shop on Saint Andrews Road, there are new beginnings for

Another trademark stitching on a new sole, cuts a groove so the thre the pavement.
Dickson's business h much of a hit during the sion; he says it's more li affected by the weather.

1. Byline font and size: These are to be determined by you. If you do some research, you will find that the size

Your notes

is often the same as the story or slightly smaller. The font can be the same, but often is bolder or italic so that the author's name is more noticeable.

– **Publication:** You will often find the type size of this element to be smaller than the name and often the type attribute is different (example: caps, italic, or some other change made).

2. Byline text composition and leading: Again, you need to determine if it is flush left, centered, etc.

– You also will need to determine the space between the lines in the byline (leading).

Creating text box with frame

There are times you might want to draw more attention to the story's other content. One method is to add a frame to the text box. You see this often when pages contain several stories or other content.

More info »

To learn about **Uniquely shaped text boxes** */ Pg. 106*

1. Create frame: With the text box selected, go to the "Control Strip" and locate the stroke weight. Next select the frame thickness (or type the specific amount).

2. Inset text: You will notice that when you added the frame, it is butted up against the text. This is uncomfortable and creates unneeded tension. The solution is to inset the text.

– **Get palette:** Go to the top and select "Object" / "Text Frame Options."

– **Inset spacing:** Next, select the amount to inset the text within the text box (and the frame in this case). Click on the arrows or enter the exact amount.

NOTE: Clicking on/off the chain icon allows you to set all the same amounts or different amounts. Also, check the "Preview" box at the bottom to see your selections before hitting "OK."

Story headline

The story's headline words, typeface, size, and placement are all left for you to design.

1. Typeface: Should reflect the tone and message of the story and also be appropriate for the style of the magazine.

2. Headline size: Treat this story as if it is the magazine's top story. If you do some research into magazine headlines, you will see that the size will range from large to very large.

3. Headline words: Consider not making all the

Cobbler saves communities' soles

Cobbler saves communities' soles

words the same size to help emphasize the key points. This is a technique used often by some of the nation's top-designed magazines.

HINT: Sometimes it is easier to create separate text blocks for some of the headline words to allow for more creative placement. When doing this, make sure you do not apply text wrap to the headline words.

Design strategy

There are several things I have learned over the years that have enabled me to produce some very effective and creative publication designs. I would like to share two of them at this time that may help.

– **Know your content:** Read the story first and then look at all the photos and captions to know how they relate to each other.

– **Research designs:** Go and look at other great publications, designs that relate to your material. Look for great headline, story, and photography uses.

– **Place best content:** Select the story and all the best photos and place them outside the print area. Why? First, this enables you to see all the content while you are making design decisions. Second, placing all the content outside the print area allows you more design freedom. Too often I have seen designs never advance past the initial placement of the content, which is often not the winning solution.

NOTE: This works best if you organize your material into most important to least (often making the best images larger at this point).

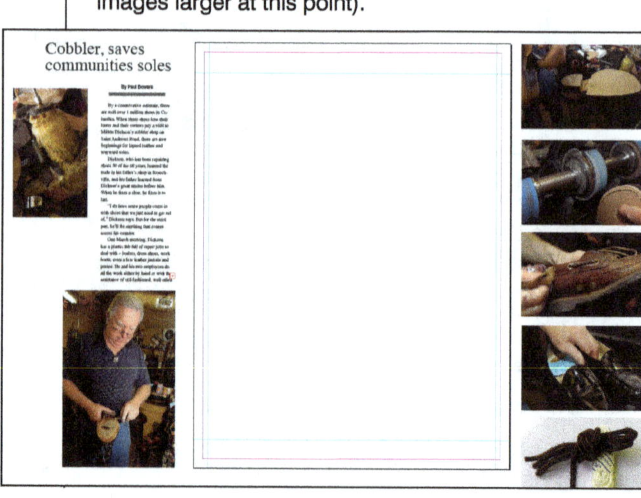

Essential knowledge for using photos in InDesign

Photographs taken directly from a camera **ARE NOT** typically ready to be used in InDesign. Those new to desktop publishing often make this mistake, which more often than not results in production and quality problems later.

Images work best when they make the trip from the digital camera to a photo editing software like Photoshop. Here, they are taken from a raw form captured in the camera and transformed into a digital image that has the correct size, mode, quality, color saturation, and format for the media and use. A photograph used for a 1 inch Web thumbnail is not the same digital image used in a centerspread of a high-quality printed magazine.

– **The solution:** Never use images directly from the digital camera or the Internet–work them in Photoshop.

More info »

Learn more about using **photographs correctly** */ Pg. 107*

- *The correct photo size does matter.*
- *Why images look poor in InDesign.*
- *How photographs are linked.*

Placing images in InDesign

Keeping the photo links working is essential. Make sure you have a copy of the "Design Photo_B Lesson" folder on your desktop. Make sure you replaced your last name with the "B Lesson" words on this folder. Last, make sure you have saved the InDesign document you created in this folder. You are now ready to successfully add photographs to your lesson!

There are several ways to get photographs and other images (which include vector graphics and other types of images) into InDesign: however, I am going to explain two of the most common techniques:

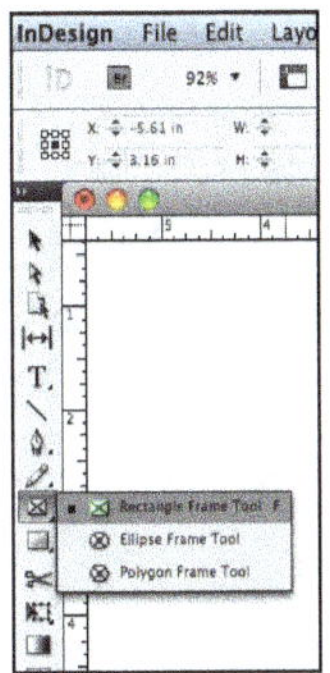

Method one

1. Select the "Rectangle Frame Tool" from the "Tool Palette." Click and drag on the document (moving the mouse diagonally) to create a container for the photograph. A box with handles (for resizing) and diagonal lines identify the type of container (these lines do not print).

NOTE: There are other picture box styles available by clicking on the small black arrow within the tool box (ellipse and polygon).

2. Place photograph: With the image box created, go to the top drop-down menu and select **"File" / "Place."** Now locate the photograph file to be placed in the box. Click on the file name and select the "Open" button.

NOTE: It is important that you know where your files are located and what they are called (organization and consistent naming is essential with large projects).

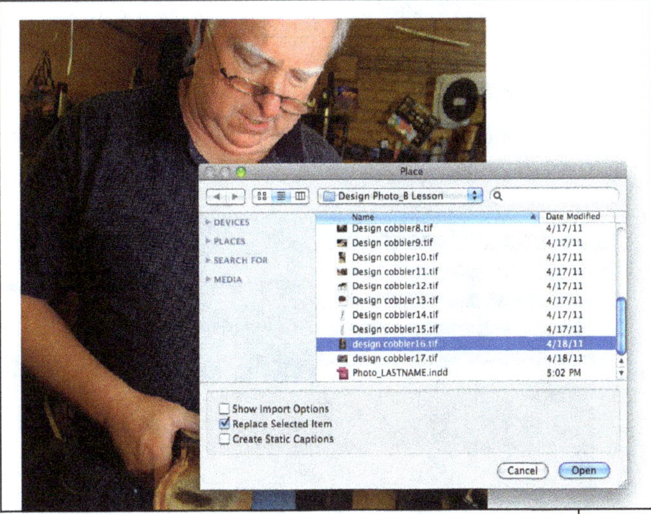

3. Image content: When you place the photograph within the rectangle frame, you will see only what is possible within the size shape you created, often not the entire image. The reason is that the image is brought in the size that it was created, often the size saved in Photoshop. Do not worry, we will address sizing and cropping later.

– **I use this method** when I need specific-sized photo images for the design because it is quicker and more accurate.

Method two

1. Place: Using the "Selection Tool" (black arrow), go to the top drop-down menus and select "File" / "Place." Here, you will navigate to your lesson folder to locate the desired image, just like the previous method.

2. Move image: Once you have selected the image, click on the "Open" button. Now you will see that your arrow / computer mouse has a very small image attached.

– **Move your mouse** to the desired location and click to release the image to the InDesign document.

3. Image content: This method brings the image in at the exact dimensions it was created.

– **I use this method** the most because it allows me to see the entire photograph's composition quickly.

By Paul Bowers

Special Editor / BigE Maga

By a conservative estimate are well over 1 million shoes i lumbia. When those shoes lose luster and their owners pay a v Milton Dickson's cobbler shop Saint Andrews Road, there are beginnings for lapsed leather a wayward soles.

Dickson, who has been rep shoes 50 of his 60 years, learn trade in his father's shop in Br ville, and his father learned fro

Your notes

Your notes

TIP photo quality hint »

If the photo does not look good when placed on a document, remember that InDesign creates a link to the image and does not actually embed the image on page.

*– **Rely on the image quality:** If the actual photo file looks great in Photoshop, then it will be great when printed in an InDesign document.*

Sizing photo frames

Changing frame dimensions:
Using the "Selection Tool," click on the photo image and then click and drag on the handles to change the size of the container.

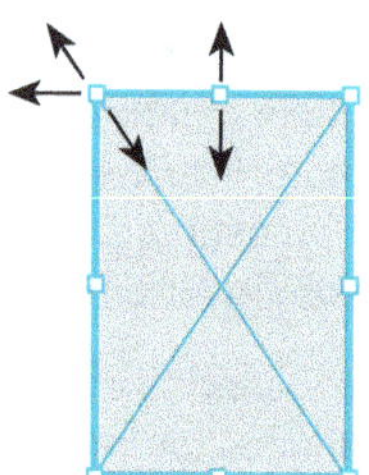

– **Change proportionally:** Holding down the "Shift" key while selecting one of the photographs' corner handles and dragging the mouse will change the frame size while maintaining the same proportions.

– **Change frame to exact size:** If you are having trouble getting the photo frame an exact size, try this method. With the image selected, go to the "Control Strip" and type the specific dimensions in the "W" (width) and "H" (height) controls.

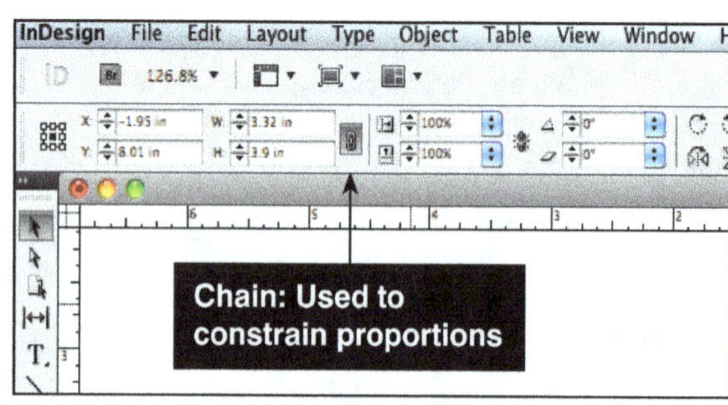

NOTE: To constrain proportions, click on the nearby chain (locks or unlocks width and height constraints).

Sizing photos to fit

Often you have created a specific size photo frame and placed the image. Now you want to quickly fit the image content to the frame. The good news is that InDesign has several features that help you do this quickly.

1. Create frame: Using the "Rectangle Frame Tool" (or any other image tool), create a shape.

2. Place photo: With the shape still selected, go to "File" / "Place" and select the photo.

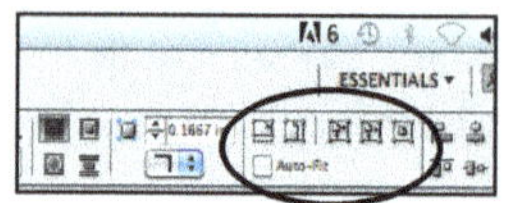

3. Resize image: Fit image content to frame using any one of the five tools located in the "Control Strip."

Example: Here is how four of the most common tools resized the image to the same-sized photo frame.

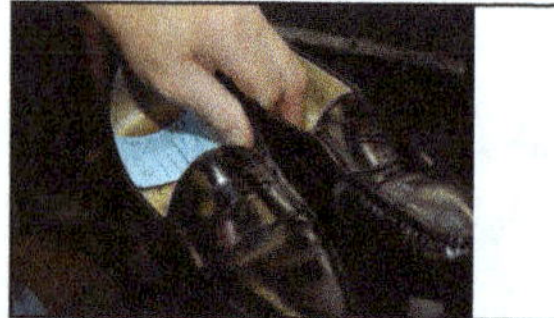

Fit content proportionally

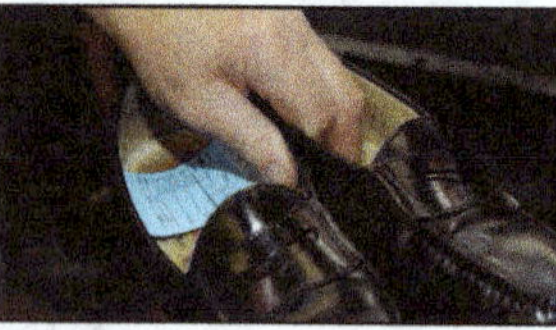

Fill frame proportionally

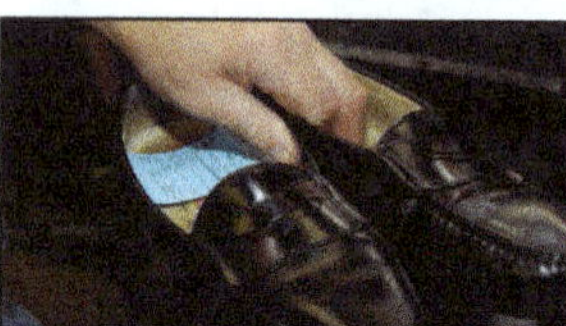

Fit content to frame

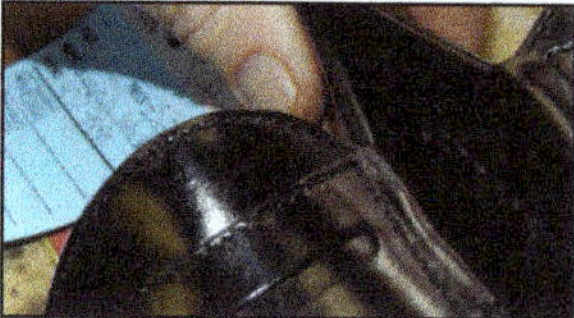

Center content

TIP editing photographs »

There are several ways to size and adjust the photograph placement within the image container.

*– **Using the "Control Strip" tools:** Once an image is placed on the page, there are five tools that quickly will resize the photo. Be careful using them, because some will distort the image.*

*– **Using the "Direct Selection Tool:"** After an image is placed, use this tool to adjust the size and image placement. Hold down the shift key when using this tool to adjust the size proportionally.*

*– **Color quality:** Editing a photograph's contrast, color quality, or other aspects would need to be done in Photoshop or another photo editing software program.*

Cropping photos

This refers to much more than changing the size or shape of the image. Cropping involves modifying the size, proportion, and composition to simplify and strengthen an image. To crop photos, you will be working with two InDesign tools:

Selection Tool – Black arrow: Used to select, move, or change the shape of the photo frame.

Direct Selection Tool – White arrow: Used to edit the content of the photograph. This tool can resize the image within the photo frame (by clicking on white handles) and will turn to the hand tool to allow you to move the image within the photo frame.

1. Place image: Place the photograph on the InDesign document using one of the two methods used earlier.

2. Crop image: Select the "Direct Select Tool" (white arrow) in the "Tool Palette." Move the tool over the pho-

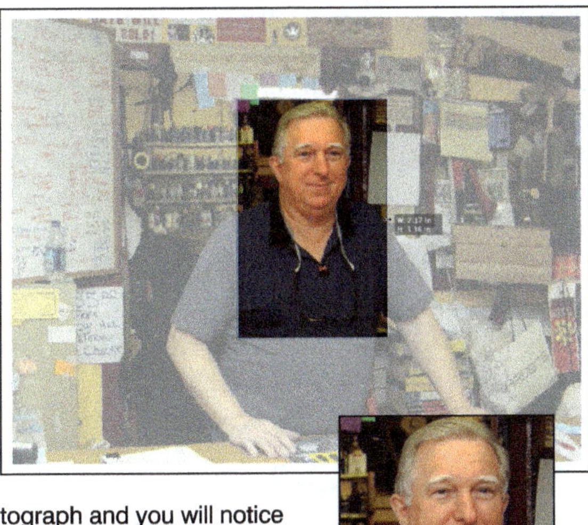

tograph and you will notice the arrow changes to a hand. Click and drag to move and change the composition (cropping) of the photograph.

NOTE: When you click and drag (the "Direct Selection Tool") on the photograph, you can see the photo (dark tones) and the cropped portion (screened tones) at the same time.

Add frames to photos

Using the the "Selection Tool," click on the photo.

– **Go to the "Control Strip"** and select the line weight. Next, select the line type (basic or one of the other many choices).

– **Select a line color** using the "Stroke" tool in the "Tool Palette." You also could use the "Swatches" palette to select a line color.

NOTE: Many newspapers and magazines use a 0.5 pt. frame on their photographs.

Wrapping text around photographs

The "Text Wrap" feature in InDesign is a very powerful and time-saving tool. This feature was created so designers could place photographs within text without manually adjusting the line returns. If used correctly, this tool does what its name implies: The type wraps around the image.

■ This section will introduce you to several different ways to use this tool. This lesson requires you to use a text wrap, so learn the steps well.

ore info »

See the different types of ***text wraps*** */ Pg. 110*

Creating bounding box text wrap

1. Place photo: Using the "Rectangle Frame Tool," create an image shape and go to the top drop-down menus and select "File" / "Place" and locate the image. The location of the image rectangle does not matter now (I place my images outside the document area.)

2. Move image: Select the photo using the "Selection Tool." Make sure that the photo is in the layer in front of the text by going to the top pull-down menus and selecting "Object" / "Arrange" / "Bring to Front." Now move the image to the desired position.

3. Text wrap palette: Open this palette by looking to the right of your InDesign document and clicking on "Text Wrap," which is within the other palettes.

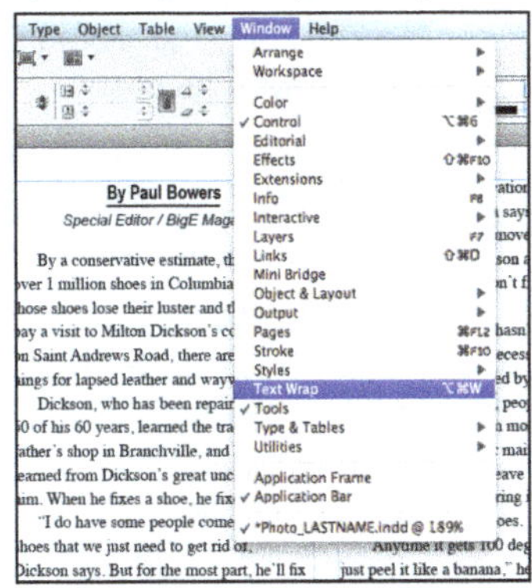

NOTE: If the palette is not visible, go to the top and select "Window" / "Text Wrap" to open this palette.

4. Type of text wrap: There are five different types of text wraps, and each makes the image and text work together in different ways.

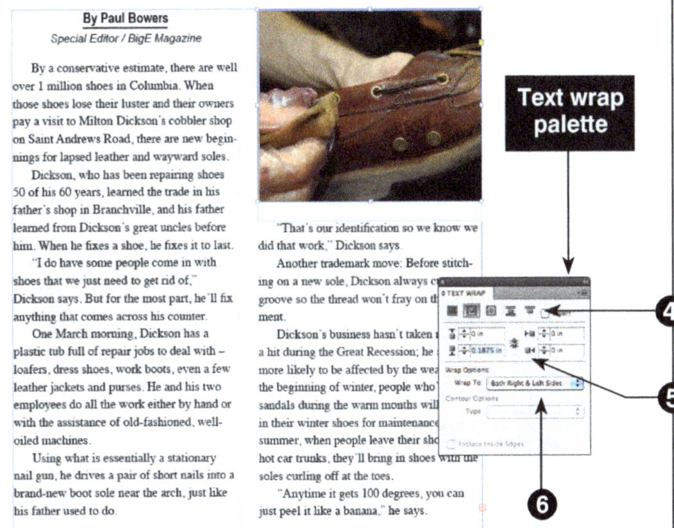

By Paul Bowers

Special Editor / BigE Magazine

By a conservative estimate, there are well over 1 million shoes in Columbia. When those shoes lose their luster and their owners pay a visit to Milton Dickson's cobbler shop on Saint Andrews Road, there are new beginnings for lapsed leather and wayward soles.

Dickson, who has been repairing shoes 50 of his 60 years, learned the trade in his father's shop in Branchville, and his father learned from Dickson's great uncles before him. When he fixes a shoe, he fixes it to last.

"I do have some people come in with shoes that we just need to get rid of," Dickson says. But for the most part, he'll fix anything that comes across his counter.

One March morning, Dickson has a plastic tub full of repair jobs to deal with – loafers, dress shoes, work boots, even a few leather jackets and purses. He and his two employees do all the work either by hand or with the assistance of old-fashioned, well-oiled machines.

Using what is essentially a stationary nail gun, he drives a pair of short nails into a brand-new boot sole near the arch, just like his father used to do.

"That's our identification so we know we did that work," Dickson says.

Another trademark move: Before stitching on a new sole, Dickson always c groove so the thread won't fray on th ment.

Dickson's business hasn't taken a hit during the Great Recession; he more likely to be affected by the wea the beginning of winter, people who sandals during the warm months wil in their winter shoes for maintenance summer, when people leave their sho hot car trunks, they'll bring in shoes with the soles curling off at the toes.

"Anytime it gets 100 degrees, you can just peel it like a banana," he says.

– With the photo still selected and the "Text Wrap" palette open, click on the "Wrap around bounding box" which is the second text wrap icon.

5. Amount of text wrap: In this step you will indicate how much space you want between the image and text.

– **Set the amount for the top, bottom, left, and right** by clicking on the arrows or typing in specific amounts. The amount to set will depend on the images, text gutters, and your design. I often set this amount to match the text gutter width. A good starting amount is 0.125.

NOTE: Not setting a text wrap amount is often the wrong choice.

– **Click on the middle chain link** (will appear as whole or broken chain link) to set all amounts the same.

6. Wrap options: This setting gives more control over how the wrap will work. Set this to "Both Right & Left Sides," which is the setting used most often.

7. Text wrap: Using the "Selection Tool," cick on the image and move it about the story and the copy will flow around the image (if not, retrace steps).

Your notes

Your notes

Creating object shape text wrap

This method allows you to flow text around the specific image within the photographic container created; however, this technique will not work on all photographs. Since InDesign must be able to identify the image within the photo box (rectangle frame) you created, content with distinctive foregrounds and backgrounds work the best.

NOTE: Often I modify the photograph's background in Photoshop, making it white, black, or some other solid color to make using this type of text wrap easier.

1. Place photo: The first two steps are the same as creating the bounding box text wrap. Using the "Rectangle Frame Tool," create an image shape and go to the top drop-down menus and select "File" / "Place" and locate the image. The location of the image rectangle does not matter at this point. I suggest placing images outside the document area to makes designing easier later.

2. Move image: Select the photo using the "Selection Tool." Make sure that the image rectangle you created is in the front layer (select "Object" / "Arrange" / "Bring to Front)."

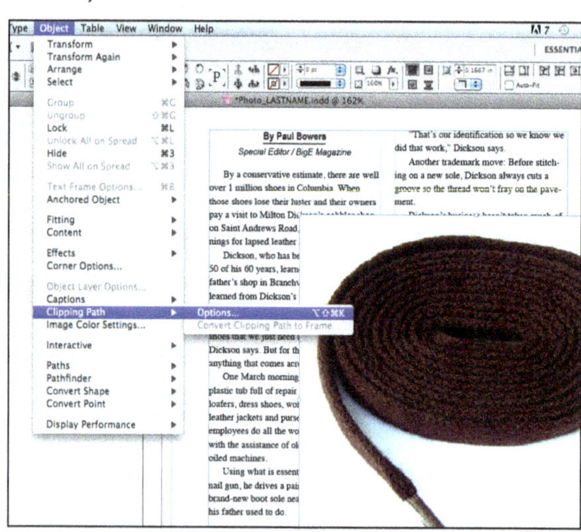

3. Clipping path: Set the photograph's clipping path, which will be used to determine the text wrap around the image. With the image still selected, go to the top and select "Object" / "Clipping Path" / "Options." This brings up the "Clipping Path" palette.

– **Now change the "Type" selection** from "None" to "Detect Edges." To see if the clipping path is detecting the outside edges, click on the "Preview" box.

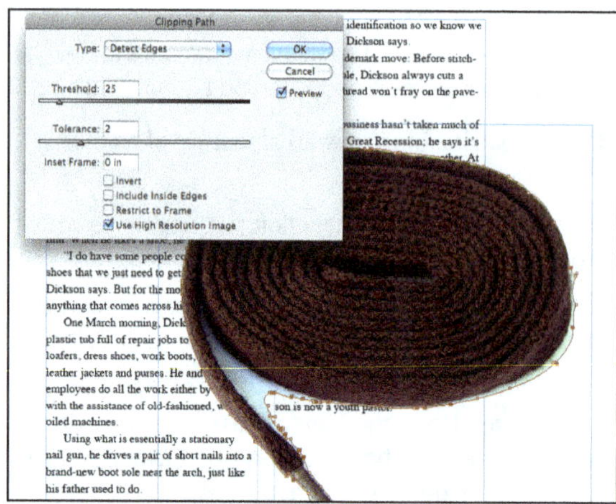

NOTE: If the edges are not defined well, it may be necessary to adjust the "Threshold" and "Tolerance" levels. In most cases when there is a well defined background color, you will not need to touch these settings.

4. Text wrap: The final step is to set the type of text wrap and the amount. With the image still selected, open the "Text Wrap" palette.

– **Select the "Wrap around object shape."**

– **Set the amount of text wrap** (amount of space between the text and the image). This amount will depend on the image, typeface, type size, and column width used in the design. I usually begin with approximately the amount of the leading used or the gutter width.

– **"Wrap Options:"** Most often I use the "Both Right & Left Sides" (often the default setting).

Modified text wrap shape

This method allows you to customize the text flow around an image container created. This is very helpful when neither the basic bounding box wrap or the object shape wrap do not give you the specific look you want.

1. Place photo: Using any of the image "Frame Tools" (such as the rectangle, ellipse, or polygon frame tools), create an image shape and go to the top drop-down menus and select "File" / "Place" and locate the image.

NOTE: This is the same start as other text wrap options.

2. Adding image frame points: Go to the InDesign "Tool Palette" and locate the "Pen Tool." Using your mouse, click / hold to locate additional tools and select the "Add Anchor Point Tool." This tool adds additional points to the

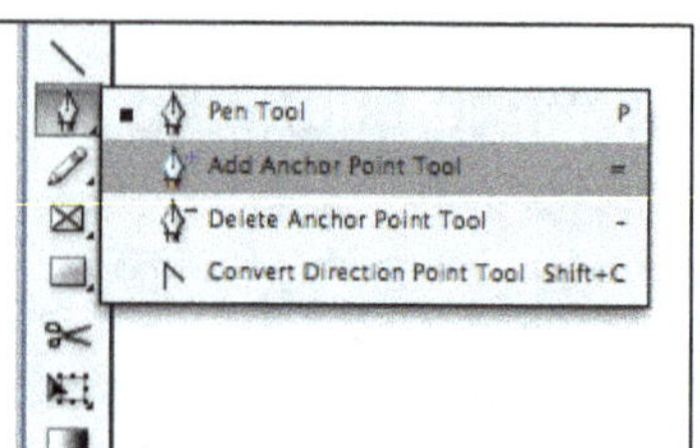

rectangle frame.

– **Using the "Add Anchor Point Tool,"** click repeatedly anywhere on the image's outside frame and add as many points as you would like. Add just a few points at first, because you can add more at any time.

By Paul Bowers

Special Editor / BigE Magazine

By a conservative estimate, there are well over 1 million shoes in Columbia. When those shoes lose their luster and their owners pay a visit to Milton Dickson's cobbler shop

"That's our identification so we know we did that work," Dickson says.

Another trademark move: Before stitching on a new sole, Dickson always cuts a groove so the thread won't fray on the pavement.

Dickson's business hasn't taken much of

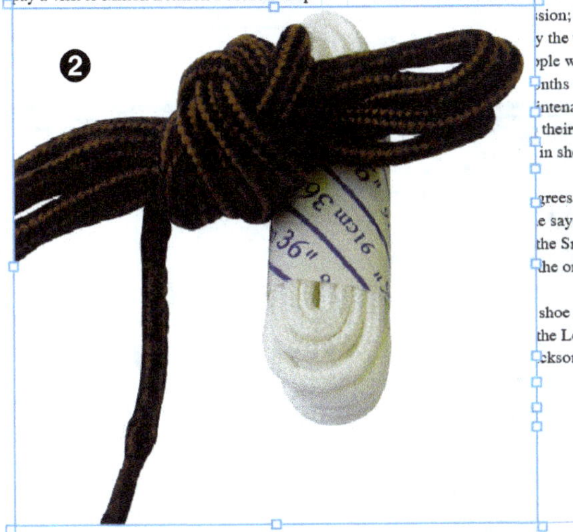

By Paul Bowers

Special Editor / BigE Magazine

By a conservative estimate, there are well over 1 million shoes in Columbia. When those shoes lose their luster and their owners pay a visit to Milton Dickson's cobbler shop

on Saint Andrews Road, there are new beginnings for lapsed leather and wayward soles.

Dickson, who has been repairing shoes 50 of his 60 years, learned the trade in his father's shop in Branchville, and his father learned from Dickson's great uncles before him. When he fixes a shoe, he fixes it to last.

"I do have some people come in with shoes that we just need to get rid of," Dickson says. But for the most part, he'll fix anything that comes across his counter.

One March morning, Dickson has a plastic tub full of repair jobs to deal with – loafers, dress shoes, work boots, even a few leather jackets and purses. He and his two employees do all the work either by hand or with the assistance of old-fashioned, well-oiled machines.

Using what is essentially a stationary nail gun, he drives a pair of short nails into a brand-new boot sole near the arch, just like his father used to do.

"That's our identification so we know we

3. Moving new points: Next, go to the "Tool Palette" and get the "Direct Selection Tool" (white arrow).

– **Click and drag any of the image frame points** to a new preferred location.

NOTE: You cannot move the points unless they are white boxes. If the box's handles are not white, use the "Direct Selection Tool" and click on any point or outline edge.

4. Adding text wrap: With the new image shape defined, you will need to add additional space between the text and the image. Open the "Text Wrap" palette and select "Wrap around object shape" icon.

TEXT WRAP ❹ Invert 0.125 in 0 in 0 in 0 in Wrap Options: Wrap To: Both Right & Left Sides Contour Options: Type: Same as Clipping Include Inside Edges

– **Next, add the text wrap amount** directly below by clicking on the arrows or entering a specific amount.

REMEMBER: Select or unselect the link in the middle to make all text wrap amounts the same or different.

Are your images linked?

InDesign and other desktop publishing programs require you to be very organized. Failing to do so will result in printing problems.

POTENTIAL PROBLEMS: When you placed a photograph onto an InDesign document, the image was not embedded, but a link to the photo was created. If you did any of the the following things while creating your project, you may have busted links:

– Moved elements outside the lesson folder.

– Changed the name of the document.

– Changed the name of any of the images.

– Added additional images to your project that are located in places outside the lesson folder.

Solution: You must fix the bad link. The easiest way to do this is to use InDesign's "Links" palette.

More info »

To learn more about
using the links palette / *Pg. 112*

Finishing this lesson

Review the lesson requirements carefully to make sure your design meets all the specifications. The goal is to produce a design that has impact and uses photographs well (sized, cropped, and placed effectively).

– **Check spelling:** Go to the top and select "Edit" / "Spelling" / "Check Spelling."

– **Edit the design:** Remember all of the design priniciples covered so far. Check to see how you did or did not apply them.

– **Edit the color:** Did you use color for a function or did you use color as decoration?

– **Edit the typography:** Did you use the correct typefaces and correct size for the content and the design?

– **Wow factor:** Does your project command attention?

Your notes

SAVE

*– **Reminder:** Do not wait until the end to save your work.*

Save often!

Your notes

Good design or bad design?

To be a successful communicator, you wil need to be able to edit and evaluate your own work. Here is an example of some problems that should be avoided in this lesson . . . hopefully you will edit your work.

Problem
Decorative border is too much. This is not an advertisement.

Problem
Trapped white space creates a significant design problem.

Problem
Image is scaled incorrectly–not proportional.

Problem
Poor wording, type size is too small, poor placement. Design and content must be edited.

Problem
Missing captions. All photographs need captions.

Problem
Text wrap problems. More space is needed between words and element.

Problem
Body text is the wrong size and has the incorrect leading.

Problem
Poor design, too many photographs being used near the same size.

Cobbler, saves communities soles

By Paul Bowers
Special Editor / BigE Magazine

By a conservative estimate, there are well over 1 million shoes in Columbia. When those shoes lose their luster and their owners pay a visit to Milton Dickson's cobbler shop on Saint Andrews Road, there are new beginnings for lapsed leather and wayward soles.

Dickson, who has been repairing shoes 50 of his 60 years, learned the trade in his father's shop in Branchville, and his father learned from Dickson's great uncles before him. When he fixes a shoe, he fixes it to last.

"I do have some people come in with shoes that we just need to get rid of," Dickson says. But for the most part, he'll fix anything that comes across his counter.

"I do have some people come in with shoes that we just need to get rid of," Dickson says.

One of Dickson's assistants rubs neutral polish on shoe leather.

One March morning, Dickson has a plastic tub full of repair jobs to deal with – loafers, dress shoes, work boots, even a few leather jackets and purses. He and his two employees do all the work either by hand or with the assistance of old-fashioned, well-oiled machines.

Using what is essentially a stationary nail gun, he drives a pair of short nails into a brand-new boot sole near the arch, just like his father used to do.

"That's our identification so we know we did that work," Dickson says.

Another trademark move: Before stitching on a new sole, Dickson always cuts a groove so the thread won't fray on the pavement.

Dickson's business hasn't taken much of a hit during the Great Recession; he says it's more likely to be affected by the weather. At the beginning of winter, people who'd worn sandals during the warm months will bring in their winter shoes for maintenance. In the summer, when people leave their shoes in hot car trunks, they'll bring in shoes with the soles curling off at the toes.

"Anytime it gets 100 degrees, you can just peel it like a banana," he says.

Aside from a stint

Dickson grinds the leather soles to fit the shoe.

DESIGNING with creativity

"**Creativity** is to design in the future, not the present or past."

Everyone in communications must become more creative to produce more sophisticated content. Why do I make such a bold statement? Look closely at those around you and you will see the answer. For the last three decades, our society has been increasingly exposed to more advertisements, more information, and more communication overall. Those who publish are creating louder messages, using more media, and creating more sophisticated content.

An example of this change can be seen in kids' Saturday morning cartoons. Get up early and take in a few hours, you will see smooth animation, rich audio, and sophisticated use of color. What do you think it will take to effectively communicate to these kids when they become adults? The message is going to have to be simple, sophisticated, creative, and have impact–the bar has been set!

Creative designers are going to have to learn to research the past, see and understand the present, and have the ability to create new ideas for the future.

What is creativity?

It's more than a feeling

When people discover what I do for a living (a graphic designer), they almost always react by saying they had always wanted to go into this field, or something like it, but they unfortunately had not been born creative. This response used to make me furious. They had no idea how many years I spent in college learning all areas of the arts, mass communication, and journalism. All the hours I have spent researching design theories and then learning the many technical skills required to produce creative answers to difficult media problems. Most think that you get this feeling that makes you creative. Wow, creativity is far more than a feeling!

The term is often defined as:
The state of being creative. The ability to go beyond traditional ideas, rules, patterns, relationships to solve a problem and create meaningful new ideas and methods.

Are you creative?

Usually, I ask my class, "Who is creative? " Out of about 100 students, only ten or so will indicate they are creative. My response is: Anyone going into media, communication, or a related field had better be creative to succeed in this fast-evolving society.

Advertising: Clients are counting on

Your notes

Your notes

you to provide them with new ideas.

Public relations: Without creativity you will keep doing the same old things over and over and never advance your company or organization.

Print journalists: You better be creative to bring new story ideas and storytelling techniques to the audiences. This is one of the reasons for the decline of newspapers and magazines.

Broadcast journalists: To get the best stories, best video shots involves more creativity than you think.

Visual communicators: Should eat and breathe creativity if you want to be a leader and not a follower.

How to be creative

First, remember that creative design is more than a gut feeling. Yes, I get that feeling, but it usually confirms that I have begun to find a good and correct design solution. Creativity involves science, theory and is a learned skill.

Over the years I have developed my own methods to be creative. My job often requires me to be creative immediately, which was hard to do for many years. While many of my techniques are similar to other designers, artists, and other creative occupations, some are different. Here are a few ideas that I hope will inspire or help you develop your creativity.

Big idea: I first start writing all the words that can be associated with my design problem. I look for the association between these words in an effort to simplify them and create a "Big Idea" or concept that frames my efforts. This step will help get me started and keep me focused throughout the project.

Research: I put a lot of emphasis (and often time) into this step because of its importance in finding

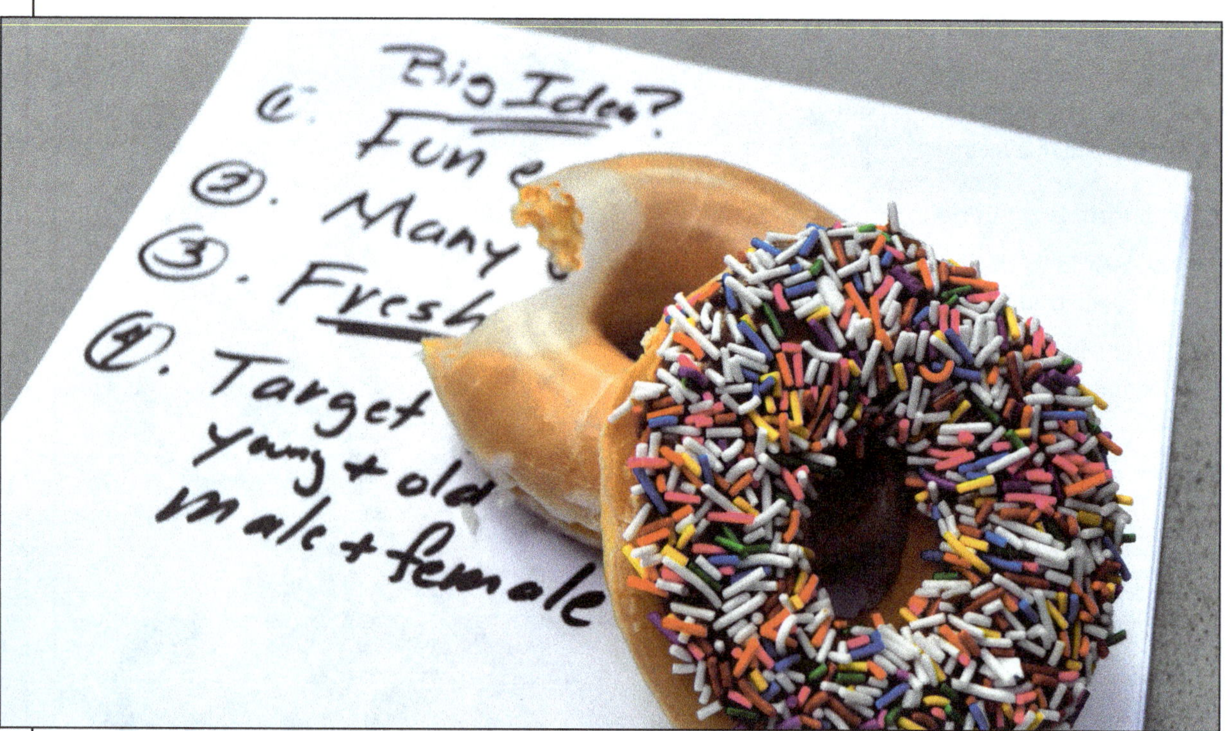

creative ideas and solutions. To give you an idea of how I approach research, let's assume I am creating a new logo for a donut company.

– Research the history of the company and branding (logos, advertising) used in the past.

– Interview the client (CEOs down to the workers).

– Research the company's or organization's product or content (in this case eat a donut!).

– Research donut competitors (even not-so-obvious competitors).

– Research donut customers and target audiences. This would involve going to the donut shop, buying donuts, and even getting behind the counter to work to see the donuts from all perspectives.

You get the idea of the many ways to look at research.

Visual research: I am out to find great ideas (sometimes current, sometimes in the past). This may involve many different media depending on the design task. I usually go through what I call a visual bombardment. I will look at hundreds of great things (often award winners or innovators work–not average or bad work) within a very short period of time looking for great image use, type use, color use, design use, and more! I will save, bookmark, or print out all those that relate to my current project.

Have fun: Designing can often be very stressful, so I find a way to relax and have fun while I am in the process of being creative. If you look at the best designers, you will notice they have one thing in common: They are all a bit weird and have toys! You have to discover what works best for you. For me, I start at 7:30 a.m., get out a few visual toys, put on some music, and proceed to begin being creative. Music is such a big part of the creative process for me that I have thousands of music selections that represent almost every music genre you can think of to use for any given project.

Keep it simple: I remind myself that creativity does not mean decorating or trying to use every great idea. Control the typography, color, images, and design. The goal is to keep simplifying until all that is left is the pureness of communication.

Edit, edit, and edit again: You will soon discover you cannot do enough editing. While I do not enjoy this step, I know it is essential in producing the most creative and effective design. I edit the words, spelling, content, tone, images, color, typography, and the design (all separately). I then enlist someone else to help me, since I know I am not the best person to be editing my own work.

Sophisticated design

Creating sophisticated colors

We have already talked about color and how important it is to communication. Remember how excited you were when a new version of a video game came out because you anticipated better graphics, animations, and colors? Well, now it is time to improve your use of color the same way . . . because the audience expects better. Here are several ways to make your use of color more sophisticated:

1. Use more tints and shades in your designs. Do not settle for just using 50% of a basic color.

– **Try using more variations of contrast.** For example, use 6% of a blue green or try 11% of a red violet instead of a basic pink.

– **Use more subtle variations of shades.** I seldom use just basic black. I will create 80% black with 20%

cyan, 10% magenta, and 10% yellow to create a softer, richer black.

2. Mix more colors instead of always using the basic 20 or so in the palette. You were not happy when your computer screen only used 256 color to display the contents. Instead, you wanted thousands of colors so everything looked good. Soon a thousand colors were not good enough, and you wanted millions of colors so everything would look rich and vibrant. So why are you not using some of those millions of colors?

– **Use a much wider and diverse range of colors.** Do not always mix your colors using percentages of ten. For example, for a sophisticated light blue green consider mixing 19% cyan, 11% yellow, and 5% red.

3. Discover muted colors. These colors have less saturation and intensity of more basic colors. To make a soft muted color ,you add a color that is the opposite of the main color. The secret is to use small amounts of the opposite color to diminish, not kill, the color's intensity. Example: I make a nice, rich blue using 80% cyan and 30% magenta. To make this a muted blue color, add a small amount of the opposite color on the color wheel (which is orange = yellow and magenta). Thus, this new muted blue color is 80% cyan, 30% magenta, and 14% yellow.

Muted blue color

4. Consider using color schemes rather than an arbitrary mix of colors. Using specific color schemes has the potential of advancing the function of color. It can bring harmony to the project.

– **Research past design and art movements** to discover color schemes that might be appropriate, such as impressionism, pop art, and the 1950s album music era.

– **Take advantage of software and Web sites** that can help you discover and create color schemes.

Software: Adobe Illustrator's swatch libraries.

Web sites: colorschemedesigner.com www.colourlovers.com kuler.adobe.com

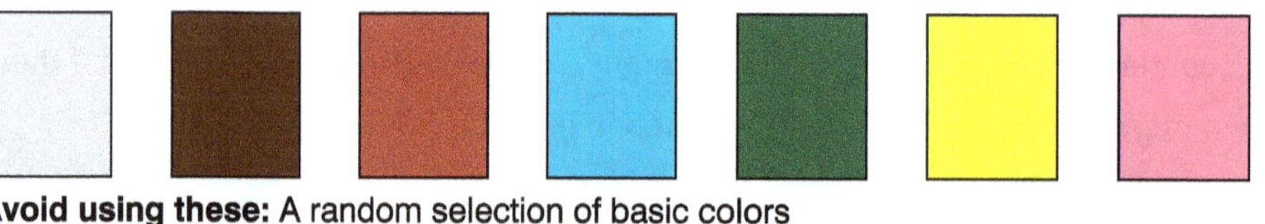

Avoid using these: A random selection of basic colors

Aspire to use these: A specific color scheme

Designing with sophisticated typography

By now you have gotten good at identifing a topography that works with specific content. The goal now is to show more restraint in using different typefaces while manipulating the typography and content together so they work in unison to create a higher level of sophistication. Here are three ways to improve your typography:

1. Try to limit your typeface use to three when possible on any given project. Often I am able to use only one type. However, there are times I might need many more.

– One typeface for the display type and other large type uses.

– One typeface for the text. Very often the display typeface does not work for small body text uses.

– One other typeface that acts as the utility typeface to categorize content and help layer the information.

2. Legibility is the key. Recently, one of my students wrote a great story and she found a typeface that was great for the subject matter. When I reviewed the project, I found she had placed a complex photo underneath the body text, making it difficult to read. I pointed out this problem, but she really liked the typeface. She assured me she would be able to make it work.
Sadly, when the project was published, the comments concerned the difficulty in reading the story instead of how fantastic the story was. This time, design and poor typography had severely damaged the content.

– **Keep body text typography simple.**

– **Consider limiting the use of display typography,** especially if you have selected a very complex or ornate typeface. You must realize that a little of a good typeface goes a long way, and too much can overpower the design and content.

– **Do not trust the computer screen.** What you see on the screen might not be what you get when a project is printed. If words are slightly difficult to read on the screen, they will most likely be impossible to read when printed. Always do an early print test before you fall in love with your design.

CAUTION: Putting type on photographs is difficult and has the potential to fail more often than succeed.

Poor type use

Home town peanut festival

Still poor type use

Home town PEANUT FESTIVAL

3. Put more emphasis on the words than the typeface.
We often spend a lot of time with selecting the correct typeface when we would have better designs if we spent more time emphasizing the words.

– **Try larger type** (200 pt. and above).

– **Make the key word or words** significantly larger than other words.

– **Art:** Consider making the display headline the main visual element in your design.

– **Experiment:** Make each of the words in your headline its own text

Better type uses

Hometown
peanut festival

Your notes

Your notes

Hometown Peanut festival

Even better type uses

box and experiment with word size and placement to make a stronger display headline. Just remember, it is all about the words and what they say that is the focus. **Remember: You must** adjust the letter spacing (most often reduce) and kern letter pairs.

Creating a sophisticated design

Creating an excellent design will require sophisticated use of typography, color, images, and the ability to effectively simplify the content to create a message with clarity and impact design. I have several suggestions that will improve your design:

1. Do more than one design. This is the difference between simple and sophisticated, and the difference between student and professional work. Do one design quickly that has all the essential content and meets all the requirements. Take that file and do a "Save As." This quickly creates a duplicate file. Now take your your design and go bigger and bolder and do a "Save As" to create a third version. The next step is to make your design even bolder and a bit crazy. Finally, open all three files side by side, and take the best of each. You will discover this takes minimal time but pays off.

2. Edit & critique your work. This sounds simple, but is too often neglected. Set aside your work and go do something completely different. Come back and edit your design.

– To take your design to the next level, get someone else to evaluate the design. Look for their reactions more than their comments. If they say they like your colors, images, or some other element of your design, you're not there yet.

3. Invisible design. The goal of any designer is to become invisible. When someone critiques or looks at your work, they should become absorbed into the material. When this happens, you have created a sophisticated design that works!

– Print out your project and get one person you casually know to look at your work (for best results do no tell them this is your work). Take a second printout and get someone who is in communications to review your work. Compare the results and decide on refinements that need to be made.

Summary

I hope I have convinced you that creativity is just not something nice, but is an element that is essential in today's communication. Creativity is not just part of your inborn DNA, it is a skill that takes hard work to achieve.

I suggest going out each day and identifying something that is a good design and something that is a bad design. Try to figure out what element made it a good or bad design. After doing this awhile, you will increase your design vocabulary and be able to quickly analyze design. Eventually, you will have refined your skill to be able to pick out the good and bad elements in your work.

The next time you are searching for that jewel of a creative idea, I encourage you to not let your guard down and succumb to making things only look nice . . . decorating. Instead, you should draw upon your design and communication knowledge and make your designs simple, functional, and speaking with authority to the audience. If you do this, you will discover your design most likely is very creative.

For this lesson I am giving you a "real life" design challenge and have included very little InDesign instructional assistance. I have included instructions on some creative uses of InDesign tools. You will have to draw upon all that you have learned about design and your InDesign skills to be successful with this project.

Your notes

DESIGNING with creativity

LESSON . . .

What InDesign skills will you learn?

- How to use the "Type on Path" tool to flow typography along any shape
- How to use opacity and effects on images and type
- Working with multiple text wraps

SCOTT FARRAND DESIGN & inDESIGN

Designing with Creativity

Magazine advertising

Overview

It is now time to prove everything that you have learned. In this lesson you will be creating an advertisement promoting all the tourist opportunities in the city of San Francisco. You will need to use all the design knowledge and computer skills you have developed to be successful.

Your design must include all of the following:

■ **Photos:** The number is up to you, but it must include at least one. You must use the images provided.

■ **Display headline:** The wording, size, and typography is up to you, but must be appropriate for ad.

■ **Text:** The ad must have at least two sentences. The wording, size, and typography is up to you, but content must be grammatically correct and contain no misspellings.

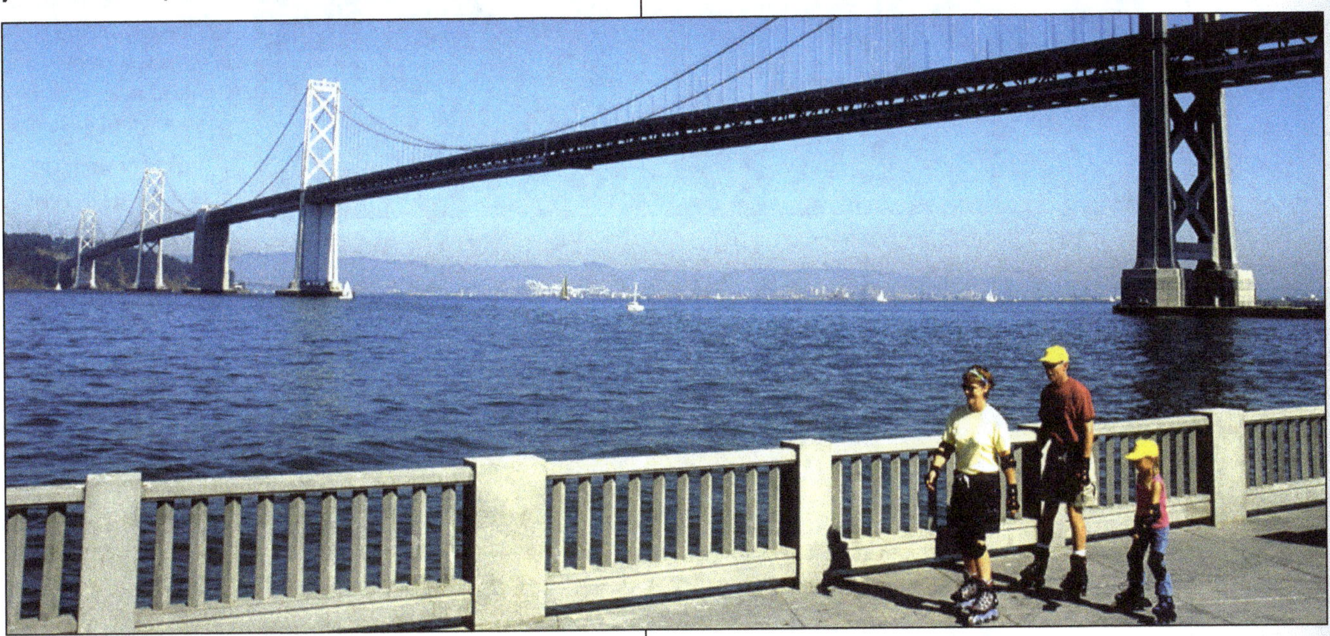

■ **Logo:** The ad must contain the campaign logo that is provided. Its size and use is up to you.

■ **Call to action:** The ad must include a call to action that encourages the target audience to go to San Francisco.

■ **Other content:** Include any other content that you deem appropriate for your design; however, all content must be of excellent quality and free of any legal issues.

Specifications

The assignment: The state of California is launching an ad campaign promoting its most popular travel destinations to the rest of the nation. Your task is to find a creative way to promote the city of San Francisco for two different target audiences: You are to pick only one.

Young professionals (ages 22–32).

Young families (one to two children under the age of 11). Your ad should grab the audience's attention!

■ **Size:** You have two sizes to pick from:

– Vertical half-page ad (4.75" wide by 9.75" deep).

– Horizontal half-page ad (7.25" wide by 4.75" deep).

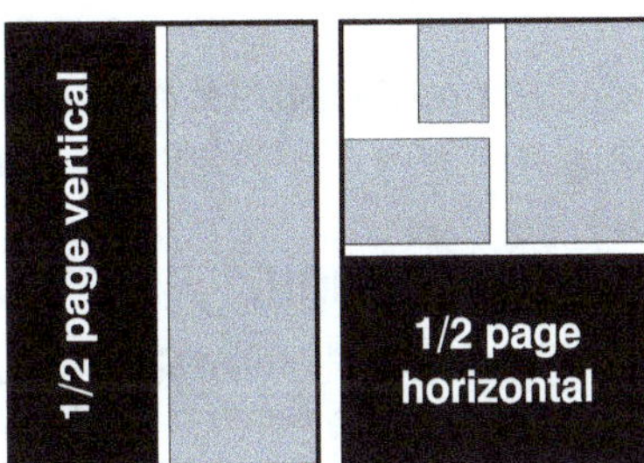

NOTE: There is no InDesign template for this lesson.

Ad content

A folder titled "Design Creativity_A Lesson" includes some content for the advertisement that includes photos, logos, and maps. You will need to create the text.

The final project

■ **Print the design** in color centered on 8.5" X 11" paper and include your name on the lower left corner of the page.

■ **PDF:** This project must also include a PDF file of your design that is suitable to send to the client in an e-mail.

Assessment criteria

■ Is the ad the correct size and centered on the page?

■ Does the project demonstrate knowledge and skill in typography, design, color, and photo use?

■ Was the PDF created correctly?

■ Is the ad complete and includes all required elements?

■ Does the ad communicate to the target audience?

■ Does the ad design demonstrate creativity?

Your notes

Instructions Designing with Creativity

stantially down since 2008, primarily from the recession and the outbreak of the H1N1 flu.

– San Francisco is one of the state's top tourism attractions and had 15.9 visitors in 2010 spending $8.3 billion.

– San Francisco, known as "the city by the bay," is well known and wants to attract the next generation of travelers.

– The client wants to attract more U.S. visitors to San Francisco, especially young professionals age 22 to 32 and young families who typically have one to two children under the age of 11.

Getting started

This lesson does not include an InDesign template and only has minimal instructions, because you now have much of the knowledge and InDesign skills to handle many projects. This lesson will challenge you to come up with an original design that is creative.

A real client's communication problem

This lesson is much like a typical day as a visual communicator. You are introduced to a new client who asks for your assistance in solving his communication problem. He gives you some background on the company or organization, which is followed by offering you some content or resources they currently have.
Finally, he asks your opinion and when he can expect to see your design as he walks out the door. You are left thinking, "What have I gotten myself into now?"

Your client: The California Department of Tourism and the city of San Francisco.

The problem: California is a state of over 37 million people, with an economy that relies on tourism. Unfortunately, California's numbers have been down the last four years. The state wants to promote more tourism to its major markets and wants your help with San Francisco.

– The client is seeking a half-page magazine print ad to be placed in tourism-related magazines.

Organization background:
Tourism accounts for $87 billion, but has been sub-

Content and resources: The lesson folder contains many photographs of San Francisco, a few maps of California, and a "San Francisco, Visit us" tourism logo. You can chose to use as little or as much as you deem appropriate to achieve your goal.

All images are copyrighted and are forbidden to be used other than for the "Design & in Design" lessons.

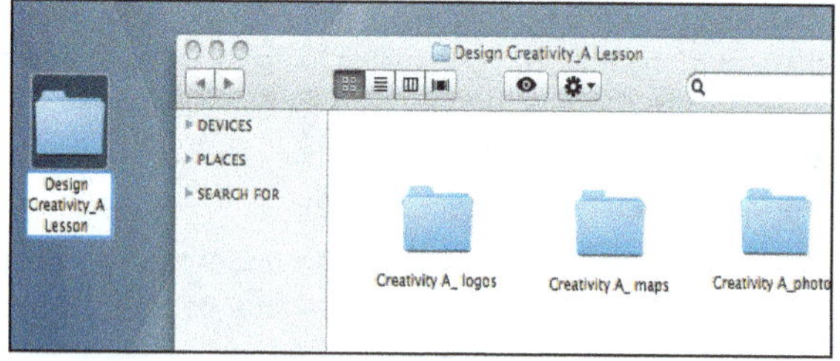

Project details: Refer to the lesson instructions for additional specific information (previous page).

Let's begin

Locate the "Design Creativity_A Lesson" folder that contains the lesson contents. Place the entire folder on the desktop of your computer.

■ **CAUTION:** Never open and work on content that is located on your thumb drive.

Highlight part of the folder's name "A Lesson" and replace it with you last name. This will ensure you are always working on your copy of the lesson and can find the folder later.

Create a new document

Have you done your research?

First: I would never think of beginning this lesson, or any other professional project that required a high level of creativity without doing research.

Second: I would never sit down in front of the computer screen without having several sketches of design ideas.

– While the computer is a great piece of technology, it is an inanimate object and will not unveil great ideas . . . you have to create them yourself!

TIP: I really want to you to do great on this lesson. I suggest that you go back to pages 130 and 131 and review the steps for creativity.

Now you can begin by creating a new document

1. Launch the InDesign program: With InDesign running, go to the top controls and select "File" / "New" / "Document" to begin creating a new document. A window will appear for you to set up the document size, type, and other specific settings.

– **Standard letter-size document** will work for this lesson; however, you will need to decide the correct orientation for your design.

2. Create ad shape: You have two very different sizes to pick from depending on what type of magazine ad you would like to design.

– Vertical half-page ad (4.75" wide by 9.75" deep).

– Horizontal half-page ad (7.25" wide by 4.75" deep).

3. Center ad shape on document: With the ad shape selected, move it to the center of your InDesign document.

4. Create guides: I would suggest this so you can be assured you do not accidentally change the size.

5. Save document: Make sure you name the file correctly ("creative design_yourlastname.indd") and save the document within your lesson folder located on your computer desktop.

IMPORTANT: Failure to save your file in the correct location can result in printing problems later!

Ad headline

What you say is up to you, but remember how important this element is in an ad. The headline gives information, supports the image, and also sets the tone.

– **Importance:** Most often the headline is the first or second thing the viewer sees. Avoid label headlines, because what the headline says is very crucial to an effective advertisement.

– **Position:** I have seen successful designs with the headline at the bottom, the middle, and even running down the side.

New technique: Type on path

Sometimes the traditional headline that follows a straight horizontal or vertical line is not what is needed. This type technique allows a headline to be any shape you can image and uses InDesign's "Type on Path Tool."

1. Create words: Using the traditional "Type Tool," create a text box and type in your headline. I suggest making the headline large at first (about 60 pts.).

– Select a typeface.

– Tighten letter spacing and kern inconsistent letter pairs.

2. Create a shape: Locate the "Rectangle Tool" and click and hold down to select the "Ellipse Tool."

– Make a large ellipse in the middle of your page.

– Give the ellipse a fill on none and a stroke of none.

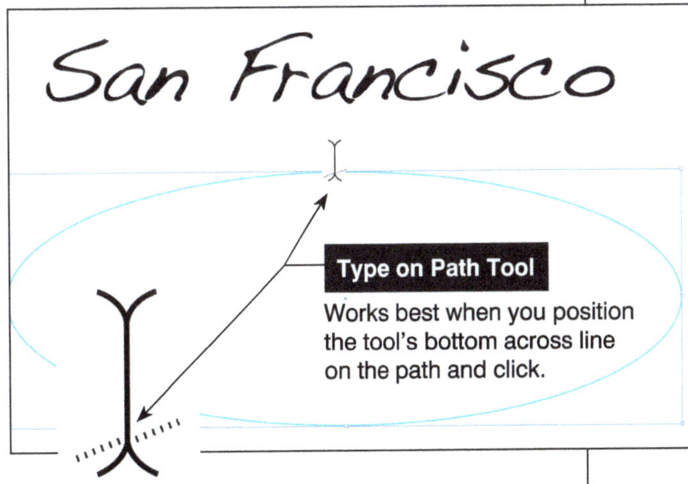

NOTE: If you can't see your ellipse, go to "View" / "Extras" and select "Show Frame Edges."

3. Copy headline: Using the "Type Tool," highlight the headline (click and drag the mouse over the letters) and go to the top and select "Edit" / "Copy."

4. Type on path: Locate the "Type Tool" and click and hold down to select the "Type on Path Tool."

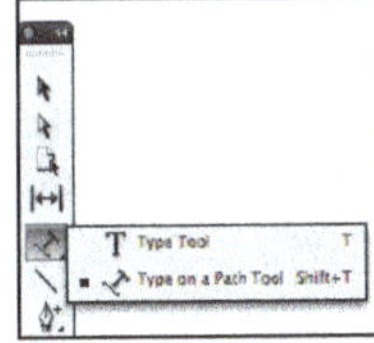

– Click on the center of the top of the ellipse you created.

Your notes

Your notes

NOTE: You will see a small diagonal line on the lower third of the "Type on Path Tool." Try to place this portion on the line when clicking on the shape.

– After clicking on the shape, go to the top and select "Edit" / "Paste."

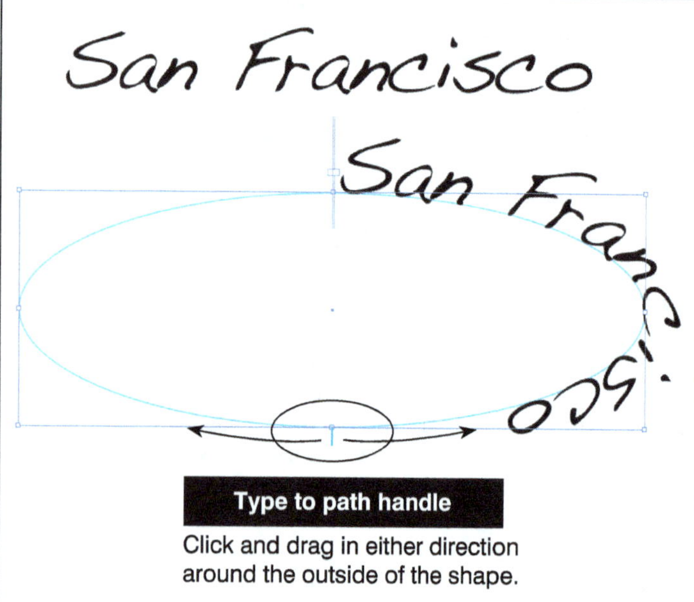

Type to path handle

Click and drag in either direction around the outside of the shape.

5. Move type on path: Using the "Selection Tool," click and drag on the small handle in the direction you would like to move the type along the path. Click and drag slowly until you get the hang of this tool.

NOTE: If you drag this small handle inside the shape, your type will go inside. If you pull the handle outside the space, the type will go outside.

6. Reshape or move: Using the "Selection Tool," click on the line of the shape to reshape the element.

7. Adjust letter spacing and kerning: Using the "Type Tool," highlight the letters or click in between letter pairs to adjust the letter spacing.

Other type to path shapes

The number of paths you can make type flow along seems endless.

– Try squares, rectangles, and polygons.

– Try using the pencil tool to create some very unusual shapes (just click and drag).

– The pen tool is also a great tool to create different shapes (click, move, click–much like dot-to-dot).

– You can also create some very sophisticated and smooth shapes with the pen by bending the line. This, however, takes a good bit of practice and is probably best left for another time.

Headlines vs. text wraps

Using multiple headlines: When your design calls for overlapping headline elements, make sure that the text wrap is turned off or you will have problems.

Headlines on photographs: When placing a headline on top of a photograph with text wrap applied, you will have problems. One quick solution is to convert the type to outlines.

To learn more about ***Outline type*** */ Pg. 146*

Ad text

This is completely your choice. Just remember everything that you have learned about typography.

– Content is everything! Create text that meets the client's needs and speaks to the target audience.

– Default type is most often the wrong font, wrong size, and wrong leading for many designs.

– Check grammar and spelling.

Ad logo

The client wanted to brand the ad campaign if possible to gain greater overall impact, so consider using the logos supplied in the lesson folder.

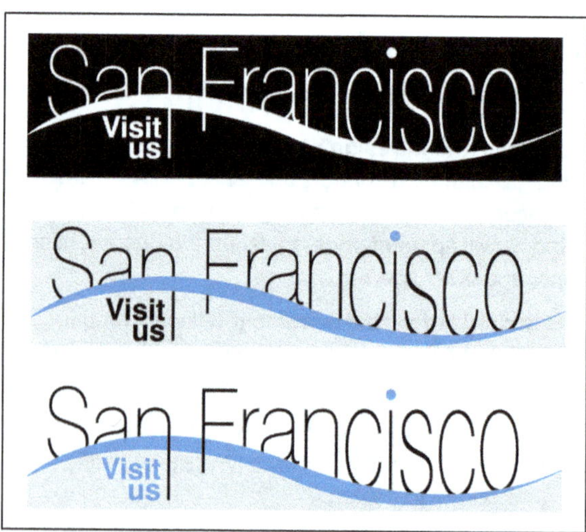

– **There are two files** that have a variety of the same logos that you could consider. Place either the "San Francisco logo 1.tif" or the "San Francisco logo 2.tif" file on your InDesign document. Size and crop out the logos you do not want.

REMEMBER: Legibility is a always a design concern, so be careful when using the logo very small.

– **San Francisco logo 1:** This is an Adobe Illustrator file that can be used by those who know the program and seek another version of the logo to use in their design.

Ad images

Within the lesson folder are many great photographs of San Francisco for you to use; just remember to crop and size them well. There is a new technique I would like to introduce you to that I have used successfully in the past.

Using opacity and effects

InDesign allows you to select an element and change its opacity and add an effect. This works well when layering multiple elements on top of each other. Here is how the example was created:

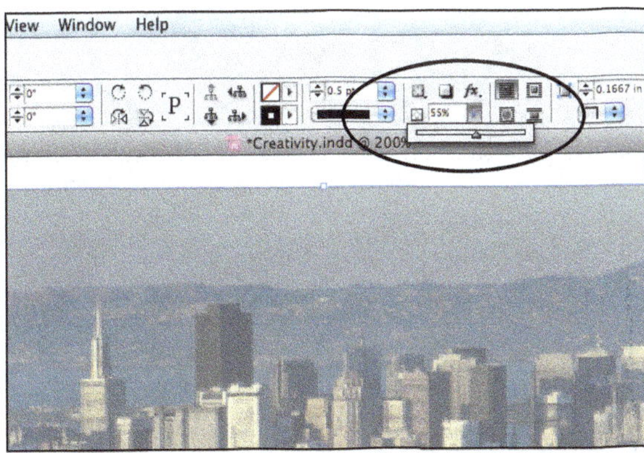

1. Place an image in your InDesign document. Using the "Selection Tool," size and move the photo into place. With the image still selected, reduce the opacity by using the "Opacity" tool in the "Control Strip" at the top.

– Use the slider or type the desired opacity amount for the element selected.

2. Place second image on top of your large image with the opacity. Notice the differences in color intensity?

3. Create headline by using the "Type Tool." Move the headline into place and give it a fill of white.

4. The headline opacity is created by selecting the headline with the "Selection Tool" and using the "Opacity" tool again.

5. Headline effect: With the headline still selected, go to the top and select "Object" / "Effects" / "Drop Shadow."

This brings up the "Effects" window. Now check the

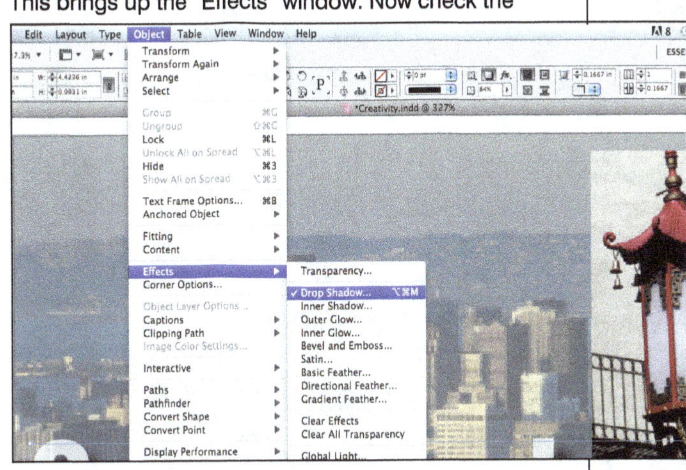

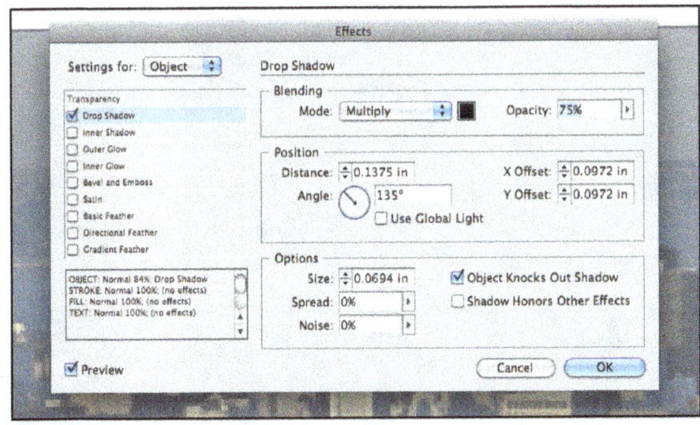

"Preview" box at the bottom and experiment with the settings to get your desired effect.

– **More effects:** There are many other effects and they can be combined to get many more different results.

Finishing the ad

Remember to consider completing the ad and doing a "Save As" to create a second, or even third, ad quickly

Your notes

DESIGNING with creativity

LESSON . . . B

What InDesign skills will you learn?

- Setting up the document when creating 3-dimensional projects
- Creating and working with outline type
- Using opacity and effects on photos and typography
- Getting quality photos prepared for the InDesign document

Music CD design

Overview

It is now time to prove all that you have learned. Your objective is to create a multi–platinum–selling CD cover, using all the design knowledge and computer skills you have developed. This is a very competitive market, and much of the success of musicians can be attributed to their CD designs.

Specifications

The assignment: Recording artist Terence Young has had four successful CDs and now it is time to produce a greatest hits CD. Research other Grammy artists to come up with a creative design that helps put him to the top of the charts.

■ **Target audience:** Gospel, jazz, and inspirational music lovers who are age 18 to 65.

Content

A folder titled "Design Creativity_B Lesson" includes photographs supplied by the artist for the CD design.

Your design must include all of the following:

■ **Design requirements:** Must design the CD cover, back, and two sides.

– Must include an image of the recording artist in some fashion on the front or the back of the CD design.

– Can include any other element or image as long as it is of high quality and does not have legal issues.

– Design must be in color (appropriate colors)

■ **CD title:** *Terence Young's Greatest Hits* (can be a variation of these words or other words that convey this idea).

■ **CD back:** Must include:

– Song titles.

– Recording label information to include "Produced by Your Name" and copyright info.

– Barcode and any other info you deem appropriate.

■ **Recordings:**

"Come with Me"
"If Only You Knew"
" Daughters"
"Groovin"
"Will Last"
"Give Yourself"
"Friday Night and Island Love"
"With Her"
"New Beginnings"
"Higher Ground"
"Silent Night"

■ **CD sides:** Must include appropriate side information.

The final project

You will need three copies of your design.

1. A quality color print of CD design.

2. A second quality print of the CD design that is trimmed and placed inside a CD case (you must supply). This will let you and the client see how your design will work.

3. The third version of your design needs to be a PDF file named "CDdesign_yourlastname.pdf." The pdf file typically would be sent to the client for approval.

Assessment criteria

■ Is the design the correct size (fits perfectly in the CD case)?

■ Does the project demonstrate knowledge and skill in typography, design, color, and photo use?

■ Was the PDF created correctly?

■ Is the design complete and includes all required elements?

■ Does the CD communicate to the target audience?

■ Does the design demonstrate creativity? Would I buy the CD?

Your notes

Instructions Designing with Creativity

Getting started

This lesson does not include an InDesign template and only has minimal instructions, because you now have much of the knowledge and InDesign skills to handle many projects. This lesson will challenge you to come up with an original music CD design that is creative enough to make this a Grammy winner.

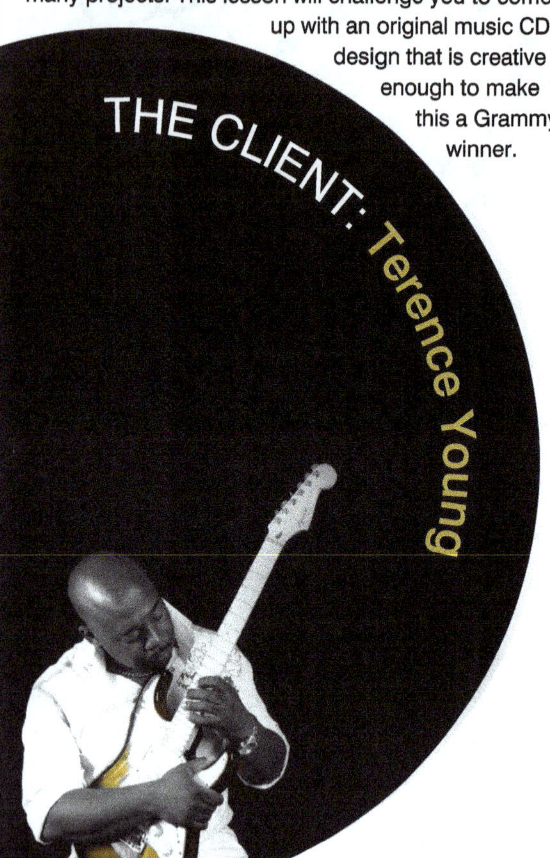

A real client's communication problem

This lesson is much like a typical day as a visual communicator. You are introduced to a new client who asks for your assistance in solving this communication problem. He gives you some background on the company or organization, which is followed by offering you some content or resources they currently have. Finally he asks your opinion and when he can expect to see your designs, as he walks out the door. You are left thinking, "What have I gotten myself into now?"

The problem: Musician Terence Young has produced four music CDs and his fan base is rapidly growing. He has almost completed new material for the upcoming CD release. Terence wants your help to take him to the next level and go multi-platinum.

– One of the biggest recording labels in the nation recently approached Terence with an offer to join them. He wants to impress them with this next release so they might sweeten the deal.

Content and resources: The lesson folder contains many images of the musician. Some of these are professional photographs, while others are images taken by friends. There is also a folder inside with various other images that might help with the project. You can choose to use as few or as many as you deem appropriate. **All images are copyrighted** and are forbidden to be used other than for the "Design & in Design" lessons.

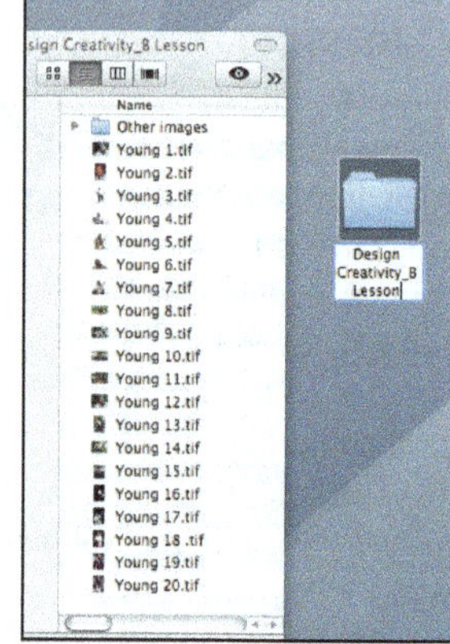

Project details: Refer to the lesson instructions for additional specific information (previous page).

Let's begin

Locate the "Creativity_B Lesson" folder that contains the lesson contents and place the entire folder on the desktop of your computer.

■ **CAUTION:** Never open and work on content that is located on your thumb drive.

Highlight part of the folder's name "B Lesson" and replace it with your last name. This will ensure you are always working on your copy of the lesson and can find the folder later.

Designing 3-dimensional projects

Taking a design from the computer to paper and then to the product can be a challenge. One of the biggest mistakes I often see people make is starting the design process before understanding the product. The first step should be to examine music CD cases and determine the exact size of the design.

NOTE: This lesson does not include a template or the size of the design. This is part of the project challenge.

1. Obtain a CD case: Looking closely at music CDs, you will find there are a good number of different ones. Some have thin front cover edges and others are significantly wider. CD cover edges come in a variety of colors, which may influence your design.

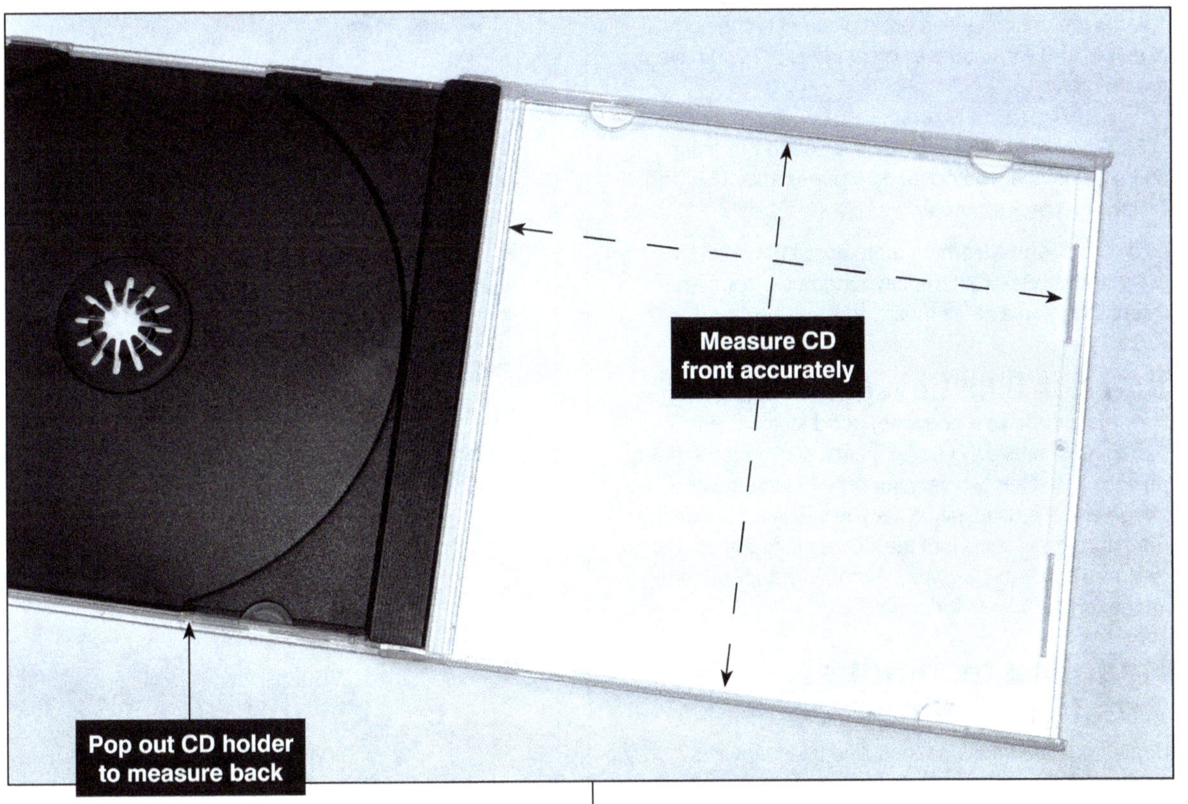

– You will need to obtain an empty music CD case now so you can continue.

2. Determine sizes: If you are using a used music CD case, you can take out the printed pieces and measure them. If you are using a new case, take a ruler and measure the dimensions from side to side. Here are the sizes you need:

– **CD front size:** Be careful, as these vary depending on the one you choose.

– **CD back size:** The same depth as the front but very different width. You will need to pull out the inside CD holder to measure correctly. The good news is that it pops out fairly easily.

– **CD side sizes.** Get these right! If you look closely, you will notice that the side is actually part of the CD's back design.

Setting up the InDesign document

1. Launch the InDesign program: With InDesign running, go to the top controls and select "File" / "New" / "Document" to begin creating a new document. A window will appear for you to set up the document size, type, and other specific settings.

– **Standard letter-size document** with vertical orientation will work for this project.

2. Create CD front shape: Using the "Rectangle Tool," create this shape at the top of the document.

3. Create CD back and sides: The secret is to create a shape that includes the back and the two sides. This shape should be placed below the cover shape so that both pieces can be printed out at the same time.

– Create two guides to indicate the CD sides.

4. Create guides: I would suggest this so you can be assured you do not accidentally change the size.

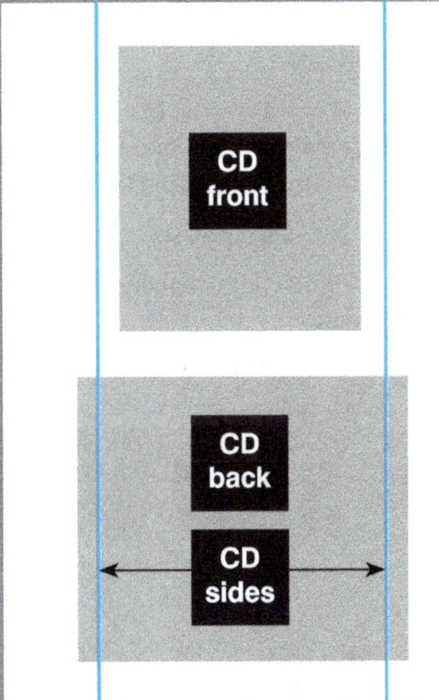

5. Save document: Make sure you name the file correctly ("creative design_yourlastname.indd") and save the document within your lesson folder located on your computer desktop.

IMPORTANT: Failure to save your file in the correct location can result in printing problems later!

Let's begin designing

With the inDesign document created, you are ready to begin bringing in all the content and create a great CD design. Are you ready?

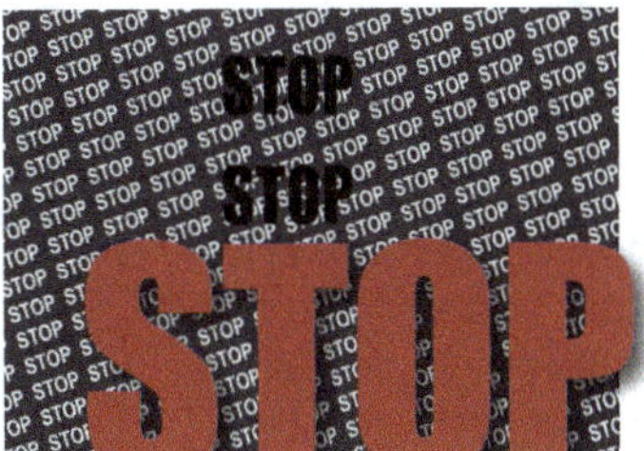

Have you done your research?

First: I would never think of beginning this lesson, or any other professional project that required a high level of creativity, without doing research.

Second: I would never sit down in front of the computer screen without having several sketches of design ideas.

Your notes

– While the computer is a great piece of technology, it is stupid and will not unveil great ideas . . . you have to create them!

TIP: I really want to you to do great on this lesson so I suggest that you go back to pages 130, 131, and review the steps for creativity.

– I would suggest learning more about the artist by going to his website (terenceyoungmusic.com) and listening to some of his music.

Now it is time to begin designing!

Now that you have a couple of good ideas, it is time to begin the music CD design. Let's start with the front design. There are two very important elements, the image and the headline. What you say is up to you, but remember how important the CD title is to the overall design. The headline gives information, supports the image, and also sets the tone.

Headline technique: Creating outline type

Sometimes the traditional headline that follows a straight horizontal or vertical line is not what is needed. This type technique using outline type will allow you to modify the typeface and provide many more creative options.

1. Create words: Using the traditional "Type Tool," create a text box and type in your headline. I suggest making the headline large at first (about 200 pts.).

– Select a typeface.

– Tighten letter spacing and kern inconsistent letter pairs.

Original typeface

Young

Reduced letter spacing and kerning

Young

2. Create outline type: Using the "Selection Tool," click on the type and go to the top and select "Type" / "Create Outlines." What this does is convert the word from a typeface to an outline drawing.

NOTE: When I use a specialty typeface that is not common, I will often create my project and then turn all the content in the specialty typeface to outline type (still filled with black or whatever color I was using). This avoids the client or the printer from needing to have the typeface to see the project or print it.

3. Reshape letters: One of the big benefits of turning type into outlines is the ability to change the shape of letters.

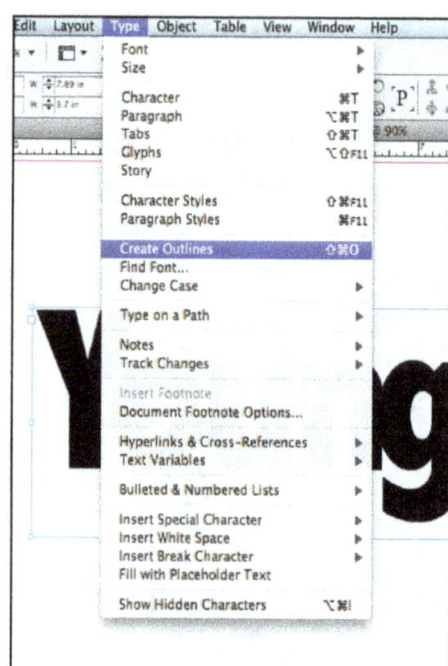

– Using the "Direct Selection Tool" (white arrow), click on a line or a corner point and drag to reshape the letter. This is a way to customize a typeface. This technique is used often when creating company logos.

4. Fill letters: You can now fill the letters with a color, gradient color, pattern, or even an image.

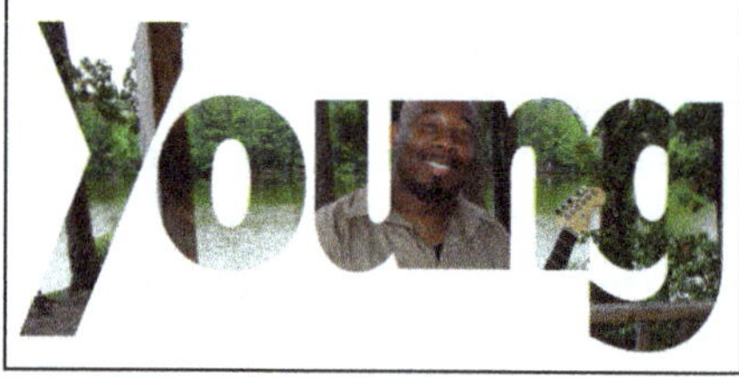

– Using the "Selection Tool," click on the type and go to the top and select "File" / "Place." Get the "Direct Selection Tool" (white arrow), and click and drag in the middle of the text to adjust size or placement of the image.

5. Add an effect: Using the "Selection Tool," select the outline type and go to the top and select "Object" / "Effects" / "Drop Shadow."

– **This brings up the "Effects" window.** Now check the "Preview" box at the bottom and experiment with the settings to get your desired effect.

– **More effects:** There are many other effects and you can even combine them to get different results.

Another creative type technique

Would you like to curve your headline? Well, InDesign's "Type on Path Tool" makes it possible to conform type along any shape you can create.

– Use traditional shapes like squares, rectangles, and polygons.

– It is possible using InDesign's pencil or pen tools to create some very usual shapes for your headline or other text to flow along.

 **ore info »**

To learn more about the **Type on Path Tool** */ Pg. 139*

Using photographs

Within the lesson folder are many great photographs of the music artist and other things for you to use. Remember to crop and size them well. You can use any other additional images as long as they are free from legal concerns (copyright, etc.) and of high quality.

Preparing quality images for InDesign

As was mentioned earlier in the book, photographs are made for many different media uses. It is possible to place an image directly into InDesign without addressing the quality and image format.

– To do this you will need to use Photoshop or some other photo manipulation software. While working in these programs can be very complicated, I have simplified the steps to produce quality images for this lesson.

NOTE: The following instructions are for the use of Photoshop, but the same steps (with possible different terminology) would need to be addressed when using other image software programs.

Step 1 – Photograph location: Make sure the image file is located on your computer's desktop.

– Why? Unlike words, photographs are made up of millions of pixels of information; therefore the file sizes can be very large. I have had many problems in the past trying to manipulate images on flash/thumb drives.

Step 2 – Image mode: Open the image in Photoshop and go to the top and select "Image" / "Mode" / "CMYK Color."

– This converts the photo from RGB, which is the color format used for digital cameras and images used on websites to the printed color format.

Step 3 – Image size: Now go to the top and select "Image" / "Image Size" which brings up the "Image Size" window.

Not linked

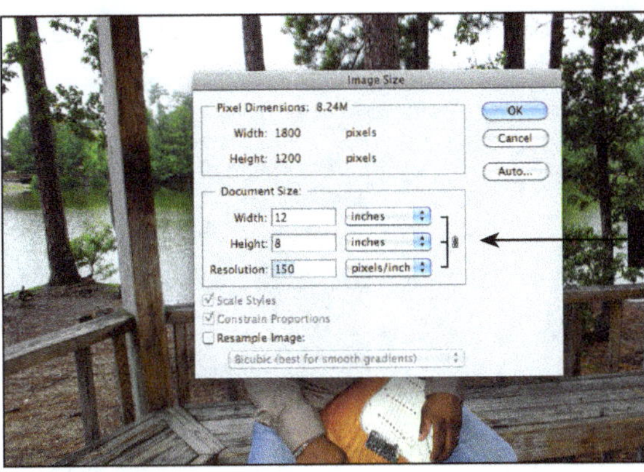

Is linked

– **Locate the "Document Size" settings** and make sure all are linked together (indicated to the right of the settings with connecting lines). To link all the settings (width, height, resolution) together, click on the "Resample Image" box if needed.

– **Locate the "Resolution" setting** and change to 150 and click on the "OK" button. This is the quality needed to produce quality images for desktop printers.

NOTE: If you are getting an image from the Web, the new size is much smaller. This new size is the maximum size you will be able to use the image in your InDesign design. If it is too small, you will need to find a larger image. I usually do searches only for large images about 1,000 pixels or larger.

Step 4 – Image format: The last step is to go to the top again and select "File" / "Save As." I always do "Save As" because I want to make a duplicate file. That way I will have the original file in case I made a mistake.

– **Change the "Format"** by clicking on the arrows to change to TIFF (puts .tif at the end of the file name).

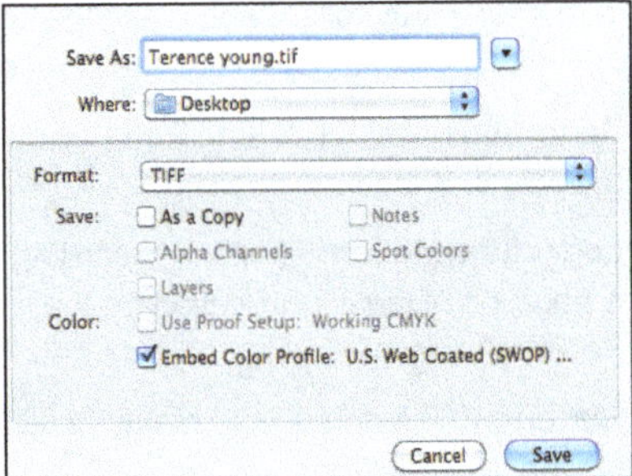

– **Give the photo a name** in the "Save As" area (leaving the software identification (.tif) at the end.

– **Click on the "Save" button.**

Your notes

Your notes

Step 4 – Image location: The last step is to make sure you have put the new image in your lesson folder so when it is placed on the design it will create and maintain a good link.

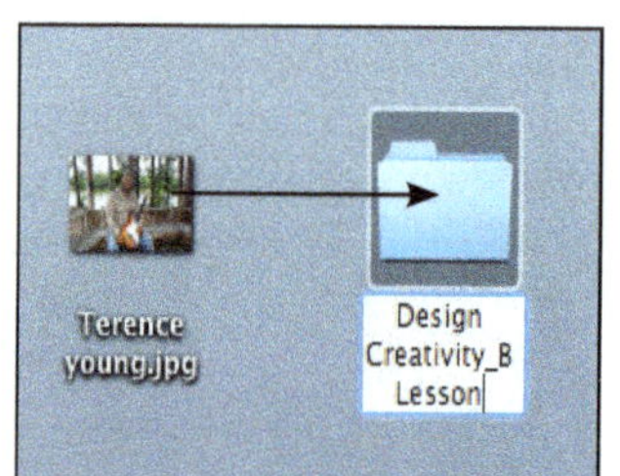

Using opacity and effects

There is another technique I would like to introduce you to that I have used successfully in the past. InDesign allows you to select an element and change its opacity and add an effect.

–This works well when placing multiple elements on top of each other, including photographs and typography.

– Also consider using this technique to increase the legibility of small text on photographs.

How it is done:

– The background image is placed and a 57% opacity applied.

– The top photograph has 100% opacity, a frame of 3 pts. white, and a drop shadow effect applied.

 **ore info »**

To learn more about ***using opacity & effects*** */ Pg. 141*

Designing the CD back

While it is similar to the front, it does have some required elements that you need to research and design carefully. The design should give information, but also complement or match the tone of the CD front. The goal is to impress the client and make the CD design look real, like it was just pulled off the shelf of a music store.

Song titles: Include them all and be careful of legibility problems. Watch the spelling.

Legal information: All major recording labels include a good bit of legal information on the back of the CD. Research this info because yours needs to look real.

Bar code: The object is to make this CD design look real so you need one!

Other info: Think smart! If you were the recording artist or representing him, what other elements or information would you want on the CD design?

Creating the barcode

Sure, you could get a barcode image from the internet, but it would not give many design options since it already comes with a background. Here is a better option:

1. Barcode shape: Using the "Rectangle Tool," create a shape that is the same as an actual barcode found on a music CD (often smaller than most).

– I suggest creating the barcode off the side of the document and move into the proper place when completed.

2. Guides: Turn document rulers on and place guides on all edges of the rectangle. This makes it easier to align barcode lines.

– Now, delete rectangle created and lock the guides. To lock the guides, go to the top and select "View" / "Grids & Guides" / "Lock Guides."

3. Snap to guides: To make it easy to align the lines, it is first necessary to turn on "Snap to Guides." To do this go to "View" / "Grids & Guides" / "Snap to Guides."

4. Draw lines: Select the "Line Tool." Click and drag from the top horizontal guide to the bottom horizontal guide. You will notice when close it will snap to the guide ensuring consistent length lines.

HINTS: Remember, holding the "Shift" key down while creating a line ensures a perfectly straight line.
Also, enlarge the view when creating the barcode.

– Vary the width and the line styles to make it look real. To do this, select "Window" / "Stroke" to open the stroke palette.

– Create another horizontal guide about an 1/8 inch from the bottom guide to help align the middle lines of the barcode.

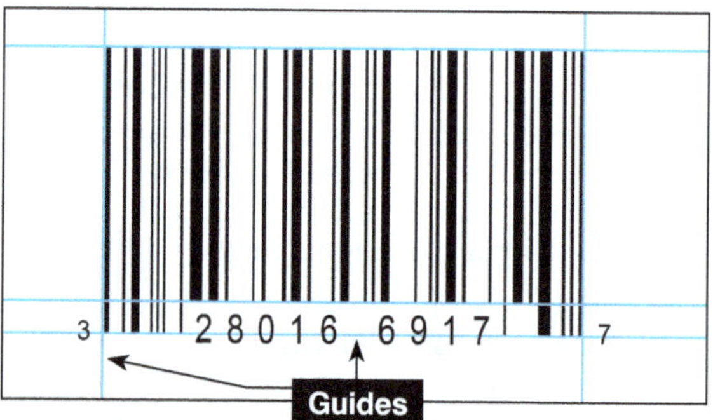

5. Barcode numbers: Create some small numbers to go at the bottom of the barcode.

NOTE: You can easily make all the lines and numbers white to use the barcode on a dark background.

6. Group: The last step is to select all the elements and group them so you can easily move them into place.

Finishing the lesson

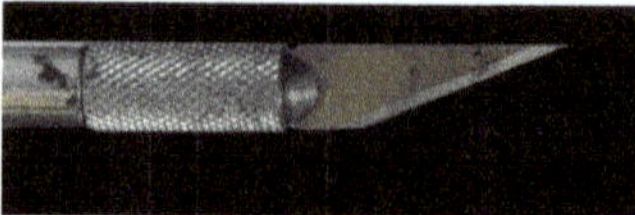

You will need to print one copy and trim it to be placed inside the music CD case. The trimed edges need to be straight and not jagged. Use an X-Acto knife and a metal ruler to trim the design. I have seen many clients pick inferior designs over great designs with poor presentation.

DESIGNING with technology

"Poor design gets in the way, average is obvious, and great is invisible."

One thing that still surprises me is how often I hear is "I am not good with technology." This usually means "I am afraid of technology." How can this be, when we are one of the most technologically advanced nations in the world? If you look closely at the people you know, you will see how little they know about the technologies they use. Most people do not know half the functions of their mobile phones, yet they now want to use smart technology phones. How does this make any sense?

Well, I too am often afraid and overwhelmed by technology. Having to learn new software and equipment each year to teach to students, I have learned that I will never know everything about technology. Yet, I also have learned I cannot avoid it. My goal now is to identify the technologies that I value as part of my personal life and career and learn those. Become a master of a few technologies and have general knowledge of many.

In the communication field it is not enough to just know how to create a message. It is essential you have the ability to create the message and often to deliver it. To do this, you will need tools. I challenge you to put fear aside and learn the communication technologies and software basics.

Digital media

Taking your files with you

Often, you will not be able to complete your project in a single session at the computer. This will require you to save and take your digital files with you so that you can complete them later. There are many file storage methods and each have their advantages and disadvantages. In recent years many backup technologies are becoming obsolete because of storage capacity, speed, and complexity of backing up the files. I will introduce you to several options:

CDs & DVDs: While these two have been used for many years and are inexpensive ways to store digital files, they have some significant disadvantages. Both of these require significant time burning the material on the disks (I do not recommend these).

Flash drives: Since IBM began selling these to the public in 2000, they have been a big hit. This portable digital memory storage device which has no moving parts is durable, portable, and easily connects to any computer's USB port to allow you to quickly add or delete files from the device. The flash drive, also known as a thumb drive or jump drive, comes in a variety of memory sizes and prices to fit many needs (highly recommend).

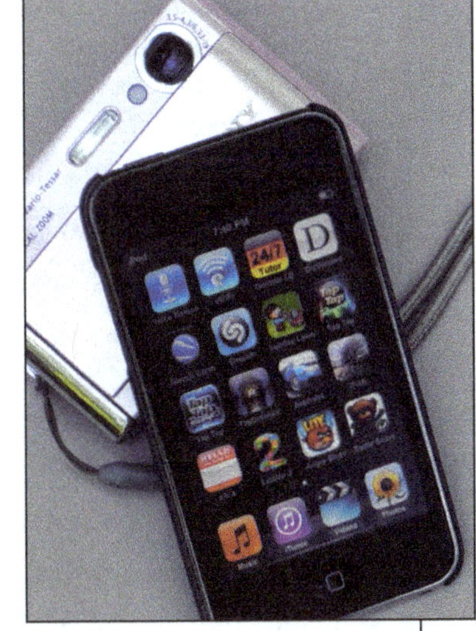

External drives: This is another excellent way to store your digital files. While theses devices are significantly larger than the flash drives, they have the ability to store larger amounts of data at quicker speeds. The disadvantage is their size. Not all devices connect to USB ports and many require an additional power supply. These are great to handle larger complex files like video, audio, animation, and website materials, which often are too much for flash drives (highly recommend for those in the visual communication field).

Other options: Any digital device that has internal memory and can connect to a computer by USB device has the potential of storing your digital files. Also, any device that has a removable memory card (used with a USB memory card reader) can store your digital files also. Such devices include smart phones, digital cameras, iPods, iPads, and the list goes on (recommended in an emergency, and short-term use).

Backing up files to the flash drive correctly

WARNING – While the flash drive is a great device, you need to know how to use this correctly or there is the potential you will damage or destroy your digital files. If you follow these easy steps you will be successful:

1. Save your file to the computer: I recommend this because it is faster and it will give you an additional backup file in case something goes wrong later.

Your notes

2. Name file correctly: Remember to create a short name, preferably with your last name or initials, and it must end with the InDesign identification (.indd).

3. Connect flash drive: Insert the drive into the computer's USB port. You can connect it to the keyboard on Apple's newest computers. On all other computers you will need to use the other USB ports.

– Shortly an icon will appear, representing your flash drive, on your computer's desktop.

NOTE: Click on the flash drive icon words and it will allow you to change the name. I suggest inserting your last name, so if it is misplaced someone might return it to you.

4. Save your file to the flash drive: Locate your digital file and drag the icon on top of the flash drive icon. Within seconds this copies the file. Double-click on your flash drive icon to make sure the file was copied correctly.

5. Eject the flash drive: Drag the flash drive icon to the trash icon (which will change to "Eject"). You can also select the flash drive icon and right-click the mouse to eject. Remember to wait a few seconds before removing the flash drive (make sure the small light on the flash drive quits flashing).

Naming your files

This seems so simple; however, giving your document a correct file name is more important than you think. Many magazines and newspapers create hundreds of files daily and many of them are handled by over a dozen people each day, so naming and organizing these important digital documents is essential to their publishing success. Here is a sampling of potential problems that can occur if you fail to name your documents correctly:

– Some computers will not be able to open the file.

– You may not be able to locate the file because you can't recall the name.

– Your file name embarrasses the client/boss–or worse, the file name becomes a concern in a court case.

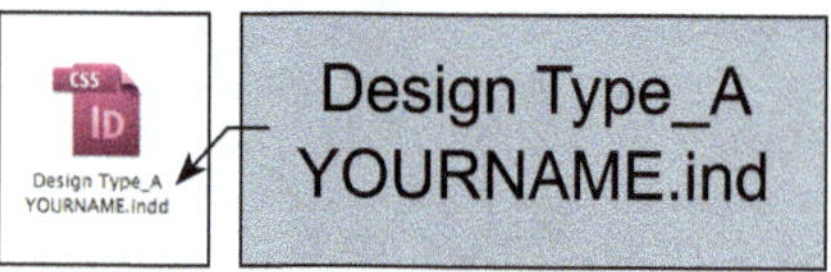

The good news is that naming files is simple and not a problem if you remember these simple suggestions:

■ **Avoid long file names:** The problem is that long names are hard to remember and difficult to read. When viewing files as icons, long file names go on multiple lines and make odd letter breaks.

– Solution: I suggest trying to keep your file names under 21 characters if possible.

■ **Include the software identification:** This is the two, three, or four letters at the end of the document name. If you always worked in the Apple computer world, this has never been a concern for you. However, with more files being shared on different computer systems and used on a variety of different digital media, this has become a problem at times. The good news is that most software programs include this at the end of the file name (but not all).

– Solution: Make sure all your files have the software identification at the end. Here are some common file identifications you will need to know:

InDesign file = .indd

Photoshop photo file = .psd or .tiff or .eps or .jpg

Microsoft Word file = .doc or .docx

Illustrator document = .ai

NOTE: It is essential that the dot at the front of the software identification be included.

■ **Include your name:** Searching for your specific file among hundreds or thousands can be frustrating. I often will forget file names, but I know there is a great chance I will remember my name.

– Solution: Include your last name or abbreviation as part of the file name. I suggest putting a space or an underscore between the file name and your initials to make searches easier.

■ **Avoid punctuation:** If you ever have to move your files to another computer system or use your files in a website, you will quickly find out that many punctuation symbols will get you into trouble.

– Solution: Use little, if any, punctuation in digital file names. I suggest using single spaces and underscores to separate specific words or letters, if needed.

Using different versions of InDesign

The good news is that using an older version of the InDesign software is OK. The only problem is that you will not have access to some of the newer tools and features. The fact is that I do most of my desktop publishing using the basic InDesign tools that were introduced with the earliest versions.

Opening an older version of InDesign with a new version:

The good news is that all of your design work will work! Even all the links will be fine as long as you stayed organized.

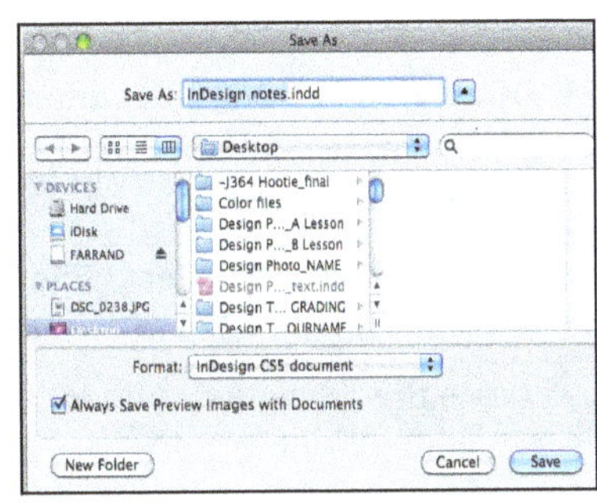

– **Launch your InDesign program.** Double-click (open) your older version InDesign document. You are working in the new program and everything should work perfectly.

– **Save file.** Go to the top and select "File" / "Save." This will bring up the "Save As" window automatically to enable you to save this document in the new version of InDesign but still retain the older version.

Using a new version of InDesign but need to save as an older version: This is something you need to learn if you have to do your work on several different computers. This is one aspect of InDesign I am very disappointed with, because I am spoiled having worked with Adobe's Illustrator program which has allowed me to save files to any older version for years. The good news is that you can save InDesign 5 to a version that can be opened and used by InDesign 4.

1. InDesign 5: Open your InDesign document on the computer on which it was created (InDesign 5).

2. Export: With the InDesign 5 file open, go to the top and select "File" / "Export." This brings up the "Export" window, where you need to set the "Format" (at the bottom) to "InDesign Markup (IDML). Make sure you have the correct file name in the "Save As" window at the top.

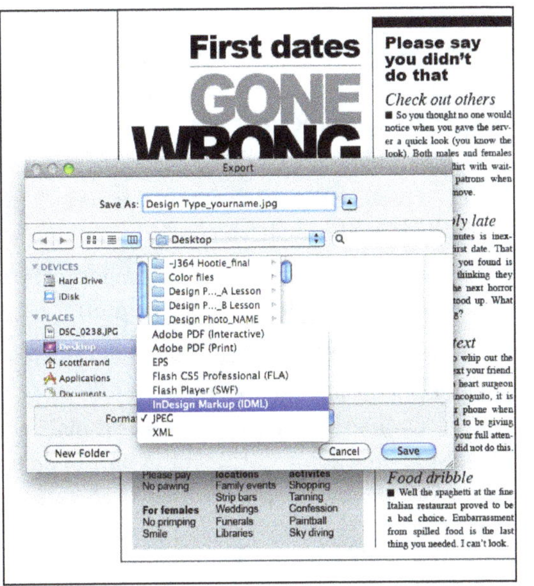

3. Create IDML file: This stands for InDesign Markup Language and is how InDesign translates the program to be opened and used by an earlier version.

– Now take this file and copy it to a flash drive so you can move it to the other computer you are using.

NOTE: If this document contains images, it is very important to name this file correctly, place it in the same location as previous InDesign 5 documents, and to include all the images. Failure to do this will result in busted links that will have to be repaired or you will have to replace all the images.

4. Convert to InDesign 4: The last step is to place the .idml file located on your flash drive to the next computer with the older version of InDesign.

Your notes

– Launch InDesign 4 and open this ".idml" file.

– Save this file, give it a new name, and it will now be an InDesign 4 document that will work perfectly.

Working with an even older version of InDesign: The good news is that it is possible. The bad news is that InDesign has often changed the export program name and it requires many more steps. InDesign only allows you to save back to one version. What does this mean?
InDesign 5 can save back to InDesign 4 (export using InDesign Markup (IDML) = ".idml")
InDesign 4 can save back to InDesign 3 (export using InDesign CS3 Interchange = ".inx")
InDesign 3 can save back to InDesign 2 (export using InDesign Interchange =".inx")

NOTE: Remember, if you use some of the new features in the newer program they could be lost when opened in the older version of InDesign. The best advice is to try to always work in one version and to finish in the newer version of InDesign. Avoid working backward when possible.

Saving InDesign documents as PDF files

You may ask your self, "Why do this?" If you want to share your work with someone who does not have InDesign, this is a great option. Also, many publishers and printers now require sending your work to be printed with them as PDF files. This reduces the software, font, and image issues they often face when working with many types of files.

How to create a PDF: This is very easy since InDesign and most other programs have built in PDF formats into their programs.

1. Open your InDesign document and make sure all your images are linked and all the typefaces (fonts) are OK.

2. Go to the top and select "File" / "Export." This brings up the "Export" window.

– Locate the "Save As" (at top) and give your file a name (keeping .pdf).

– Locate the "Format" (at bottom) and select "Adobe PDF Print."

– Now click on "Save."

3. Export Adobe PDF window: This widow that appears lets you select the proper PDF settings for your needs

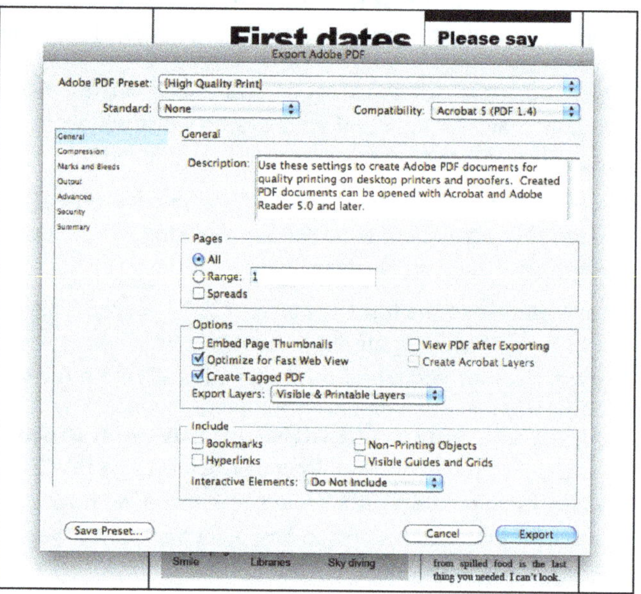

– Adobe PDF Preset: This setting allows you to pick the PDF quality. I suggest selecting "High Quality Print" for printing needs or select "Smallest File Size" if you just want to e-mail the PDF so someone can see your work.

– Compatibility: If someone can't see or use your work, you can change the PDF version. I usually leave it at the default unless I have problems.

– Description: This gives you information about the selections you have made (very helpful).

– Pages: Select specific pages of a multipage document.

– Option: I usually do not change this setting. However, select "Optimize for Fast Web View" if placing on a website or sending document as part of an e-mail.

– Include: Rarely use this section, so you can skip.

4. Select Export.

5. Preview: Double-click on the PDF file created. This usually will open the file in the PDF reader (comes with most computers), which is how those who do not have InDesign or other programs will view your document.

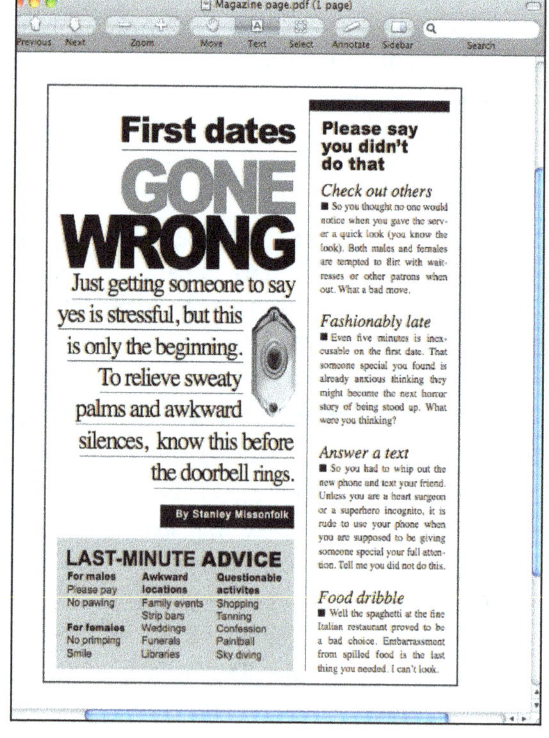

Magazine page.pdf (1 page)

First dates GONE WRONG

Just getting someone to say yes is stressful, but this is only the beginning. To relieve sweaty palms and awkward silences, know this before the doorbell rings.

By Stanley Missonfolk

LAST-MINUTE ADVICE

For males	Awkward locations	Questionable activites
Please pay	Family events	Shopping
No pawing	Strip bars	Tanning
For females	Weddings	Confession
No primping	Funerals	Paintball
Smile	Libraries	Sky diving

Please say you didn't do that

Check out others
■ So you thought no one would notice when you gave the server a quick look (you know the look). Both males and females are tempted to flirt with waitresses or other patrons when out. What a bad move.

Fashionably late
■ Even five minutes is inexcusable on the first date. That someone special you found is already anxious thinking they might become the next horror story of being stood up. What were you thinking?

Answer a text
■ So you had to whip out the new phone and text your friend. Unless you are a heart surgeon or a superhero incognito, it is rude to use your phone when you are supposed to be giving someone special your full attention. Tell me you did not do this.

Food dribble
■ Well the spaghetti at the fine Italian restaurant proved to be a bad choice. Embarrassment from spilled food is the last thing you needed. I can't look.

NOTE: Look over the PDF file content closely, because if you had font, image or other unknown problems, the content may be missing or have quality issues.

Your notes

Printing your document successfully

It surprises me how many people do not know how to print a document successfully. What do I mean by this? Well, recently one of my students showed me an e-mail he received from an angry printing company that refused to print his work because of so many problems. He did not understand what the problem was! He proceeded to show me his documents on the computer and exclaimed how good it looked on the screen. I calmly told him it did not matter what it looked like on the computer screen, it mattered what it looked like when it printed. I asked him to hit the print button. What came next was one warning popup window after another, which he said he had ignored.

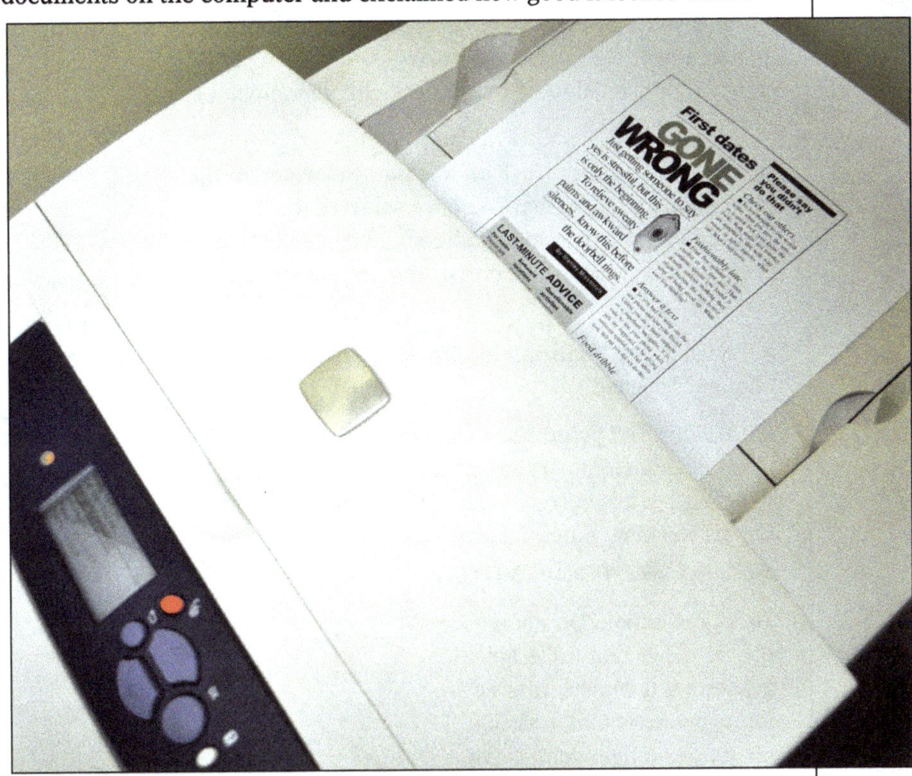

Well, it matters what your project looks like when it is printed and it is not hard to print, but it does involve more than hitting the print button to be successful. I know technology and printers can be intimidating. I know it seems all print settings are different (well, they often are but, you are looking for the same print settings. Here are some steps I have simplified to cover most types of desktop printers.

Printing instructions

1. Document location: Make sure your InDesign documents and all other content (to include images) are sitting on your computer's desktop. I have seen numerous printing problems when files are located on flash drives.

2. Open InDesign document: Look to be sure you are opening the document on your computer's desktop. Also, make sure you have saved your file before printing. If there is a chance of losing a document, it often seems to appear when printing.

3. Print: Go to the top and select "File" / "Print." This will bring up a print dialog box that you must not ignore to print successfully.

DO NOT hit the print button now!

4. Print settings (General): Address these settings.
– Printer: Select the correct printer. In many environments you will have access to many printers and each has different quality it can produce.

– Copies: Enter how many you want. When needing many copies I print one at first to makes sure it prints well (this helps avoid wasting paper).

– Pages: Nothing (Only use this when printing multipage projects).

– Option: Nothing (Only use on specialty printing projects).

DO NOT hit the print button yet!

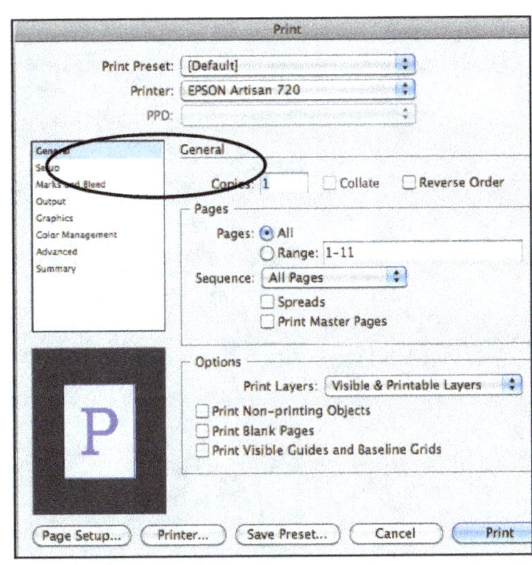

5. Print settings (Setup): Address these settings. Often you will have to select the setup button to get to these settings.

– Paper size: Select the paper size that best fits your project. In most cases it is "US Letter."

Your notes

– Orientation: Select the icon that is correct for your project.

– Scale: If you have created your document in the correct size, make sure it is set at "100%" and you have checked the "Constrain Proportions" box.

– Page Position: Select the correct position of your work. I use "Centered" most often.

Are you ready to print yet? . . . NO!

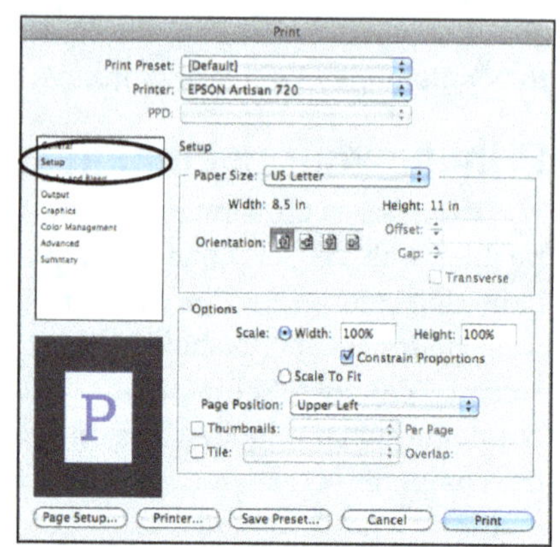

6. Print settings (Others): Marks & Bleeds, Output, Graphics, Color Management, Advanced, Summary.
You will only need to address these with very advanced specialty projects.

7. "Printer" button: Click on this button located at the bottom and confirm that you have selected the correct printer. In some printing conditions I have had to select the printer again at this point or the project will not print correctly.

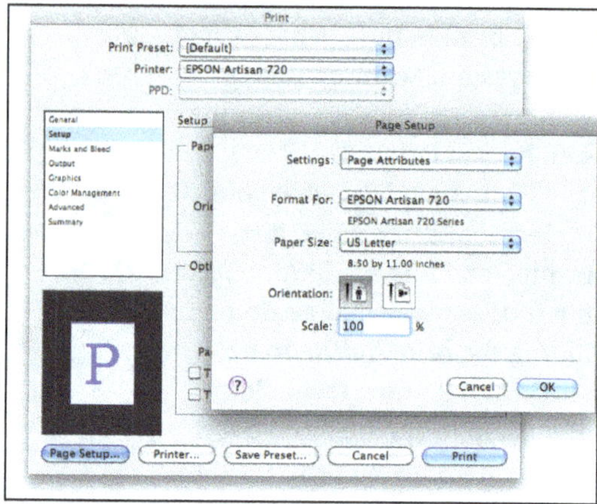

8. "Page Setup" button: Confirm these settings and change if needed.

9. Confirm and print: Examine the visual representation of the document on "Print" window (lower left) and determine if it is correct (should not contain red, which means warning: potential problem).

NOW HIT THE "PRINT" BUTTON!

10. Big problem: Do not ignore the warnings that InDesign will give you if it detects missing fonts, overflow text, missing images, or other problems that will be given. You need to address each of these problems to produce a successfully designed and printed project.

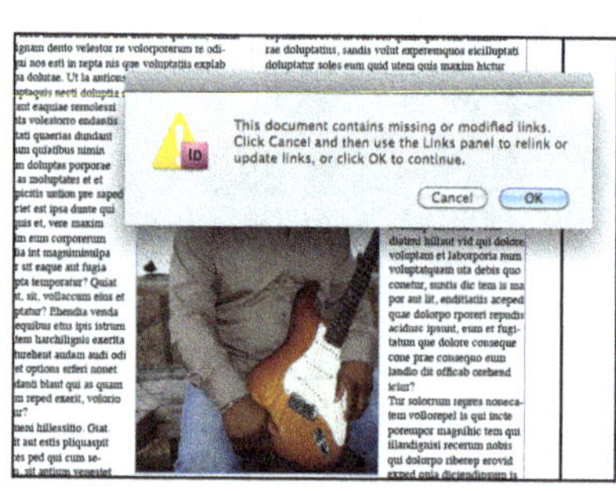

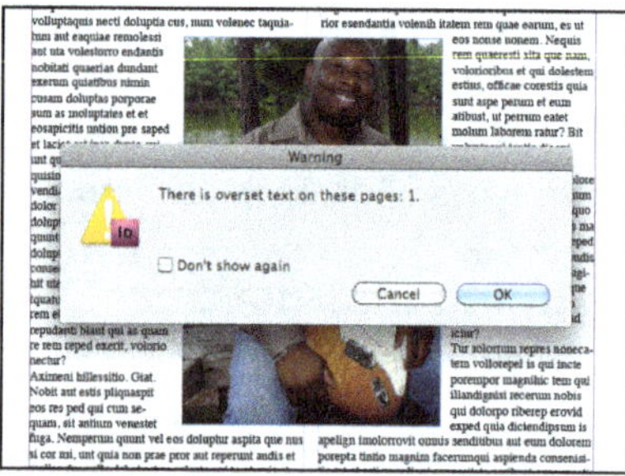

Summary

Trying new things the first time is scary for people of all ages. Learning new technologies is intimidating to even the scholarly. But the fact is that most of the fear is exaggerated and you really cannot afford to not learn technology. So, if you made it this far, you have learned a lot, and hopefully I have helped you become a bit more confident. Now you will not be one those people I meet who say "I am not good with technology" . . . because you have learned the basics.

www.ingramcontent.com/pod-product-compliance
Lightning Source LLC
LaVergne TN
LVHW081653180126
830141LV00009B/295

* 9 7 8 1 6 0 9 2 7 0 2 0 9 *